The Poultry and Game Cookbook

The Poultry and Game Cookbook

Jill Graham

HAMLYN

For my mother

Published 1985 by The Hamlyn Publishing Group Limited
London • New York • Sydney • Toronto
Astronaut House, Feltham, Middlesex, England
By arrangement with Lansdowne Press
© Copyright Jill Graham 1985
ISBN 0 600 32448 6
Printed in Hong Kong by Everbest Printing Co. Ltd.

CONTENTS

INTRODUCTION

The art of cooking has developed over thousands of years and the most beautiful part of that process is that it is still developing, still changing, and will continue to do so for as long as we do.

One of the reasons that poultry and game are so interesting is that they exemplify this process of change so well. Their geographical distribution knows few barriers and they have been cooked by people of so many different cultures, using local methods and produce, that an enormous fund of recipes is available to test, exchange and adapt. A present-day South American recipe, for example, may well need to be adapted because the variety of chillies — and the corresponding understanding of their use and blending — is not readily available. Similarly, a recipe from the sixteenth or seventeenth century will need modification: the spicing will need to be reduced because we no longer have to hide the taint of unrefrigerated meat. A blender or food processor readily changes a texture too coarse for our taste (a taste shaped, perhaps, by those very appliances). And so new dishes result from the overlay of culture and time.

Commercial farming of poultry and game has, I think, suffered much unwarranted criticism. We have at least given up eating flamingos, nightingales, peacocks, swans, and practically everything else that flies, and if intensive farming has brought chicken within the reach of everyone, made the most expensive game birds cheaper and more plentiful than they were fifteen years ago, and given us a wider range of food to choose from, that is a reasonable exchange.

Cooking is alive and there is always something new to learn, to try, and, best of all, to taste. Eating is essentially a sharing process and the person who sits at my table is more important to me than what is on it. Nevertheless, that food should be as good and interesting as we can make it.

I see a cookery book as a basic kitchen appliance, but also as an instrument to set you thinking, rather than as a set of rules to be slavishly followed. You should, for instance, feel free to change an ingredient you dislike. This collection of recipes ranges between the simple and the elaborate, not necessarily haute cuisine, but designed for modern life. Most have been collected over many years, some have been adapted particularly for the book, and some have been given to me by friends — these are special gifts and each time I cook them I am reminded of that person. I hope there is a gift for you among these pages.

Chicken Liver and Ham Gougère, page 243

HOW TO USE THIS BOOK
Weights and Measures

I have made every effort to ensure that this book will be useful to all readers by making clear the differences between the weights and measures of various countries. Gertrude Stein's 'Rose is a rose is a rose' does not apply to the vagaries of international food measurements, thus 'cup is a cup is a cup' does not mean the same in the United Kingdom, North America, and Australia. For that matter neither does a pint or a tablespoon, but at least we all share a 5-millilitre teaspoon.

The recipes in this book have all been tested using the Australian Standard 250-millilitre cup, 20-millilitre tablespoon, and 5-millilitre teaspoon but are designed to be usable by cooks using measures of different volume. In all recipes metric measures are shown followed, where necessary, by imperial equivalents in parenthesis; for example:

> *1 ½–2 cups (14–18 fl oz) aspic*
> * jelly*
> *3 hard-boiled eggs, sliced*
> *375 g (12 oz) chopped cooked*
> * chicken*
> *185 g (6 oz) lean ham*
> *1 tablespoon chopped parsley*

By combining expressions of weight — mainly for ease of marketing — and volume, the recipes will work as well whether you use the British 300-millilitre cup or the North American 8-fluid-ounce cup, as the proportions remain the same within each system. The tablespoon volume of the United Kingdom, North America, and New Zealand is smaller than that of Australia, having a capacity of 15 millilitres or 3 teaspoons. Generally speaking, however, tablespoon measurements are not critical within the recipes but for complete accuracy use four 5-millilitre teaspoons to equal the Australian tablespoon. The Australian, British, and New Zealand pint has a capacity of 20 fluid ounces whereas the North American pint has a capacity of 16 fluid ounces.

For successful results use either all metric measures or all imperial measures but not a mixture of the two. When using metric measures the yield will be approximately 10 per cent greater than that of the imperial equivalents.

Note: All cup and spoon measurements are level.

Oven Temperature Guide

Description	Celsius (°C)	Fahrenheit (°F)	Regulo
Cool	100	200	¼–½
Very slow	120	250	1
Slow	150–160	300–325	2
Moderately slow	160–170	325–350	3
Moderate	180–190	350–375	4–5
Moderately hot	190–200	375–400	6
Hot	200–230	400–500	7
Very hot	230–250	450–500	8–9

Note: Where two temperatures are listed in the table above, the lower temperature refers to gas ovens, the higher to electric ovens. It is impossible to give exact figures for every cooker as different makes vary, but these figures give a reliable average in most cases. If in doubt follow the manufacturer's temperature chart for your oven.

Raised Pigeon Pie, page 132

International Terminology

Wherever practical the recipes I have followed characteristically Australian/British names and terms with the American equivalents in parenthesis; for example, grill (broil), spring onion (scallion), frying pan (skillet). The following list sets out a number of these terms but is by no means an exhaustive glossary as there is much overlapping between our various traditions as well as a shared vocabulary of common sense!

Aust./U.K.	American
bicarbonate of soda	baking soda
boiling chicken	stewing fowl
cake tin	cake pan
capsicums	sweet or bell peppers
castor sugar	superfine sugar
celery stick	celery rib
cornflour	cornstarch
desiccated coconut	shredded coconut
essences	extracts
frying pan	skillet
glacé fruits	candied fruits
greaseproof paper	wax paper
green prawns	raw shrimp
grill	broil
ground rice	rice flour
hard-boiled egg	hard-cooked egg
icing sugar	confectioner's sugar
kitchen paper/absorbent paper	paper towels
mince/minced	ground
oven tray	cookie sheet
(a) pinch	dash
plain flour	all-purpose flour
pork fat	fat back
(bacon) rasher	slice
scone	biscuit
self-raising flour	self-rising flour
(to) shell	shuck/hull
spring onions	scallions
stock cubes	bouillon cubes
(to) stone, seed	pit
(to) whisk	whip

Game Seasons

Closed seasons — when hunting is not permitted — are imposed in order to conserve game stocks. These vary from one country to another and, indeed, in some countries from State to State, but the closed season is usually when the birds are breeding. The United Kingdom seasons are given in the relevant chapters. Quite a variety of frozen game birds are now available out of season.

Hanging Game

The flesh of game — furred or feathered — is distinguishable in several ways from that of domesticated birds and animals: stronger flavour, darker, and much tougher, meat (although toughness is generally related to the age of the game). Young birds shot early in their season can be eaten immediately — in fact this is traditional for grouse shot on the 'Glorious Twelfth', the opening day of the grouse season in the United Kingdom.

It is not essential to hang game if you object to the flavour it then acquires, but most game is improved by this process, during which protein is metabolised by tissue enzymes, thus tenderising the flesh and developing the flavour. The table below gives approximate hanging times for freshly killed game. Purchased game should have been prepared and hung to your requirements.

Grouse	2–4 days	Quail	Do not hang
Hare	2–3 days	Rabbit	
Pheasant		(farmed)	Do not hang
(young)	3–4 days	(wild)	1–3 days
(old)	8–10 days	Venison	7–21 days
Pigeon		Woodcock	2–4 days
(farmed)			
Do not hang			
(wild)	2 days		

PLUCKING

First ensure that there are adequate waste containers available to catch the feathers.

Hold the bird by the legs and begin with the tail end. Pull out the feathers, a few at a time, using a quick jerk in the opposite direction to which the feathers lie.

Care must be taken when plucking to avoid tearing the skin which will be soft and tender after hanging.

Wing feathers are removed by gripping all of the main feathers in one hand and pulling sharply. Stubborn feathers may require the use of pliers.

The down of the bird is best removed by singeing. This is done by placing 2 tablespoons of methylated spirits in an enamel plate and lighting it. Hold the bird at each end and rotate. The wide area of the plate makes the job much easier than over a narrow gas flame. After singeing the down is easily removed.

DRAWING

Enlarge the vent opening and carefully remove the organs which consist of the gizzard, intestines, heart, and liver with the gall bladder attached. Do not break the gall bladder as it makes everything it touches bitter. Remove the lungs from under the ribs. Clean the gizzard, heart, neck and liver in cold water.

Make an incision down the length of the neck, then pull out the windpipe and the crop. Cut off the neck leaving the skin flap intact to fold over the back. Cut off the feet and lower legs. Pheasant and other small birds are sometimes trussed with the head intact.

Wipe the bird inside and out with a damp cloth.

TRUSSING
Chicken

Pull the neck skin over the back then run the string across the flap and under the wings.

Tuck the wings under the back and cross the string over the back.

Turn the bird breast·up·and·bring·the·string·up, crossing at the leg bones, down and crossing under the tail and back up to tie off.

The bird will now retain its plump shape while cooking.

Duck, Goose, Pheasant (see also pages 75, 108)

Tie the legs together and then truss the wings to the body by bringing the string up from the back and around the wings to tie off at the breast.

Note: If the head of the pheasant remains on then twist the neck back and tuck the head under the wings. The breast of pheasant and other small game birds is usually covered with goose fat (as shown) or lard to prevent the breasts drying out.

Turkey

Tie the legs together. Place a fine skewer through the wing joint and into the bird. Then place a second skewer at the end of the wing pinion, through the bird to keep it close to the body for roasting.

BONING
Chicken, Duck, Goose, Turkey

Make a cut along the back bone and using a sharp knife scrape the flesh away from the bone.

Pare the flesh from one side of the rib-cage, working down and toward the tail. Repeat on the other side. Lift out the rib-cage.

Grasp the thigh joint and scrape the flesh away from the thigh bone until the leg joint is reached. Pull the bone out of the remaining flesh. Repeat with the wings if desired. In some cases it is simpler to remove the whole wing.

JOINTING
Chicken, Duck, Goose, Turkey

Split the bird by cutting through the breast bone and down one side of the back bone.

Note: Small birds are usually served whole or split in half.

Cut the back bone off the side and use for stock.

Grasp the leg and cut under the joint and down towards the board, removing the leg and thigh in one piece. Cut the leg from the thigh at the joint.

Cut off the wing with a portion of breast.
This yields eight even-sized pieces.

Rabbit, Hare

Cut off the legs through the back bone, then separate. Cut off the saddle through the back bone.

Split the rib-cage and back bone to give two equal portions.

CARVING
Chicken, Turkey, Duck, Goose
(see also page 75)

Remove the leg, thigh and wing. Make a cut parallel to the rib-cage across the breast.

Continue in this manner to produce even slices containing stuffing. The meat may be carved from legs and served separately thus giving guests a choice of white or dark flesh.

Duck and Goose have only dark flesh.

FIRST COURSES

Most of us enjoy those preliminaries, which should never do more than tantalise our appetites for the main event.

Chosen carefully, the first course should harmonise with what follows; individual dishes may be fine, but a bad combination will detract from each.

Cock-a-Leekie, page 20; Samoosas, page 26

Soups

Soups are essentially either light or substantial. Light soups, hot or cold, may precede most main dishes to their and the diners' mutual advantage. More substantial soups can be meals in themselves or balance a light main course.

Chicken Consommé

My first experience of consommé was in Switzerland. There it was always served piping hot, clear as crystal, and very frequently, but over a period of several weeks never with the same garnish — sometimes the tiniest slices of cucumber, the finest strips of carrot, or perhaps a single slice of hard-boiled egg. The aesthetic was pleasing, the soup light and not damaging to the appetite. Today I serve it chilled as well as hot and either way it is superb with sliced avocado.

Serves 4–6

4–6 cups (1³/₄–2³/₄ pt) jellied chicken stock, strained
2 eggs
salt
white pepper
3 tablespoons dry sherry
1 ripe avocado

Put the stock in a fairly large saucepan. Separate the eggs (store the yolks covered in water for other use), crush the shells, and add to the stock. Beat the whites until just foamy, pour into the stock, and set the pan over moderate heat. Whisk the stock constantly until it comes to the boil. By rotating the whisk towards you, anti-clockwise, the eggs will be more thoroughly pushed through the stock. Reduce the heat as soon as the stock boils, stop whisking, and simmer for 2 minutes. The egg-whites will coagulate and rise to the surface. Remove from the heat and strain through a closely woven cloth (a scalded linen tea-towel will do). Allow the clarified stock to drip through without disturbing the eggs.

Reheat the clear soup, season with salt and pepper to taste, and add the sherry. Peel the avocado, remove the stone, and cut the flesh into thin slices. Put the avocado in a heated tureen and pour the very hot soup over.

Note: To serve cold, leave a little of the stock until quite cold. If it sets firmly, clarify as described above; if not, add ¼ to ½ teaspoon of agar-agar or gelatine before clarifying. Cool the clarified soup before adding the avocado.

Cream of Chicken Soup

I always make my own cream of chicken soup. I have a lot of time for canned soups — particularly if you add a dash of this or a handful of that — but I maintain that canned chicken soup does not measure up, no matter what you do to it.

Serves 4–8

1 kg (2 lb) chicken wings
6–8 cups (2³⁄₄–3¹⁄₂ pt) water
2 medium onions, each studded with 4 cloves
2 celery stalks, quartered
1 bay-leaf
salt
white pepper
2 tablespoons cornflour (cornstarch)
3 tablespoons milk
¹⁄₂ cup (4 fl oz) cream
1¹⁄₄ cups (11 fl oz) milk
snipped chives

Put the chicken wings in a large pan and add the water, vegetables, and bay-leaf. Bring to the boil, removing any scum that rises to the surface. Reduce the heat, cover, and simmer for 1 to 1¹⁄₂ hours, adding salt and pepper after the first hour.

When the chicken is falling from the bones, strain the stock into a large bowl and set aside. Skin the wings and remove any meat. Purée the meat in a blender or food processor with a little of the stock. Pour the strained stock into a pan and stir in the cornflour, which has been mixed to a smooth paste with the 3 tablespoons of milk. Continue to stir until the soup thickens. Add the cream and milk and heat slowly until the soup is very hot. Stir in the puréed chicken and adjust the seasoning. Serve very hot, garnished with the chives.

Chicken Soup with Beans and Avocado

This is another chicken and avocado combination, but so unlike consommé with avocado (page 18) that I could not leave it out. Serve before a light meal or with hot crusty bread for a winter luncheon or supper dish.

Serves 6

1·5 kg (3 lb) chicken pieces
6 black peppercorns
2 sprays of celery leaves
1¹⁄₂ teaspoons salt
white pepper
1 large onion, coarsely chopped
2 medium carrots, sliced
1 leek, split and sliced
1 green (bell) pepper, seeded and diced
1 medium can red kidney beans, rinsed and drained
1 ripe avocado

Put the chicken in a heavy pan with the peppercorns, celery leaves, salt, and pepper to taste. Add enough water to cover the chicken. Bring to the boil, reduce the heat, and simmer for 15 minutes. Remove any scum from the surface and add the onion, carrots, and leek. When the stock returns to simmering-point, cover, and cook for 1 to 1¹⁄₂ hours, until the chicken is very tender.

Remove the chicken from the pan and leave to cool. Strain the stock into another saucepan and discard the vegetables and herbs. Remove the chicken from the bones, discarding the skin, and chop the meat into small pieces. Return to the stock with the beans. Bring to the boil and adjust the seasoning. Reduce the heat and simmer for 5 to 10 minutes. Peel the avocado, remove the stone, and cut the flesh into thin slices. Add to the simmering soup and heat through. Pour the soup into a heated tureen.

Cock-a-Leekie

This traditional Scots fare, made with a boiling fowl, is simple and very good.

Serves 4–6

1 boiling fowl, untrussed
2 bacon rashers, roughly chopped, with rind removed
4 leeks, split and cut into 2·5 cm (1 inch) lengths
6–7 (2¾–3¼ pt) cups chicken or veal stock
salt
freshly ground black pepper
4 parsley sprigs
12 prunes, stoned and roughly chopped

Put the fowl and the bacon in a large saucepan with the leeks and enough stock to cover the bird. Season lightly with salt and pepper and bring slowly to the boil. Reduce the heat, cover, and simmer until the chicken is falling from the bones.

Remove the chicken from the stock, discard the skin and bones, and chop the meat. Return the meat to the soup with the prunes. Adjust the seasoning and simmer for 15 minutes longer.

Mulligatawny Soup

The original Indian version of this soup was a thin, curry-flavoured consommé. The colonial English, with their fondness for thick soup and stews, gradually introduced the chicken and vegetables. This is now a soup of distinction throughout the world. A small portion is enough for a first course; a generous serving, accompanied by crusty bread, makes a hearty supper.

Serves 4–8

1 small boiling fowl, cut into serving portions
1 medium onion, quartered
1 small carrot, cut into chunks
1 celery stalk, quartered
1 teaspoon salt
2 parsley sprigs or ½ teaspoon dried parsley
2 thyme sprigs or ½ teaspoon dried thyme
2 tarragon sprigs or ½ teaspoon dried tarragon
2 small bay-leaves
3 bacon rashers, chopped, with rind removed
1 tablespoon ghee or butter
1 tart cooking apple, peeled, cored, and chopped
3 medium tomatoes, peeled, seeded, and chopped
3 teaspoons (approx.) curry powder
4 tablespoons plain (all-purpose) flour
cayenne or red pepper
salt
⅓ cup (3 fl oz) cream

Put the fowl in a large pan with the vegetables and salt. Tie the parsley, thyme, and tarragon together in a piece of muslin and add to the pan with the bay-leaves. Cover with cold water and bring slowly to the boil, removing scum from the surface if necessary. Reduce the heat and simmer until the meat is tender. Remove the chicken from the pan and leave to cool. Strain the stock into a large jug and discard the vegetables and herbs.

Sauté the bacon in the same pan until the fat starts to run, adding the ghee or butter if more fat is needed. Stir in the apple and tomatoes and cook for 1 or 2 minutes, turning to coat well with the fat. Sprinkle with the curry powder and flour, mixing thoroughly. Gradually add the reserved stock, stirring constantly between each addition, until the soup is smooth and thick (a little more or less stock can be added to produce the consistency you prefer). Simmer the soup very gently for 10 to 15 minutes.

Remove and discard the skin and bones of the cooled chicken; cut the meat into strips or cubes, add to the soup, and heat through. Add cayenne or red pepper and salt to taste, bring to the boil, and then remove from the heat immediately. Stir in the cream and transfer the soup to a heated tureen.

Pâtés, Terrines, and Moulds

Among the waxing and waning fashions in food, pâtés and terrines have remained popular because they are easy to make, easy to eat, and are always different; the slightest variation in their ingredients will alter the subtle balance of flavours.

Chopped Liver

This is one of the most famous chicken liver dishes and probably the most simple. It is the traditional recipe, which I do not think can be improved. Serve on small lettuce leaves.

Serves 4–6

2–3 tablespoons chicken fat
1 large onion, finely chopped
250 g (8 oz) chicken livers,
  trimmed and chopped
salt
white pepper
3 hard-boiled eggs
1 tablespoon finely chopped parsley
lettuce leaves

Heat 2 tablespoons of the fat in a shallow pan and cook the onion until transparent. Add the livers and turn with the onions until they are just cooked, 2 or 3 minutes. Season with salt and pepper to taste. Purée the mixture in a blender or food processor. Remove the yolk from one of the eggs and set it aside. Chop the egg-white and the remaining eggs and fold into the chicken paste, adding a little more of the fat if the mixture is too stiff. It should be of a spreading consistency.

Sieve the reserved egg-yolk and mix lightly with the parsley. Arrange the chopped liver on lettuce leaves and garnish with the parsley mixture.

Chopped Goose Liver
Goose livers and fat can be used in place of chicken — prepared and served in the same way. The flavour is slightly stronger but also very good.

Chicken Liver Pâté de Luxe

There is no delicate nuance of taste in this pâté. A smooth blender pâté, it is crammed with such flavour that it is hard to resist. Serve with crisp toast triangles or, even better, with hunks of crusty French bread.

Serves 10

60 g (2 oz) butter
500 g (1 lb) chicken livers, skinned
   and trimmed
1 large onion, chopped
2 celery stalks, chopped
2 cloves of garlic, crushed
3 tablespoons chopped parsley
1 – 1 ¼ teaspoons salt
1 teaspoon cracked black
   peppercorns, or ground black
   pepper
2 teaspoons dry mustard
¼ teaspoon ground cloves
¼ teaspoon ground allspice
¾ cup (⅓ pt) goose fat or melted
   butter
1 teaspoon Tabasco sauce
2 tablespoons brandy
½ cup (4 fl oz) aspic jelly (page
   95, but optional)

Melt the butter and when sizzling add the chicken livers. Cook for 3 minutes only, turning them until they are sealed on all sides. Remove the livers from the pan with a slotted spoon and set aside. Add the onion, celery, and garlic to the pan and cook gently until softened but not brown. Transfer the contents of the pan to a blender or food processor and purée. Mix the parsley with the salt, black pepper, mustard, and spices in a small bowl and blend gradually into the pâté. Lastly blend in the goose fat or butter, Tabasco, and brandy.

Turn the mixture out of the blender into a lightly oiled pâté mould or terrine. Level the surface with a palette knife and chill in the refrigerator for an hour or so before coating the surface with the liquid aspic.

Chicken Liver Pâté de Luxe

Game Pâté en Croûte

shortcrust pastry (page 201) made
with 185 g (6 oz) butter
250 g (8 oz) minced (ground)
mixed game trimmings
250 g (8 oz) minced (ground) belly
of pork
125 g (4 oz) minced (ground)
chicken livers
1 medium onion, minced (ground)
2 cloves of garlic, crushed
60 g (2 oz) fresh breadcrumbs
2 teaspoons finely chopped fresh
thyme or ¹⁄₂ teaspoon dried thyme
1 tablespoon finely chopped parsley
¹⁄₄ teaspoon ground mace
1–1 ¹⁄₄ teaspoons salt
¹⁄₂ teaspoon white pepper
2 tablespoons brandy
2 eggs
1 tablespoon butter
2 bacon rashers, cut into strips, with
rind removed
125 g (4 oz) mushrooms, sliced
185 g (6 oz) lean veal, cut into
thin strips
90 g (3 oz) lean ham, cut into thin
strips
egg glaze (page 205)

A mixture of any game trimmings can be combined to make the total weight. You will need a terrine or loaf tin of 1 litre (2 pint) capacity. The hinged loaf tins that open flat are perfect.

Make the pastry and leave to chill while you prepare the filling. Mix the minced meats and livers with the onion, garlic, breadcrumbs, herbs, and mace. Season with salt and pepper to taste. Beat the brandy with the eggs and stir into the mixture. Set aside.

Melt the butter in a small pan and quickly sauté the bacon strips until the fat starts to run. Add the mushrooms and cook for 1 minute. Remove from the heat and leave to cool. Pre-heat the oven to moderate.

Cut off a quarter of the pastry and roll the rest to about 5 millimetre (¼ inch) thickness and use to line a terrine or loaf tin. Put half of the game mixture into the tin, pressing it gently into the corners. Mix the mushroom mixture with the veal and ham and use half of it to form a layer on top of the game. Add the remaining game mixture and top with the rest of the mushroom mixture.

Roll out the reserved pastry, brush the edges lightly with water, and cover the game mixture, pressing the edges together to seal. Decorate the top with the pastry trimmings and brush lightly with the egg glaze. Bake in the centre of the oven for 1½ hours. Cover the top with paper or foil halfway through the cooking time to stop the pastry from becoming too brown. Allow the pâté to cool in the tin before removing. Chill before serving.

Game in Aspic

In spite of all the hoo-ha talked about aspic, it involves no real mystery. It is only a savoury jelly and I think it matters little whether you make it from scratch, or pep up a commercial product with wine and herbs. What does matter is the bejewelling effect that aspic has on food. The simplest example is the ordinary hard-boiled egg ('ordinary' being the point). Set a single slice, or a whole quail egg, in aspic and it is magically different. As in this recipe the smallest amount of chopped game, or poultry, becomes a treat as a first course or with a salad for a superb lunch.

Serves 4–8

*1¹/₂–2 cups (14–18 fl oz) aspic
jelly (page 195)*
3 hard-boiled eggs, sliced
60 g (2 oz) unsalted pistachios
1 small dill pickle, thinly sliced
185 g (6 oz) chopped ham
375 g (³/₄ lb) chopped cooked game

Pour a thin layer of cool aspic over the base of a 23 centimetre (9 inch) mould or loaf tin. Arrange in a pattern over the aspic a few slices of egg, pistachios, dill pickle, and some neatly trimmed pieces of ham. Cover with aspic and allow to set. Chop the remaining slices of egg and spread some over the set jelly with some of the chopped game. Add just enough aspic to cover and leave to set. Continue layering the ham and pistachios, game and eggs, between aspic until the mould is full, allowing each layer to set before adding the next. Finish with aspic. Chill before serving.

To remove the mould, dip it quickly into warm water, invert a plate over it, and turn out.

Note: If you do not have the full quantity of cooked game, make it up with a little more ham.

Variations
The rather non-specific game ingredient is deliberate because any poultry or game can be used. They all marry well with ham and the only point to make is that goose or duck skin should be discarded.

Canapés and Finger Food

Croustades

These Melba toast patty cases are my favourite standby for easy appetisers. They can be stored in airtight containers, filled well in advance without losing their crispness, and served hot or cold.

If you are making a few dozen use an uncut sandwich loaf, which will give you twenty-four to thirty cases. Trim the crusts from the whole loaf and cut the bread lengthwise into thin slices, using an electric carving knife if you have one. If the bread is difficult to slice, chill it thoroughly in the freezer for about 1 hour. Cut circles of bread with a 6- to 8-centimetre (2½ to 3 inch) pastry cutter.

Pre-heat the oven to slow. Lightly brush the patty tins with butter and press the circles firmly into the tins. Brush the edges of the bread with butter and dry out in the oven for 20 to 25 minutes until just crisp.

Cool before storing or filling.

Mazagrans

These are small patty cases made with a potato base and served hot, filled with any of the mixtures below. The cases can be flavoured in a variety of ways — for example, add finely chopped fresh herbs, spices, or ground nuts to the basic mixture.

Makes 24

220 g (7 oz) mashed potatoes
30 g (1 oz) plain (all-purpose) flour
1 egg, separated
salt
white pepper
oil

Combine the dry, mashed potatoes with 2 tablespoons of the flour and the lightly beaten egg-yolk. The mixture should form a fairly dry, rather soft dough. Add a little more flour if the mixture is at all sticky. Season with salt and pepper to taste and knead on a lightly floured board. Pre-heat the oven to moderate.

Brush patty tins lightly with oil. Roll the dough out to about 5 millimetre (¼ inch) thickness and use a 6- to 8-centimetre (2½ to 3 inch) pastry cutter to make circles to fit the patty tins. Lift the circles with a palette knife and line the tins, pressing the dough carefully into place.

Beat the egg-white until foamy and use to glaze the inside of the mazagrans. Dry in the centre of the oven for 20 to 25 minutes. Spoon the filling into the cases and serve hot.

Fillings for Croustades and Mazagrans

This quantity is sufficient for 24 to 30 cases

Filling 1

185 g (6 oz) finely chopped cooked poultry or game
¾ cup (⅓ pt) heavy béchamel sauce (page 196)
4 spring onions (scallions), very finely chopped
salt
white pepper
approx. 2 tablespoons cream
cayenne or red pepper

Filling 2

⅓ cup (3 fl oz) mayonnaise
⅓ cup (3 fl oz) sour cream
185 g (6 oz) finely chopped cooked poultry or game
1 medium dill pickle, finely chopped
1 tablespoon finely chopped fresh herbs

Almost any combination of poultry or game can be blended with a fairly heavy sauce and seasoned with chopped herbs, spices, or various pickles to make an excellent filling. The cases can simply be filled with chopped spinach and served as a hot garnish with roast goose or duck. Filled with redcurrant jelly or cranberry sauce, they can accompany cold poultry or game.

Filling 1
Fold the chopped meat into the sauce with the spring onions (scallions). Season with salt and pepper to taste and add enough cream to bring the sauce to a rich but not runny consistency. Divide between the cases, sprinkle lightly with cayenne or red pepper, and serve hot or cold.

Filling 2
Mix the mayonnaise with the sour cream and fold the meat and pickle in. Divide between the cases, sprinkle lightly with the herbs, and serve hot or cold.

Variations
To either of the above recipes add to taste: finely chopped and cooked onion, mushrooms, bacon, celery, or seafood. Chopped pimiento, nuts, capers, and olives add flavour, colour, or texture. Curry powder or paste and cheese also add a new dimension.

Samoosas

These triangles of pastry have a spicy Indian filling. Make a good number because they freeze well, take only a few minutes to cook, and are perfect for all sorts of occasions.

Makes 30–36

125 g (4 oz) plain (all-purpose) flour
½ teaspoon salt
1 tablespoon ghee or butter
3–4 tablespoons lukewarm water
oil for deep-frying

Filling
30 g (1 oz) ghee or butter
1 small onion, finely chopped
2 sweet green chillies, seeded and finely chopped
2 cloves of garlic, crushed
2.5 cm (1 inch) piece of fresh ginger, peeled and grated
½ teaspoon ground bird's eye chilli
½ teaspoon turmeric
375 g (12 oz) minced (ground) raw chicken
2 teaspoons garam masala
juice and finely grated rind of ½ lemon
salt

Sift the flour with the ½ teaspoon of salt into a mixing bowl. Rub in the ghee or butter and mix to a dough with the lukewarm water. Turn on to a lightly floured board and knead until the dough is elastic and shiny. Set aside while you make the filling.

Divide the dough into twelve or fifteen pieces and roll each to a 10-centimetre (4 inch) circle. Cut each circle in half and put a little of the filling on one side of each piece of pastry. Fold into a roughly shaped triangle, pinching to seal (use a little water on the edges only if necessary). Flatten each samoosa slightly and set aside until ready to cook.

Pre-heat the oil for deep-frying to 190°C (375°F) and fry the samoosas for 2 to 3 minutes. Drain on paper towels and serve while very crisp.

Filling
Melt the ghee (or butter) in a frying pan (skillet) and fry the onion, chillies, garlic, and ginger over moderate heat until the onion is the colour of pale straw. Sprinkle with the chilli powder and turmeric and mix together. Stir the chicken into the pan, breaking up any lumps with a fork and turning until it is lightly coloured. Cook over low heat until most of the moisture in the pan has evaporated. Add the garam masala, lemon juice, and rind, mixing all the ingredients thoroughly. Season to taste with salt and put the mixture aside to cool.

Chicken Quiche

Serves 4–6

250 g (8 oz) shortcrust pastry (page 201)
1 tablespoon butter
2 bacon rashers, chopped, with rind removed
6 spring onions (scallions), chopped
125 g (4 oz) button mushrooms, thinly sliced
250 g (8 oz) chopped cooked chicken
2 eggs
¾ cup (⅓ pt) cream
salt, white pepper
1 tablespoon finely snipped chives

These individual quiches are as good hot as cold and suitable for many occasions.

Chill the pastry. Pre-heat the oven to hot. Roll the pastry thinly and use to line individual flan rings. Prick the bases lightly with a fork and line with foil. Bake blind (empty) for 15 minutes. Reduce the temperature to moderate.

Melt the butter and fry the bacon until the fat starts to run. Add the spring onions (scallions) and mushrooms and cook until just softened. Cool slightly before mixing with the chicken. Beat the eggs with the cream and season with salt and pepper to taste. Divide the chicken mixture between the flan cases and pour some of the cream mixture over each. Bake for 15 to 20 minutes until set. Sprinkle with the chives and serve hot or chilled.

Chinese Dishes

The following group of recipes gives only an indication of the style, variety, and range of Chinese cookery. You can, of course, use one dish as part of a full Chinese meal, but any of these recipes can be taken completely out of that context. Each makes a light and interesting first course.

Top: *Peking Drumsticks, page 30;*
centre: *Canton Fruit Chicken;*
foreground: *Threaded Chicken with Peppers, page 30*

Canton Fruit Chicken

Serves 4

½ cup (4 fl oz) fresh orange juice
8 fresh or canned lychees, stoned
* and quartered*
1 tablespoon tomato paste
3 teaspoons light soy sauce
3 tablespoons water
2 tablespoons vegetable oil
250 g (8 oz) boneless chicken,
* thinly sliced across the grain*
1 tablespoon cornflour (cornstarch)
1 teaspoon salt

The abundance of fruit grown in this fertile, subtropical area of China has produced many fruit and savoury combinations. This is typical of the Cantonese style.

Mix the orange juice with the lychees, tomato paste, soy sauce, and water and set aside. Heat the oil in a wok or frying pan (skillet). Dust the chicken slices with the cornflour (cornstarch) seasoned with the salt and lay them in the hot oil. Turn almost immediately and then stir-fry for 2 minutes. Pour the fruit mixture over the chicken and stir gently until the sauce has thickened. Serve at once.

Threaded Chicken with Peppers

Serves 4

3 tablespoons cornflour (cornstarch)
1 teaspoon salt
185 g (6 oz) boneless chicken, cut
    into matchstick strips
2 tablespoons vegetable oil
2·5 cm (1 inch) piece of fresh
    ginger, peeled and halved
1 tablespoon butter
1 dried red chilli, seeded and finely
    chopped
1 red (bell) pepper, seeded and cut
    into matchstick strips
1 green (bell) pepper, seeded and
    cut into matchstick strips
1 teaspoon sugar
2 teaspoons vinegar
2 teaspoons light soy sauce
2 tablespoons chicken stock
1 tablespoon dry sherry

The chicken and peppers for this dish are cut into matchstick-thin strips. As in most Chinese cookery, the preparation takes the time; the cooking process takes a bare 5 minutes.

Put the cornflour (cornstarch) and salt in a bag, add the chicken strips, and shake until they are lightly coated. Heat the oil in a wok or frying pan (skillet), add the ginger, and cook for 1 minute to flavour the oil. Discard the ginger and add the chicken strips to the hot oil. Stir-fry for 1 minute, then remove the chicken and set aside.

Add the butter to the oil with the chilli and toss for 1 minute. Add the strips of red and green (bell) pepper and stir-fry for 1 minute. Sprinkle with the sugar, stir in the vinegar, soy sauce, and stock and cook for 1 minute. Return the chicken to the pan, add the sherry, and stir the mixture for a minute or so until the chicken is very hot. Serve immediately.

Peking Drumsticks

These drumsticks are marinated and steamed before being deep-fried. As a result they are not only very tender but full of flavour, and good hot or cold.

Serves 4

8 small drumsticks
2–3 tablespoons cornflour
    (cornstarch)
oil for deep-frying
Marinade
2 cloves of garlic, crushed
2·5 cm (1 inch) piece of green
    ginger, peeled and finely grated
2 medium onions, chopped
1 teaspoon salt
¼ teaspoon five spice powder
1 tablespoon brown sugar
3 tablespoons soy sauce
2 tablespoons dry sherry

Arrange the drumsticks in a shallow dish and pour the marinade over, turning the chicken until well coated. Cover and leave at room temperature for 2 to 3 hours, turning the drumsticks occasionally.

Put the marinated chicken in a steamer and cook over rapidly boiling water for 20 minutes. Remove from the steamer and leave to cool.

Pre-heat the oil to 185°C (365°F). Dust the drumsticks lightly with the cornflour (cornstarch) and deep-fry until crisp and golden.

Marinade

Mix the garlic with the ginger, onions, salt, spice, sugar, soy sauce, and sherry.

Szechwan Chicken

The Szechwan cuisine goes hand in hand with chillies and spice. This dish is delicious served in Mexican chilli style with crackers.

Serves 4

4 teaspoons cornflour (cornstarch)
1 teaspoon salt
250 g (8 oz) boneless chicken, cut into small cubes
1 teaspoon chilli sauce
¹/₃ cup (3 fl oz) chicken stock
2 tablespoons water
3 teaspoons tomato paste
2 teaspoons wine vinegar
4 tablespoons vegetable oil
1 small onion, minced (ground) or very finely chopped
2 dried red chilli peppers, seeded and finely chopped

Put 2 teaspoons of the cornflour (cornstarch) in a bag with the salt. Add the chicken cubes, and shake until they are lightly coated. Mix the chilli sauce with the remaining cornflour, the stock, water, tomato paste, and vinegar. Heat 2 tablespoons of the oil in a wok or large frying pan (skillet). Add the chicken and stir-fry for 2 minutes. Remove the chicken from the pan and keep hot.

Add the remaining oil to the pan, heat, and stir-fry the onion and chilli peppers for 2 minutes. Pour the chilli sauce mixture over the onion and cook, stirring constantly until the sauce thickens. Return the chicken to the pan and mix with the sauce for a minute or so until very hot. Serve immediately.

Lemon Chicken Wings

These crisp chicken wings are good as appetisers, as part of a smorgasbord or buffet, and as picnic food.

1 kg (2 lb) chicken wings
140 g (4¹/₂ oz) cornflour (cornstarch)
juice and finely grated rind of 1 lemon
1 tablespoon light soy sauce
1 tablespoon maple syrup
oil

Trim the tips from the chicken wings. Mix the cornflour (cornstarch) and lemon rind to a paste with the lemon juice, soy sauce, and maple syrup. Brush the wings with the paste, arrange on a rack, and leave for an hour or so to dry.

Pre-heat the oven to moderately hot. Space the chicken over baking trays brushed with oil. Cook for 20 to 30 minutes, turning once, until the wings are crisp and well browned.

CHICKEN

Chicken, now a staple part of our diet, is still a much-maligned bird, the butt of that hoary old chestnut 'chicken isn't what it used to be' and surrounded by mumblings about battery hens and no flavour. Well, it has been a long time coming and we have had plenty of time — two generations — to get used to it. Intensive poultry farming began as an experiment in the 1920s and was in full swing in 1950.

So, rather than look back, why not look objectively at what we have? Here is an inexpensive and excellent table bird, albeit a bit pale and a bit lacking in flavour, but that is very easily fixed. We have an abundance of herbs, spices, vegetables, and liquors to counterbalance those minor shortcomings.

If you are still not convinced that chickens are not what they used to be — and perhaps distance lends enchantment — consider this: the Romans bred chickens for their tables. Presumably they were free-range birds, the sort that some yearn for, and yet the Romans used to drown their chickens in red wine in order to add flavour.

Black Velvet Chicken, page 36

Roasts

Roast Chicken

Today's quickly bred chickens need careful roasting. Overcooking so ruins the texture that carving them becomes virtually impossible; the fibres split and separate into shreds. I find the following recipe the most satisfactory way of cooking a simple roast chicken. Serve the chicken with your favourite vegetables, bread sauce (page 196) and giblet gravy (page 197) made with the reserved stock.

Serves 4–6

1·5–2 kg (3–4 lb) chicken, with
   giblets
stuffing (optional)
salt
freshly ground black pepper
1 small onion, peeled
a small bunch of fresh herbs — e.g.
   parsley, thyme, rosemary,
   tarragon
3–4 tablespoons butter

Put the giblets (not the liver) in a pan with 2½ cups (1⅛ pints) of water and simmer for 30 minutes. Strain and reserve for gravy. If stuffing the bird, choose one of the recipes on page 206 or use your own favourite version. Loosely fill the neck cavity with the stuffing. Fold the skin over the stuffing, moulding it into a nice plump shape. Secure the skin with tiny poultry pins or coarse thread.

Pre-heat the oven to very hot. Season the bird inside and out with salt and black pepper to taste. Put the whole onion in the cavity of the bird with the herbs and a good tablespoon of the butter. Tie the legs together and fold the wings under the body. Fix the wings securely with pins (which are easier) or string. Spread the remaining butter over the bird and put it, breast side down, on a rack in a roasting dish. Cook in the centre of the oven for 15 minutes. Reduce the temperature to moderate. Turn the bird on to its back and roast for 50 to 60 minutes longer, basting occasionally with the pan-juices. The juices should run clear from a thigh when pierced with a skewer and a leg should rock easily in the socket.

Transfer the bird to a heated dish and leave to stand for a few minutes before carving.

Chicken with Tarragon

Tarragon butter is spread over the breasts, beneath the skin, and inside the bird, so that the flavouring permeates the whole of the chicken. Fresh tarragon really should be used to show the true affinity of this herb with chicken — use the dried leaves only as a last resort. Serve with simple vegetables that do not detract from the chicken; tiny new potatoes, parboiled and finished off in the buttery chicken sauce are particularly good.

Serves 4

125 g (4 oz) butter, softened
1 teaspoon salt
freshly ground black pepper
4 tablespoons chopped fresh tarragon
*   or 1 tablespoon dried tarragon*
*   leaves*
1·5—2 kg (3—4 lb) chicken
tarragon sprigs

Pre-heat the oven to moderately hot. Cream the butter with the salt, lashings of black pepper, and the tarragon. Carefully lift the skin of the chicken, at the neck end, and with your hand loosen the skin over the breast. Spread half of the butter mixture over the breasts, under the skin. Put the remaining butter in the neck cavity, fold the skin over, and secure with small poultry pins or coarse thread. Tie the legs loosely together and fold the wings under the body of the bird.

Put the chicken, breast side down, on a rack in a roasting dish and cook in the centre of the oven for 30 minutes. Carefully turn the bird on to its back, using two spoons to avoid breaking the skin. Cook for 30 to 40 minutes longer, basting occasionally with the pan-juices.

Transfer the chicken to a heated serving dish, pour the pan-juices over, and garnish with the tarragon sprigs.

Chicken with Tarragon

Casseroles, Stews, and Party Pieces

Black Velvet Chicken

Chicken casseroled in champagne and Guinness or dark ale is no longer an extravagance (unless you choose Dom Pérignon) but it does add a special touch to what is now an everyday bird. This quantity serves eight; quarter the recipe for a great dîner à deux. Serve with game chips (page 184), green beans, or Brussels sprouts.

Serves 8

60 g (2 oz) butter
2 large onions, halved and thinly sliced
2–3 kg (4–6 lb) chicken thighs or other pieces
1 teaspoon salt
1 teaspoon freshly ground black pepper
60 g (2 oz) plain (all-purpose) flour
1 cup (9 fl oz) Guinness or dark ale
1 ³/4 cups (³/4 pt) champagne
¹/2 teaspoon ground nutmeg
1 teaspoon dried thyme
2 bay-leaves
250 g (8 oz) small button mushrooms, larger ones halved
1 ¹/4 cups (11 fl oz) cream

Pre-heat the oven to very hot. Melt the butter in a large flameproof casserole and gently fry the onions until they are transparent. Add the chicken pieces and brown lightly on all sides. Season with the salt and black pepper. Put the uncovered casserole in the oven and roast the chicken for 30 minutes.

Remove the casserole from the oven. Sprinkle the flour over the chicken, on top of the stove, and turn the pieces in the pan-juices until the flour is the colour of pale straw. Gradually add the Guinness or dark ale and champagne, stirring until the sauce simmers. Add the nutmeg, thyme, and bay-leaves. Cover and return to the oven for 30 minutes, or until the chicken is tender.

Shortly before the chicken is cooked, simmer the mushrooms in the cream for 3 or 4 minutes, until they are just tender. Strain the cream into the casserole. Arrange the chicken pieces on a heated serving dish and keep hot. On top of the stove, bring the sauce just to the boil, whisking constantly until slightly thickened. Adjust the seasoning and spoon the sauce over the chicken.

Golden Chicken Casserole

This attractive casserole is good cooked the night before needed. The sauce should be finished just before serving.

Serves 4–6

1.5 kg (3 lb) chicken, cut into serving pieces
90 g (3 oz) plain (all-purpose) flour
60 g (2 oz) butter
4 medium onions, peeled and quartered
2 celery stalks, cut into 2 cm (³/4 inch) pieces

Pre-heat the oven to moderate. Remove any skin from the chicken pieces. Put the 90 grams (3 ounces) of flour in a paper bag or plastic bag, add the chicken, and shake until well coated.

Melt the 60 grams (2 ounces) of butter in a large frying pan (skillet) and lightly cook the chicken pieces until they are the colour of pale straw. Transfer them from the pan to a casserole. Add the onions and celery to the pan and sauté for 3 or 4 minutes. Add the peppers and cook for 3 minutes. Stir in the mushrooms and sprinkle with the turmeric, stirring until the mushrooms are lightly coated

*2 red (bell) peppers, seeded and
    coarsely chopped*
*125 g (4 oz) button mushrooms,
    halved*
¼ teaspoon ground turmeric
½ cup (4 fl oz) white wine
1 cup (9 fl oz) chicken stock
salt and pepper
½ cup (4 fl oz) cream
1 tablespoon softened butter
*1 tablespoon plain (all-purpose)
    flour*

with the pan-juices. Add the wine and half the chicken stock; bring gently to the boil. Reduce the heat and season with salt and pepper to taste. Pour the mixture over the chicken, add the cream, and cover. Cook in the centre of the oven for 45 minutes, or until the chicken is tender. Remove the casserole from the oven and strain off the cooking liquid; keep the chicken and vegetables warm while you finish the sauce.

Melt the 1 tablespoon of butter in a small pan. Add the 1 tablespoon of flour, and stir into the butter to form a smooth paste. Cook for 1 minute. Add a quarter of the reserved chicken liquid, stirring well. Repeat until all the liquid is used and a smooth sauce is formed. If the sauce is too thick, thin with the remaining chicken stock — it should just coat the back of the spoon. Adjust the seasoning and pour the sauce over the chicken and vegetables.

Rhubarb Chicken Masaryk

This recipe was given to me many years ago by a member of the Masaryk family living in London. It is unusual and interesting. Serve with tiny, crisp Brussels sprouts or a green salad.

Serves 4–6

*2 tablespoons goose fat or chicken
    fat*
1·5–2 kg (3–4 lb) chicken
1 large onion, halved and sliced
*1 bunch of rhubarb, trimmed and
    sliced*
½ cup (4 fl oz) chicken stock
salt
freshly ground black pepper
*4 medium potatoes, peeled and
    thickly sliced*
*125 g (4 oz) button mushrooms,
    halved*
2 teaspoons cornflour (cornstarch)

Heat the fat in a deep flameproof casserole and brown the chicken on all sides, starting with the breasts. Lift the chicken from the pan and set aside. Pre-heat the oven to moderate. Add the onion to the pan, lightly brown, and spread evenly over the base of the pan. Return the chicken to the pan and pack the sliced rhubarb around the sides. Pour in the stock and season to taste. Cover and cook in the centre of the oven for 50 minutes.

Parboil the potatoes in lightly salted water for 6 or 7 minutes. Add to the casserole with the mushrooms, cover, and cook for 30 minutes, until the chicken is tender. Transfer the bird to a heated serving dish and keep hot. Mix the cornflour to a smooth paste with a little cold water and stir into the casserole. Simmer on top of the stove until the sauce clears and thickens. Adjust the seasoning and serve with the chicken.

Trapper's Stew

Serves 4–6

60 g (2 oz) butter
1 tablespoon vegetable oil
1.5–2 kg (3–4 lb) chicken pieces
1 large onion, halved and thinly sliced
2 large potatoes, peeled and cut into 2 cm (³/4 inch) dice
1 small green (bell) pepper, seeded and coarsely chopped
3 tomatoes, peeled and quartered
1 ½ cups (14 fl oz) chicken stock
¼–½ teaspoon cayenne or red pepper
1 ½ tablespoons Worcestershire sauce
salt
250 g (8 oz) frozen or canned lima beans, thawed and drained
250 g (8 oz) sweetcorn kernels
1 tablespoon plain (all-purpose) flour
1 tablespoon softened butter

This is one of many traditional dishes created by pioneers, hunters, and trappers, who, when forced to live off the land, developed all-in-together pot meals. They used possum, squirrel, rabbit, or any large or small game they could hunt or trap. This version, using chicken, is hearty and very good, even better if made a day ahead.

Melt the 60 grams (2 ounces) of butter with the oil in a large flameproof casserole over fairly high heat. Brown the chicken on all sides, without overcrowding the pan, removing the pieces as they are finished.

Fry the onion in the pan until it is transparent. Add the potatoes and pepper and toss with the onion until lightly browned. Return the chicken to the casserole with the tomatoes, stock, cayenne or red pepper to taste, and Worcestershire sauce. Bring to the boil, season with salt, and reduce the heat until the sauce is barely simmering. Cover and cook for 45 to 50 minutes. Add the beans and corn, cover, and cook for 15 minutes, or until the chicken is tender. Work the flour with the 1 tablespoon of butter and add to the pot in small pieces, whisking or stirring between each addition. Adjust the seasoning and cook for 5 minutes longer before serving.

Prairie Steamer

Originally the corn husks were used as dividers between each layer of food, keeping moisture and steam in the pot. This is not necessary today; cook on top of the stove or over hot coals and serve with crusty bread and salads.

Serves 4–6

8 corn cobs, halved
salt
2 kg (4 lb) chicken pieces
1 tablespoon Spanish paprika
16 small or 8 large frankfurters
freshly ground black pepper
12 spring onions (scallions), chopped
12 small potatoes, unpeeled
2 cups (18 fl oz) chicken stock
1 teaspoon Tabasco sauce or chilli sauce

Arrange eight of the halved corn cobs over the base of a deep pot and sprinkle lightly with salt. Rub the skin of the chicken with the paprika and salt and put half of the pieces in a layer on top of the corn. Cover with the frankfurters and season with black pepper. Sprinkle the spring onions (scallions) over the top with the potatoes. Season lightly, add the rest of the chicken pieces, and pack the remaining halved corn cobs over the top. Mix the stock with the Tabasco or chilli sauce, pour into the pot, and cover tightly, using foil or paper if necessary to make a good seal. Cook on top of the stove, over gentle heat, for 1½ to 2 hours, until the chicken is tender. Serve straight from the pot.

Chicken Italienne

Prepare the sauce 24 hours before using, to give the flavours time to blend. The sauce keeps well in the refrigerator and is also useful for basting barbecued or grilled poultry and game. Serve with a mixed green salad.

Serves 4

3 tablespoons dry red wine
1/3 cup (3 fl oz) wine vinegar
3 tablespoons olive oil
1 small onion, finely chopped
1 clove of garlic, crushed
1/2 teaspoon ground chilli
1/2 teaspoon ground rosemary
1/2 teaspoon dried oregano
1 teaspoon salt
2 tablespoons olive oil
1 large onion, halved and sliced
1·5 kg (3 lb) chicken, quartered

Mix the wine with the vinegar, 3 tablespoons of olive oil, chopped onion, garlic, chilli, rosemary, oregano, and salt in a glass jar. Shake well and refrigerate for at least 24 hours. Heat the 2 tablespoons of olive oil in a heavy-based frying pan (skillet) and sauté the sliced onion until golden. Reduce the heat and brown the chicken evenly on all sides. Pour the chilled sauce over the chicken and bring to simmering-point. Cover and cook for 30 to 40 minutes, until tender. Turn the chicken in the sauce once or twice during the cooking time.

Transfer to a heated serving dish and coat with the sauce.

Note: The quantity of sauce is just enough to cook a double quantity of chicken.

Cumin Chicken

The spicing in Indian cookery is so perfectly balanced that it is rare to find a dish with one dominant flavour. Cumin chicken is one of these rarities — the undertones of the other ingredients are apparent, but allow the cumin to have centre stage. Serve simply with rice, mild chutneys, and sambals.

Serves 4–6

1·5–2 kg (3–4 lb) chicken pieces
juice of 1 large lemon
30 g (1 oz) plain (all-purpose)
   flour
1 teaspoon salt
1 teaspoon cayenne or red pepper
60 g (2 oz) ghee or butter
1 large onion, finely chopped
2 cloves of garlic, crushed
2·5 cm (1 inch) piece of fresh
   ginger, peeled and finely grated
2 teaspoons cumin seed
1 cup (9 fl oz) cream
1 cup (9 fl oz) natural yogurt
2 strips of lemon rind, pared very
   finely
lemon twists (page 209)

Brush the chicken pieces liberally with the lemon juice and set aside for 15 minutes. Mix the flour with the salt and cayenne or red pepper. Drain excess lemon juice from the chicken and dry with paper towels before lightly dusting with the seasoned flour.

Melt the ghee or butter in a heavy frying pan (skillet) over moderate heat. Lightly brown the chicken pieces on all sides. Remove them from the pan and set aside. Add the onion, garlic, ginger, and cumin seed to the pan and cook fairly quickly until the onion is straw-coloured but not browned. Add the cream, yogurt, and lemon rind, stirring in well. Return the chicken to the pan, turning the pieces in the sauce until they are coated. Cover and simmer gently for 45 to 50 minutes, or until the chicken is tender.

Lift the chicken from the sauce, arrange on a heated serving platter with rice, and keep hot. Increase the heat and reduce the sauce by boiling rapidly for a few minutes. Adjust the seasoning, discard the lemon rind, and pour the sauce over the chicken. Garnish with lemon twists.

Cumin Chicken

Chicken Sarma

This Balkan dish of well-seasoned, minced (ground) chicken wrapped in cabbage-leaves or vine-leaves, is inexpensive and good enough for a party. The recipe is easily doubled or trebled. Serve it very hot with a crisp green salad.

Serves 4

8 large cabbage-leaves, or 16–20 vine-leaves
3 tablespoons butter
1 large onion, finely chopped
1 clove of garlic, crushed
375 g (12 oz) raw chicken, minced (ground)
90 g (3 oz) seedless raisins
salt and pepper
2 tablespoons finely chopped parsley
1 egg, lightly beaten
3/4 cup (1/3 pt) chicken stock
1 tablespoon tomato paste
1/2 teaspoon dried oregano
2 tablespoons butter
30 g (1 oz) fresh breadcrumbs

Use a sharp knife to pare down any thick stalk on the cabbage. Blanch the leaves in boiling salted water for 5 minutes. Drain and then spread the cabbage-leaves or vine-leaves on a board.

Melt the 3 tablespoons of butter and gently fry the onion until transparent. Add the garlic and chicken and cook until the chicken is lightly browned, stirring to break up any lumps. Mix in the rice and raisins, seasoning with salt and pepper to taste. Set aside to cool before adding the parsley and egg.

Divide the cooled filling between the leaves, folding and rolling each one into a parcel. Arrange the rolls in a flameproof serving dish or casserole. Mix the chicken stock with the tomato paste and oregano, bring quickly to the boil, and season to taste. Pour over the rolls, cover, and simmer for 15 minutes.

In the meantime, melt the 2 tablespoons of butter, add the breadcrumbs, and turn in the butter until they are crisp and golden. Sprinkle over the rolls and serve immediately.

Chicken Russus

Serves 4

3 large tomatoes, peeled, seeded, and chopped
3 tablespoons tomato paste
2 bay-leaves
3 cloves
1 small onion, halved
1 cup (9 fl oz) water
salt
freshly ground black pepper
2 slices of bread, with crusts removed
500 g (1 lb) finely minced (ground) chicken
1 large onion, finely minced (ground)
1/2 teaspoon turmeric
1/2 teaspoon dried chervil or tarragon
1 egg, lightly beaten

These spicy golden chicken balls are simmered in a rich Algerian sauce. Serve them with potatoes and a salad or green vegetable.

Put the tomatoes and paste in a smallish saucepan with the bay-leaves, cloves, and halved onion. Add the water and bring to the boil. Reduce the heat, season with salt and pepper to taste, and simmer very gently, uncovered.

While the sauce is cooking, soak the bread in a little water. Mix the chicken with the minced (ground) onion, turmeric, and chervil or tarragon. Season with about 1/2 teaspoon of salt and plenty of black pepper. Squeeze the water out of the bread. Mix the bread thoroughly with the chicken mixture. Add only enough of the egg to bind the ingredients firmly together. Form the mixture into 2·5-centimetre (1 inch) balls.

Discard the onion, bay-leaves, and cloves from the sauce and transfer it to a shallow pan, adding a little more water if the sauce is very thick — it should just coat the back of a spoon. Put the chicken balls in the sauce, cover, and simmer for 20 minutes.

Chicken Russus

Boiling Fowl

Chicken with Lemon Sauce

When I began this book, lemon chicken was on my 'not to be included' list. In the middle of the time I spent testing chicken recipes I was invited out to dinner and to my dismay the main course was chicken. The dismay was short lived, however, as the chicken was deliciously different, and the Stavros family only too happy to share the recipe. Serve with rice and a crisp salad.

Serves 4–6

2 lemons
1·5–2 kg (3–4 lb) boiling fowl
2 medium carrots, sliced
2 medium onions, sliced
2 celery stalks, sliced
salt
60 g (2 oz) butter
250 g (8 oz) button mushrooms
125 g (4 oz) slivered almonds
2 egg-yolks
3 tablespoons cream
3 tablespoons dry sherry
white pepper

Squeeze the juice from the lemons and put the lemon halves in the cavity of the bird. Tie the legs together, fold the wings under the body, and put the bird in a deep casserole. Pour the lemon juice over the fowl and pack the carrots, onions, and celery around the sides. Add 1½ teaspoons of salt and just enough boiling water to cover the bird. Pre-heat the oven to moderately slow. Bring the liquid back to boiling-point on top of the stove. Cover the casserole with foil and the lid and cook in the centre of the oven for 1½ to 2 hours, until the bird is tender.

Lift the fowl from the stock, tipping to drain the liquid from the cavity. Discard the trussing string and the lemon halves. Transfer the bird to a heated serving dish and keep hot. Melt the butter in a small pan and quickly sauté the mushrooms and almonds until the mushrooms are tender and the almonds lightly browned. Arrange around the chicken.

Measure 1 cup of the cooking liquid and bring to the boil in a small pan. Beat the egg-yolks with the cream, add 2 tablespoons of the hot stock, and mix until smooth. Whisk the egg mixture into the pan, reduce the heat, and stir until the sauce thickens. Add the sherry, adjust the seasoning, and simmer for 2 minutes. Pour the sauce over the bird.

Berber Chicken

This treatment of boiling fowl is distinctly north African in origin and flavour. The short roasting to finish the cooking completely eliminates that dreadful 'grey bird' syndrome. Serve with braised chicory (page 181) and potato balls (page 185).

Serves 4–6

2 kg (4 lb) boiling fowl
2 tablespoons softened butter

Make the stuffing and leave it to cool. Spoon the cooled stuffing loosely into the body and neck cavities of the fowl. Secure the openings with coarse thread, tie the wings and legs, and put the bird

Stuffing

3 tablespoons olive oil or vegetable
    oil
1 medium onion, chopped
1 small clove of garlic, crushed
375 g (12 oz) minced (ground)
    lean lamb
60 g (2 oz) slivered almonds
60 g (2 oz) pinenuts
75 g (2½ oz) cooked long-grain
    rice
½ teaspoon ground nutmeg
½ teaspoon mixed spice
juice and grated rind of 1 lemon
salt
freshly ground black pepper

in a wok or saucepan. Add barely enough cool, lightly salted water to reach three-quarters of the way up the side of the fowl. Bring to the boil, remove any scum from the surface, and reduce the heat until the water is just simmering. Cover and simmer for 1¼ hours until the bird is almost tender but not completely cooked.

Pre-heat the oven to hot. Lift the bird carefully from the stock. Pat dry with paper towels and rub all over with the butter. Put the bird in a roasting dish and cook in the centre of the oven for 25 to 30 minutes, until crisp and golden. Remove the trussing string, transfer the bird to a heated serving dish, and garnish with the vegetables.

Stuffing

Heat the oil in a large frying pan (skillet) and gently cook the onion and garlic until the onion is transparent. Stir in the lamb and cook gently until it begins to change colour, breaking it up with a fork. Add the nuts, rice, spices, and the lemon juice and rind. Season with salt and black pepper to taste. Simmer for 4 or 5 minutes, remove from the heat, and leave to cool.

Ivory Chicken

Serves 4–6

1·5–2 kg (3–4 lb) boiling fowl
1 lemon, halved
2 large carrots, cut into chunks
2 large onions, quartered
1 celery stalk, quartered
1 spray of celery leaves
salt
white pepper
185 g (6 oz) mushroom caps,
    turned (page 209)
3 tablespoons water
2 teaspoons lemon juice
1½ tablespoons butter
1½ tablespoons plain (all-purpose)
    flour
3 egg-yolks
3 tablespoons cream

There is nothing drab about this slowly simmered fowl, coated with the palest sauce and garnished with mushrooms and bacon rolls. Serve with Portuguese cucumber (page 181).

Rub the skin of the fowl with the cut lemon. Put the bird in a large saucepan with the carrots, onions, celery, and celery leaves. Add enough warm water barely to cover the bird and season lightly with salt and pepper. Bring the water to a slow simmer (it should just shimmer). Remove any scum from the surface and cover the pan tightly, using foil or greaseproof paper to ensure that it is well sealed. Simmer for 2 hours, or more, until the bird is tender (this will depend on the size and age of the fowl).

Remove the pan from the heat and allow the bird to cool slightly in the stock. Simmer the prepared mushrooms in the water and lemon juice for 2 or 3 minutes, until they are just tender. Strain and keep hot. Carefully lift the chicken from the stock, transfer to a heated serving dish, and keep hot. Reserve 1½ cups (14 fluid ounces) of the stock. The remaining stock may be strained and frozen for future use.

Melt the butter in a heavy pan, stir in the flour, and cook for 1 or 2 minutes over low heat without browning. Gradually add the reserved stock, stirring or whisking between each addition until the sauce is smooth. Simmer for 3 or 4 minutes. Beat the egg-yolks with the cream. Remove the pan from the heat and whisk the yolk mixture into the sauce. Reheat to just below boiling-point and pour over the chicken. Garnish with the mushroom caps.

Poached Chicken

Gently poached chicken served with similarly cooked vegetables and a sauce, can be one of the simplest ways to cook and enjoy a young bird or fowl. Without care it can be that most dreadful chicken dish, the grey offering. This recipe involves no fuss and minimum care. If you want to stuff the bird choose one of the recipes on page 206. A good sauce to accompany the chicken is a simple velouté (page 198). Prepare it shortly before the end of the cooking time.

Serves 4

1.5–2 kg (3–4 lb) chicken or fowl
1 tablespoon Angostura bitters
1 quantity of stuffing (optional)
chicken stock or water
4 medium onions, peeled
4 small leeks, trimmed and split
4 celery stalks, cut into equal
  lengths
4 medium carrots, trimmed
1 bay-leaf
a small parsley sprig
2 cloves
½ teaspoon dried thyme or sage
salt
freshly ground black pepper

Brush the chicken evenly with the bitters and put aside to dry. Brush again. If you wish, stuff the bird, filling the cavity loosely. Sew the opening with coarse thread, tie the legs together, and fold the wings neatly under the body, securing with poultry pins. Choose a wide pan that is not too deep and which has a lid — the ideal vessel is a wok. Put the bird in the pan and add enough warm stock or water to reach just halfway up the sides of the chicken. Put the pan over a low to moderate heat and add the onions, leeks tied in a bundle, celery tied in a bundle, and the carrots. Bring the stock or water almost to boiling-point, remove any scum from the surface, and immediately reduce the heat until the water is barely shimmering. Add the bay-leaf, parsley, cloves, and herbs, seasoning with a little salt and pepper. Cover and simmer for 1½ to 2 hours, depending on the age of the bird. The legs should move very easily when the chicken is cooked.

Carefully lift the bird on to a heated serving dish and remove the trussing string. Arrange the vegetables around the chicken before serving. Coat lightly with sauce or serve separately.

Note: If the chicken has been cooked in water, you will now have a well-flavoured stock. Strain the liquid, freeze it, and use to poach the next bird, and the next ... The stock and the poached chickens will become better and better.

Chicken with Seafood

Chicken Pebane

Most continents seem to have a dish that combines chicken and seafood. There is the French chicken Marengo (page 48), the Spanish paella, and the Creole jambalaya. This African version has a touch of fire about it and needs no more than a crisp salad to make it complete. Cook and serve from the same pan.

Poached Chicken

Serves 4–6

500 g (1 lb) potatoes, peeled and
    cut in 1-cm (½ inch) slices
1·5–2 kg (3–4 lb) chicken pieces
salt
1 tablespoon butter
1 tablespoon vegetable oil
1 large onion, finely sliced
2 large cloves of garlic, crushed
½ cup (4 fl oz) tomato paste
approx. ½ teaspoon ground bird's
    eye chilli
1¼ cups (11 fl oz) chicken stock
185 g (6 oz) green prawns, peeled
    and deveined

Cover the potatoes with iced water and set them aside. Lightly season the chicken joints with salt. Heat the butter with the oil in a large pan over moderate heat. Fry the chicken pieces on all sides until they are golden. Remove the chicken from the pan and set aside.

Add the onion to the pan and cook fairly quickly until it is still crisp but lightly browned. Reduce the heat, add the garlic, and cook for 2 minutes without browning the garlic. Stir the tomato paste in and allow the sauce to simmer. Add the ground chilli (you may prefer to use less or more, but beware of adding too much). Stir the stock into the sauce and when it is simmering adjust the salt and chilli seasoning, remembering that the potatoes will absorb some of the flavour. Return the chicken to the pan and spoon some of the sauce over each piece. Cover and simmer for 20 minutes.

Drain the potatoes and add to the pan, pressing the slices lightly into the sauce. Cover and simmer for 10 minutes. Add the prawns, laying them over the surface of the sauce to steam. It may be necessary to add a little more chicken stock if the sauce has reduced too much. Cover and cook for 10 minutes longer, or until the potatoes are tender.

Chicken Marengo

Serves 4–6

1·5–2 kg (3–4 lb) chicken pieces,
    skinned
salt
freshly ground black pepper
2 tablespoons butter
2 tablespoons olive oil
2 medium onions, finely chopped
2 cloves of garlic, crushed
1 tablespoon plain (all-purpose)
    flour
approx. 1½ cups (14 fl oz) chicken
    stock
3 tablespoons dry sherry or white
    wine
3 tablespoons tomato paste
4 parsley sprigs
2 bay-leaves
2 sprays of celery leaves
125 g (4 oz) button mushrooms,
    halved if large
6–8 green prawns or yabbies
    (écrevisses), peeled, but with the
    heads left on
juice of ½ lemon
cayenne or red pepper
4–6 eggs (optional)

Napoleon's Swiss cook improvised this dish in 1800, after the Battle of Marengo. Legend has it that Napoleon would not eat until a battle was over, by which time I imagine he would have been mighty hungry. Soldiers were sent out to find food on near-by farms and came back with chicken, olive oil, tomatoes, eggs, and crayfish — not a bad haul. Put together with a short cut here and there, this is one of the best-ever chicken dishes. While eggs are traditionally served with chicken Marengo, I think that they add nothing worthwhile to the flavour.

Season the chicken pieces with salt and black pepper. Melt the butter with the oil in a large, heavy casserole. Quickly sauté the chicken pieces until golden on all sides. Lift the chicken from the pan and set aside.

Add the onions and garlic to the pan and cook over gentle heat until the onions are transparent. Sprinkle the flour into the pan, stirring into the pan-juices, and cook for 1 minute without browning. Gradually add the stock, stirring between each addition, until a smooth sauce is formed. Stir in the sherry or wine and the tomato paste. Adjust the seasoning and simmer gently for 3 or 4 minutes. Tie the parsley, bay-leaves, and celery leaves together and add to the pan with the chicken, turning the pieces in the sauce until they are well coated. If the sauce is too thick, add a little more stock. Cover and simmer for 40 minutes.

Add the mushrooms to the casserole and simmer for 15 minutes. Lay the prawns or yabbies on the chicken. Cook for 10 minutes. Lift the chicken, mushrooms, and prawns from the pan, arrange on a heated serving dish, and keep hot. Bring the sauce to the boil and discard the herbs. Add the lemon juice and cayenne or red pepper to taste. Pour the sauce over the chicken and garnish, if you wish, with the eggs, which have been lightly fried or poached.

Chicken Marengo

Chicken and Seafood Fondue

Another of the many chicken and seafood combinations, this is a Japanese fondue. All the food is prepared and laid out for cooking by each person — an easy way to entertain. Use a fondue dish or even a controlled-heat deep-frier to keep the stock simmering. Each person has chopsticks or fondue forks.

Serves 4–6

2 whole chicken breasts, skinned, boned, and cut across the grain into 2·5 cm (1 inch) strips
12 green prawns, shelled and deveined
24 fresh oysters
1 medium white radish, thinly sliced
12 spring onions (scallions), cut into 2·5 cm (1 inch) lengths
125 g (4 oz) button mushrooms
2 celery stalks, cut into 2·5 cm (1 inch) lengths
4 cups (1 3/4 pt) chicken stock
250 shirataki noodles, drained
315 g (10 oz) cooked long-grain rice (optional)
1/3 cup (3 fl oz) light soy sauce
1/4 cup (2 fl oz) sake or dry sherry

Arrange the prepared chicken, seafood, and vegetables attractively on a large platter within easy reach of everybody. Bring the chicken stock to the boil, add the shirataki noodles, and heat thoroughly. Strain the stock into the fondue dish and serve the noodles and rice on heated plates. Add half of the soy sauce and the sake or sherry to the chicken stock. Serve the remaining soy sauce in a small dish for dipping.

Note: Shirataki noodles are available from Asian supply stores.

Chicken Smothered with Oysters

Serve this rich but simple dish with a crisp green vegetable — green beans or broccoli — and a mixed salad.

Serves 4–6

1·5–2 kg (3–4 lb) chicken pieces
salt
white pepper
3–4 tablespoons vegetable oil
3/4 cup (1/3 pt) milk
24 fresh or bottled (not canned) oysters, drained
3/4 cup (1/3 pt) cream

Season the chicken pieces with salt and pepper. Heat the oil in a shallow pan and pre-heat the oven to moderately hot. Quickly brown the chicken in the hot fat, transferring the pieces to a baking dish as they are browned. Pour the milk over the chicken, cover, and bake in the centre of the oven for 40 minutes.

Mix the oysters with the cream and pour over the chicken. Cover and cook for 15 to 20 minutes longer, until the chicken is tender. Transfer the chicken to a heated serving dish. Adjust the seasoning of the sauce and pour over the chicken. Serve immediately.

Chicken Amager

This Danish chicken and prawn casserole is spicy (but not overly so), rich, and delicious. I think it is at its best served simply with noodles and a crisp green salad or vegetables.

Serves 4

2 tablespoons butter
1 tablespoon vegetable oil
1.5–2 kg (3–4 lb) chicken pieces
1 large onion, chopped
1 clove of garlic, crushed
1 ½ tablespoons plain (all-purpose)
  flour
¼ teaspoon cayenne or red pepper
½ teaspoon Hungarian paprika
1 teaspoon finely chopped fresh dill
  or ½ teaspoon dried green dill
  tips
2 cups (18 fl oz) chicken stock
salt
white pepper
2 tablespoons Madeira
1 large bay-leaf
250 g (8 oz) green prawns, peeled
  and deveined
250 g (8 oz) fresh asparagus,
  blanched, or 340-g (11 oz/picnic
  size) can asparagus spears,
  drained
½ cup (4 fl oz) cream

Pre-heat the oven to moderately hot. Melt the butter with the oil in a frying pan (skillet). Brown the chicken pieces on all sides, without overcrowding the pan, and transfer to a casserole. Add the onion to the frying pan (skillet) and cook gently until transparent. Add the garlic and cook for 1 minute. Sprinkle the flour, cayenne or red pepper, paprika, and dill over the onion mixture and stir for 1 or 2 minutes. Add the stock gradually, stirring constantly between each addition, until the sauce is smooth. Season with salt and pepper to taste. Stir the Madeira into the sauce and pour it over the chicken. Add the bay-leaf to the casserole, cover, and cook for 40 minutes.

Add the prawns and asparagus and cook, still covered, for 20 minutes, or until the chicken is tender. Stir the cream into the sauce, discard the bay-leaf, and adjust the seasoning before serving.

Spatchcocks

Spatchcocks, the tiniest of the chickens, are very young and tender. They are usually cooked with fairly delicate flavouring and plenty of butter.

Caucasian Fried Chickens

These tiny pressed chickens are lightly roasted and then fried until crisp and golden. Serve hot or cold with salad or vegetables and sour plum sauce (page 197).

Serves 4

4 spatchcocks, boned
1 large clove of garlic, halved
salt
½ cup (4 fl oz) natural yogurt
butter
watercress

Pre-heat the oven to slow. Bone and flatten the birds, following the directions on page 13. Rub both sides of the spatchcocks with the garlic and salt. Lay, cut side down, on a baking tray. Brush with the yogurt and roast for 15 minutes.

Melt the butter in a large frying pan (skillet) over moderate heat. Place as many birds as the pan will hold, skin side down, in the hot butter. Press the chickens while they are frying. Cover with foil, put another pan on top, and weight with anything heavy — old-fashioned flat-irons or a couple of bricks are perfect. Reduce the heat until the chickens are gently sizzling. Fry for 8 to 10 minutes, turn the birds, replace the weight, and cook for 10 minutes longer, until crisp and brown.

Keep the cooked birds hot at the bottom of the oven and finish cooking the other birds in the same way. They will need a shorter frying time because of their longer pre-cooking — 5 to 6 minutes on each side. Arrange the birds on a heated serving platter and garnish with watercress.

Caucasian Fried Chickens

Gingered Spatchcocks

There are many ways to use ginger with chicken, and it is a good combination. This is the easy way and I think it is as good as any of the more elaborate versions. Serve with braised celery (page 180) and a crisp green salad or vegetable.

Serves 4

2 spatchcocks, halved and trimmed
1 teaspoon salt
½ teaspoon freshly ground black pepper
1 teaspoon ground ginger
90 g (3 oz) butter
2·5 cm (1 inch) piece of fresh ginger, peeled and finely grated
1 small clove of garlic, crushed
juice of 1 lemon

Pre-heat the grill (broiler) to high. Season the spatchcock halves on each side with the salt, black pepper, and ground ginger, rubbing the seasoning well into the skin. Melt the butter in a small pan, add the fresh ginger and garlic, and cook over very low heat for 3 or 4 minutes.

Put the spatchcocks, skin side up, in the grill (broiler) pan. Stir the lemon juice into the butter mixture and pour over the chicken. Grill (broil) for 2 minutes, reduce the heat to medium, and cook for 5 minutes longer. Turn the birds and baste with the sauce. Grill (broil) for 3 or 4 minutes, until tender. Transfer to a heated serving dish, season the sauce if necessary, and spoon over the chicken.

Honey Lemon Spatchcocks

Baby chicken halves are grilled (broiled) and brushed with a piquant sauce. Serve with tiny new potatoes and a very crisp salad.

Serves 4

oil
2 spatchcocks, halved
360 g (11½ oz) honey
juice of 1 lemon
2 teaspoons Dijon mustard
½ teaspoon salt
4 thin slices of lemon

Pre-heat the grill (broiler) to medium and lightly brush the pan with oil. Arrange the spatchcock halves, skin side down, in the pan. Brush the cut side of the birds with oil. Grill (broil) at the furthest point from the heat for 10 to 15 minutes. Brush the birds with oil again, if necessary.

Mix the honey with the lemon juice, mustard, and salt. Brush the cooked sides of the chicken liberally with the honey mixture, turn them skin side up, and grill (broil) for 5 minutes until golden. Baste with the honey sauce and cook for 5 to 10 minutes, until tender. The juices should run clear when the birds are pierced with a skewer. Serve garnished with the slices of lemon.

Note: The honey-lemon mixture makes a very good barbecue sauce.

Grilled (Broiled) Spatchcocks with Wine Sauce

Tender to start with, these baby chickens are drenched with the full flavour of the herbs and wine before and after grilling (broiling). Serve with a crisp green vegetable or salad.

*Grilled (Broiled) Spatchcocks with Wine
Sauce*

Serves *4*

2 *spatchcocks*
125 *g (4 oz) pale button
   mushrooms, sliced*
1 *small onion, finely chopped*
¹/₂ *teaspoon salt*
freshly ground black pepper
2 *tablespoons vegetable oil or olive
   oil*
1 *cup (9 fl oz) red wine*
2 *parsley sprigs*
2 *bay-leaves*
2 *sprays of celery leaves or 1 celery
   stalk, quartered*
vegetable oil
1 *teaspoon arrowroot*
¹/₂ *cup (4 fl oz) chicken stock*
watercress (optional)

Use kitchen snips or poultry shears to halve the spatchcocks. Cut first through the breastbone and then the spine. Trim away any small backbones and discard. Lay the birds in a shallow dish and set aside.

Mix the mushrooms in a small bowl with the onion, salt, black pepper, oil, and wine. Pour over the spatchcocks. Tie the parsley, bay-leaves, and celery leaves or celery stalk together and bury among the spatchcock halves. Cover and leave at room temperature for at least 2 hours, turning the spatchcocks occasionally. The longer you leave them marinating the better — all day if you can, in which case marinate in the refrigerator. When ready to cook, pre-heat the grill (broiler) to high. Lift the spatchcock halves from the marinade and pat dry with paper towels. Brush each side lightly with oil. Arrange the birds, skin side down, on a rack and grill (broil) them for 4 to 5 minutes on each side, at the furthest point from the heat.

Slip the spatchcocks from the rack into the grill (broiler) pan. Discard the herbs and pour the marinade over the chicken. Lower the heat slightly and continue to cook the chicken, skin side up, for 10 to 12 minutes, basting frequently with the marinade. Arrange the cooked spatchcocks on a heated serving dish and keep hot.

Pour the marinade into a saucepan. Mix the arrowroot with the chicken stock and stir into the pan. Cook, stirring constantly, until the sauce is clear and slightly thickened. Adjust the seasoning and spoon over the spatchcocks. Garnish with the watercress and serve immediately.

Note: To marinate eight halved spatchcocks, it is necessary to increase the marinade ingredients only by half.

Chicken Fillets

Viennese Fried Chicken

Serve with coffee pot asparagus (page 178) and a potato dish.

Serves 4–6

1 tablespoon Hungarian paprika
60 g (2 oz) butter
1 small can anchovy fillets, drained
6 chicken thighs, skinned and boned
salt
30 g (1 oz) plain (all-purpose) flour
2 eggs
1 tablespoon vegetable oil
125 g (4 oz) dry breadcrumbs
oil

Combine the paprika with the butter and anchovy fillets in a blender or food processor until smooth. Shape the flavoured butter into a roll or rectangle and wrap in foil. Chill thoroughly in the refrigerator.

Cut through the centre of each piece of chicken to form two thin slices. Season lightly with salt and dust with the flour. Beat the eggs with the 1 tablespoon of oil. Dip the chicken slices in the egg mixture and coat with the crumbs. Put aside to allow the coating to set.

Heat oil to a depth of 1 centimetre (½ inch) in a shallow pan and fry the chicken over moderately high heat until crisp and golden, turning once. Transfer the chicken to a heated serving dish. Slice the anchovy butter into pats and serve on top of the chicken.

Chicken Suprêmes Madeira

Serve this simple but elegant dish, with Seville potato cakes (page 186) and a crisp green vegetable.

Serves 4–8

3 tablespoons butter
4–8 chicken fillets
salt
white pepper
½ cup (4 fl oz) strained orange juice
3 tablespoons chicken stock
3 tablespoons dry Madeira
finely grated rind of 2 oranges
60 g (2 oz) pâté
extra Madeira
½ teaspoon arrowroot
pimiento-stuffed olives, sliced (optional)

Melt the butter over low heat and fry the chicken fillets for 3 or 4 minutes on each side. They should be very lightly coloured, not brown. Season with salt and pepper to taste and pour the orange juice, stock, Madeira, and half of the orange rind over. Cover and simmer very gently for 20 minutes, until the fillets are tender. Turn the chicken once during this time.

Beat the pâté until creamy, adding 1 or 2 teaspoons of Madeira, if necessary to soften it. Set aside. Transfer the cooked chicken to a heated serving dish and top each fillet with some of the creamed pâté. Sprinkle lightly with the remaining orange rind and keep hot.

Mix the arrowroot to a smooth paste with 1 teaspoon of water and stir into the pan-juices. Simmer for 2 minutes, adjust the seasoning, and spoon a little over each fillet, serving the rest separately. Garnish the chicken with the sliced olives.

Chicken Suprêmes Madeira

Chicken Livers

Chicken Livers Flambé

Serves 4

220 g (7 oz) long-grain rice
2 tablespoons butter
2 tablespoons vegetable oil
6 spring onions (scallions), chopped
250 g (8 oz) button mushrooms, sliced
500 g (1 lb) chicken livers, skinned and trimmed
2 tablespoons sultanas (sultana raisins)
salt
freshly ground black pepper
1 teaspoon Angostura bitters
2 tablespoons brandy

Serve the chicken livers with a mixed green salad.

Boil the rice in salted water until tender. In the meantime, melt the butter in a pan with the oil, over medium heat. Stir the spring onions (scallions) and mushrooms into the fat and cook for 2 or 3 minutes. Add the chicken livers and sultanas and turn the livers carefully until sealed on all sides. Lower the heat, season with salt and black pepper to taste, and add the bitters. Cover and cook for 5 minutes.

Drain the rice and transfer to a heated shallow bowl. Make a well in the centre and fill with the liver mixture. Just before serving, warm the brandy, flame, and pour over the livers.

Chicken Livers with Avocado

Serves 4

2 tablespoons butter
1 tablespoon vegetable oil
1 small clove of garlic, crushed
1 medium onion, quartered and sliced
375 g (12 oz) chicken livers, skinned and trimmed
salt
freshly ground black pepper
a pinch of cayenne or red pepper
2 tablespoons Madeira
2 tablespoons tomato paste
Avocado Sauce
1 large ripe avocado
2 teaspoons lemon juice
2–3 drops of Tabasco sauce
2–3 drops of Worcestershire sauce
2–4 tablespoons cream
salt

This is a magnificent combination — rich chicken livers and a simple dressing of avocado. Serve with crisp potato balls (page 185) or tiny new potatoes.

Make the sauce. Melt the butter with the oil in a large frying pan (skillet). Add the garlic and onion and fry over low heat until the onion is transparent. Add the chicken livers and cook for about 5 to 7 minutes, until they are firm but still slightly pink in the centre. Season to taste with salt, black pepper, and cayenne or red pepper. Fold in the Madeira and tomato paste. Simmer very gently for 2 or 3 minutes, until very hot.

Transfer the chicken livers to a heated serving dish, spread the sauce along the centre, and top with the sliced, reserved avocado. Serve immediately.

Avocado Sauce

Peel the avocado and remove the stone. Cut a small quarter from it and sprinkle it with the lemon juice to prevent it from discolouring. Set aside to use for the garnish. Purée the rest of the avocado in a blender or food processor or mash with a fork until it is very smooth. Blend with the Tabasco and Worcestershire sauces and enough cream to give a consistency just heavy enough to fall from the spoon. Season with salt to taste and set aside.

Chicken Livers with Avocado

Chicken Livers Creole

Serve with boiled rice and a crisp green salad.

Serves 4–6

3 tablespoons butter

3 tablespoons olive oil

500 g (1 lb) chicken livers, skinned and trimmed

2 hot red chilli peppers, seeded and finely chopped

2 cloves of garlic, finely chopped

2 tablespoons water

salt

freshly ground black pepper

4 large tomatoes, peeled and thickly sliced

1 tablespoon chopped fresh coriander

Melt half of the butter with half of the oil in a shallow pan. Add the livers, chillies, and garlic. Cook for 2 to 3 minutes, turning the livers until they are sealed on all sides. Add the water and season with salt and black pepper to taste. Cover and simmer over very low heat while you cook the tomatoes.

Melt the remaining butter and oil in a frying pan (skillet). Quickly sauté the sliced tomatoes, turning once, until they are just softened. Season to taste, arrange on a heated serving dish, and sprinkle with the coriander. Stir the livers, adjust the seasoning, and spoon over the tomatoes. Serve immediately.

DUCK

I would rather eat duck at home than out, with the possible exception of Chinese or Italian restaurants.

To begin with I hate battling with all those bones, and it is a bony bird. Cooked at home, most of the bones can be extracted before serving. Moreover, the restaurant offering of duck almost invariably partners it with cherries or oranges (of course I have included both!).

As duck has now come out of the luxury class and we can afford to experiment with it, the recipes chosen offer a broad range of approaches.

Duck with Honey, page 62

GENERAL INFORMATION

Duck is cooked, trussed, and carved in the same way as goose (see pages 13, 15 and 75).

To thaw a frozen duck, remove the wrapping, put it on a plate, and cover loosely with paper. Defrost in the refrigerator for 12 to 14 hours, depending on size.

Most of the recipes call for a 2-kilogram (4 pound) duck, a fairly average size. A little more or less will just feed four people.

Duck with Honey

In this recipe, ducks are marinated for 48 hours before being roasted with oranges, herbs, and honey. Be really extravagant and serve them with wild rice (page 191) or down to earth and accompany them with cross-hatched potatoes (page 185) and Brussels sprouts. This quantity serves eight, on the principle that if you are marinating one duck for several days, you might as well double quantities, and share the experience.

Serves 8

2 × 2 kg (4 lb) ducks, marinated
   in game marinade (page 198)
2 teaspoons salt
1 tablespoon chopped fresh basil or
   1 teaspoon dried basil
freshly ground black pepper
125 g (4 oz) butter
juice and finely grated rind of
   1 large orange
juice of ½ lemon
2 teaspoons Dijon mustard
½ teaspoon salt
720 g (1 lb 7 oz) honey
2 large oranges, quartered
2 teaspoons cornflour (cornstarch)
2 tablespoons water
4 tablespoons brandy (optional)

Pre-heat the oven to moderate. Remove the ducks from the marinade and pat dry with paper towels. Mix the salt with the basil and about ½ teaspoon of black pepper in a paper bag. Melt the butter and, off the heat, add the orange juice and rind, the lemon juice, mustard, salt, and honey. Put 2 tablespoons of this honey mixture and a quartered orange into each duck cavity. Secure the opening with small poultry pins and lay the ducks side by side in a large roasting dish. Pour the remaining honey mixture over the birds and sprinkle with the herb mixture. Cover the dish completely with foil and cook the ducks in the centre of the oven for 1¼ to 1½ hours. Remove the foil and roast the birds for 20 to 30 minutes longer, basting them frequently with the pan-juices.

Remove the cooked ducks to a heated serving dish and keep hot. Mix the cornflour (cornstarch) to a smooth paste with the water and stir into the pan-juices. Bring to the boil on top of the stove and adjust the seasoning. Pour a little of the sauce around each bird and serve the rest separately. Warm the brandy, ignite, and pour over the birds just before serving.

Note: Wild ducks prepared in the same way can be marinated for three or four days.

Roast Duck with Potatoes

The duck is filled with tiny whole potatoes and roasted over a dish containing an assortment of vegetables, spices, and wine, which is then served with the duck.

Serves 4

2 kg (4 lb) duck
12–16 tiny new potatoes
salt
freshly ground black pepper
*4 medium tomatoes, peeled and
   halved*
*1 red (bell) pepper, seeded and
   sliced*
1 large onion, halved and sliced
¼ teaspoon ground chilli
2 bay-leaves
1 cup (9 fl oz) red wine

Pre-heat the oven to moderate. Fill the duck cavity with as many small seasoned potatoes as it will hold. Secure the opening with poultry pins, fine skewers, or coarse thread and fold the wings under the body. Put the duck on a rack and prick the skin all over. Sprinkle more pepper over. Put the remaining ingredients in a roasting dish and place the rack on top. Roast in the centre of the oven for 1½ to 1¾ hours, until the duck is cooked. Baste the duck occasionally with some of the pan-juices, adding a little more wine if necessary.

Transfer the duck to a heated serving dish, remove the pins or thread, and leave to stand in a warm place. Adjust the seasoning of the vegetables and spoon around the duck or serve separately.

Duck with Oranges

This remains one of the greatest duck dishes. Serve with roast potatoes and crisp green beans.

Serves 4

2 kg (4 lb) duck
salt
freshly ground black pepper
4 medium oranges
1 tablespoon white vinegar
1 tablespoon castor (superfine) sugar
3 tablespoons brandy
1 tablespoon cornflour (cornstarch)
2 tablespoons water

Pre-heat the oven to moderate. Season the duck inside and out with salt and black pepper. Prick the skin all over with a fine skewer. Squeeze the juice from three of the oranges and set aside; put the skins in the duck cavity. Put the bird on a rack set over a roasting dish and cover the breast loosely with foil. Roast in the centre of the oven for 1¼ hours, basting occasionally with the pan-juices.

While the duck is cooking, grate the rind of the remaining orange and set aside. Discard any white pith, slice the orange thinly, and reserve for garnish. Heat the vinegar and castor (superfine) sugar together in a small pan until the mixture is golden. Add the reserved orange juice with the brandy and grated rind. Simmer for 4 or 5 minutes, and set aside.

Remove the foil from the duck and cook for 15 to 30 minutes longer, until tender and well browned. Transfer the duck to a heated serving dish and keep hot. Skim excess fat from the surface of the pan-juices. Stir the orange sauce into the pan and simmer gently. Mix the cornflour (cornstarch) to a smooth paste with the water, add to the sauce, and stir until smooth and thickened. Add the sliced orange and simmer for a few minutes. Arrange the sliced orange over or round the duck and serve the sauce separately.

Roast Duck with Horseradish

This is a refreshingly different recipe. The style is Finnish and needs only a simple vegetable — chopped spinach, broccoli — to make it complete.

Serves 4

2 kg (4 lb) duck
juice of 1 lemon
1/2 teaspoon salt
freshly ground black pepper
8 parsley sprigs
1/2 cup (4 fl oz) dry red wine
1 tablespoon plain (all-purpose) flour
3/4–1 cup (7-9 fl oz) cream
1 duck liver, or 2 chicken livers, trimmed and finely chopped
3 tablespoons horseradish sauce or 1 1/2 tablespoons freshly grated horseradish
a pinch of dried fennel
white pepper

Pre-heat the oven to hot. Fold the wings under the body of the duck and place it on a rack set over a roasting dish. Pour some of the lemon juice into the cavity and the rest over the skin. Sprinkle the bird with salt and pepper and push the parsley into the cavity. Roast for 20 minutes, until the fat starts to run. Reduce the heat to moderate. Pour the wine over the duck and continue to cook, basting occasionally, for 1¼ to 1½ hours, or until cooked.

Transfer the bird to a heated serving dish and keep hot while you finish the sauce. Skim 2 tablespoons of fat from the surface of the pan-juices and mix to a smooth paste with the flour. Remove any remaining fat from the pan, pour the pan-juices into a measuring jug, and add enough cream to make 1½ cups (14 fluid ounces). Stir the chopped liver into the roasting dish and cook for 1 or 2 minutes over gentle heat. Add the blended flour to the pan, stir in the liver and cook for 2 minutes. Gradually add the cream mixture, stirring constantly until the sauce is smooth. Stir in the horseradish and fennel, seasoning with pepper to taste, and salt if necessary. Simmer for 2 or 3 minutes and serve with the duck.

Roast Duck with Barley Stuffing

Partly cooked barley is mixed with vegetables to make a stuffing that is moist and delicious. The barley absorbs both flavour and some of the fat from the duck. Serve with fennel peas (page 181) and carrots.

Serves 4

105 g (3 1/2 oz) barley
salt
1 large onion, chopped
1 large carrot, coarsely grated
235 g (7 1/2 oz) shredded cabbage
freshly ground black pepper
1/4 teaspoon ground sage
2 kg (4 lb) duck
3 tablespoons dry red wine

Pre-heat the oven to moderate. Put the barley in a saucepan with ½ teaspoon of salt and 3 cups (1⅓ pints) of water. Bring to the boil, simmer for 6 or 7 minutes, and drain. Repeat with fresh salt and water. Strain the barley and put it in a bowl with the vegetables and seasonings. Mix together thoroughly and spoon into the body cavity of the duck. Use any excess in the neck cavity. Secure the opening with poultry pins or coarse thread and fold the wings under the body. Prick the skin all over with a skewer, season with salt and pepper, and cook on a rack set over a roasting dish for 20 to 25 minutes. When the fat starts to run, sprinkle the skin with 1 tablespoon of cold water. Roast for 1 hour. Prick the duck again and sprinkle with another tablespoon of water. Cook for 5 to 10 minutes longer, or until cooked.

Transfer the duck to a heated carving dish. Skim excess fat from the pan-juices and stir in the wine. Bring to the boil on top of the stove, adjust the seasoning, and serve separately.

Duck Catherine

Sour cream is used in the stuffing and gravy of this roast duck, counteracting the richness without detracting from the flavour. Serve simply, with roast potatoes and peas.

Serves 4

2 kg (4 lb) duck
2 tablespoons butter
salt and pepper
3 tablespoons dry red wine, water,
  or vegetable stock
2/3 cup (6 fl oz) light sour cream

Stuffing

1 tablespoon vegetable oil
1 small onion, finely chopped
250 g (8 oz) finely minced
  (ground) veal
90 g (3 oz) chopped mushrooms
60 g (2 oz) fresh breadcrumbs
salt
freshly ground black pepper
3 tablespoons light sour cream
1 egg, lightly beaten

Make the stuffing. Pre-heat the oven to hot. Spoon the stuffing loosely into the cavity of the bird and close the opening with small poultry pins or coarse thread. Fold the wings under the body and put the duck on a rack in a roasting dish. Prick the skin all over with a skewer. Rub the skin lightly with the butter and season with salt and pepper. Roast the duck for 20 minutes, reduce the temperature to moderate, and cook for 1½ hours, or until the juices run clear when a thigh is pierced with a skewer.

Transfer the duck to a heated carving dish, remove the pins or thread, and keep hot. Allow the pan-juices to settle, skim the fat from the surface of the roasting dish, and add the wine, water, or stock. Bring the pan-juices rapidly to the boil, reduce the heat, and stir the sour cream into the simmering liquid. Heat through gently, without boiling, and adjust the seasoning. Serve the sauce separately.

Stuffing

Heat the oil in a frying pan (skillet) and cook the onion until transparent. Mix in the veal and cook until it changes colour, breaking up any lumps with a fork. Add the mushrooms and breadcrumbs, stirring together. When all the pan-juices have been absorbed, remove the pan from the heat, season the mixture with salt and black pepper, and leave to cool slightly. Stir in the sour cream and bind with the egg.

Duck Melissa

This is a much-travelled recipe given to me in London by a visitor from Johore. She found the recipe in Singapore originally, and doubtless made a few changes herself. I have certainly done so over the years. Changed or travelled, it is still good. It needs frequent basting and goes very well with a variety of salads. You will need two long wooden skewers to hold the duck flat.

Serves 4

1·5–2 kg (3–4 lb) duck
90 g (3 oz) coconut cream
1 tablespoon water
2 small cloves of garlic, crushed
¹/₂ teaspoon salt
¹/₄ teaspoon ground mace
¹/₄ teaspoon ground cinnamon
1 teaspoon turmeric
¹/₄ teaspoon ground cardamom
¹/₄ teaspoon ground cloves
1 ¹/₄ teaspoons ground fenugreek
1 ¹/₂ teaspoons ground cumin
3 teaspoons ground coriander
freshly ground black pepper
2·5 cm (1 inch) piece of fresh
    ginger, peeled and finely grated
1 large onion, finely minced
juice of 1 lemon
2 teaspoons mild chilli sauce

Cut through the breastbone and open the duck. You will have to break the ribs here and there to press the duck flat. Thread one wooden skewer through the second wing joint on one side and out through the same joint on the other side. Push the other skewer through the legs in the same way, to keep the bird flat. Prick the skin all over with a skewer and pre-heat the oven to moderately hot.

Melt the coconut cream with the water in a small pan over low heat. Cool slightly and stir in the garlic, all the dry ingredients, and then the ginger, onion, lemon juice, and chilli sauce. Spread this paste over both sides of the duck and cook, skin side down, on a rack in a roasting dish. Cook for 1¼ to 1½ hours, basting every 15 minutes or so with the pan-juices. Turn the bird halfway through the cooking time.

When the duck is cooked, remove as many of the small bones as you can before transferring it to a hot serving dish. Skim as much fat from the surface of the sauce as possible. Either pour the sauce over the bird or serve it separately.

Note: This is a very good sauce for barbecued duck. Prepare the duck for roasting flat, mix the sauce ingredients, add ¾ cup (1/3 pint) of chicken stock and 3 tablespoons of redcurrant jelly, and simmer for 2 or 3 minutes. Use to baste the bird frequently over the coals.

Peking Duck

This is one of the best-known duck dishes in the world. Purists maintain that it cannot properly be prepared at home. This is, however, a very acceptable method of enjoying the variety of texture and flavour which is the essence of Peking Duck.

Serves 4

2 kg (4 lb) duck
185 g (6 oz) sugar
1 cup (9 fl oz) water
salt
1 quantity of crêpe batter
*   (page 200)*
1 tablespoon sesame oil
12 spring onions (scallions), cut into
*   12 cm (5 inch) lengths*
1 cucumber, peeled and cut into
*   strips*
Chinese plum sauce
Hoisin sauce

Put the duck in a bowl, pour boiling water over it, and leave for a few seconds. Drain and dry the duck and tie the legs together. Hang the bird in a cool, airy place overnight.

The following day, put the sugar and water in a small pan and boil rapidly until syrupy but not caramelised. Brush the duck liberally with the syrup, sprinkle with salt, and hang again until it is dry.

Pre-heat the oven to hot. Put the duck on a rack set over a roasting dish and cook for 1 to 1¼ hours, until the skin is very crisp.

While the duck is cooking, make thin 12-centimetre (5 inch) crêpes, including 1 teaspoon of the sesame oil in the batter. As the crêpes are cooked, brush each one lightly with sesame oil and stack them one on top of the other.

When ready to serve, peel the crisp skin from the duck, slice the meat thinly, and arrange on a hot platter. Serve with the stack of crêpes and dishes of spring onions (scallions), cucumber, and the sauces. Each pancake is then spread with sauce, crisp skin, duck, and vegetables before being rolled.

Note: Hoisin sauce and Chinese plum sauce are readily available at Asian supply stores.

Peking Duck

Duck with Almonds

Serve with rice or buttered noodles.

Pre-heat the oven to very hot. Mix the garlic, salt, and black pepper smoothly with the soy sauce. Brush the duck inside and out with this mixture, fold the wings under the body, and secure with small poultry pins. Prick the skin of the bird all over and place it, breast side down, on a rack in a roasting dish.

Roast the bird for 20 minutes, until the fat starts to run. Reduce the temperature to moderately slow and cook for 1 hour, basting the duck occasionally and at the same time removing some of the fat accumulating in the dish. Turn the duck on to its back and finish cooking for 20 to 30 minutes. Transfer the duck to a heated carving dish, cover, and leave to stand in a warm place.

Drain the excess fat from the collected pan-juices. Put the chopped ginger in the roasting dish with the syrup and wine. Mix the cornflour (cornstarch) to a smooth paste with the brandy, stir into the pan, and simmer until the sauce is smooth and thickened. Add the almonds and simmer for 2 or 3 minutes.

Carve the duck, arrange on a heated serving dish, and spoon the sauce over.

Duck and Apple Flan

This is superb summertime food and not difficult to make. The duck is set in aspic — whether homemade or commercial makes little difference to the finished result. If you use a commercial aspic powder, mix it with a dry Marsala or Madeira instead of water. Serve with assorted salads.

Pre-heat the oven to very hot. Prick the duck all over with a skewer and put it on a rack in a roasting dish. Cook in the centre of the oven for 15 to 20 minutes, until the fat starts to run. Mix the orange juice and soy sauce together and pour over the duck. Roast the bird until cooked, about 50 to 60 minutes, basting occasionally with the pan-juices.

While the duck is cooking make the pastry and chill before rolling. Prepare the aspic and leave to cool.

When the duck is cooked, remove from the oven and leave until quite cold.

Roll the pastry out to line a 23-centimetre (9 inch) flan tin or ring. Prick the base lightly with a fork and cover with foil, pressing it well into the corners. You can weight it with beans before baking blind (empty) but I find that the foil works well on its own. Bake the flan case for 10 minutes until the base is firm. Reduce the temperature to hot, carefully remove the foil, and finish cooking the pastry. Remove from the oven and leave to cool.

Melt the butter and simmer the onion until softened. Add the apples and cook until tender. If using canned apples, add them to the softened onion and heat through. Stir in the sugar until it has dissolved. Remove the pan from the heat. Add the sage, ginger, and cream, beating until smooth. Season with salt and pepper to taste and leave until cold.

Spread the apple mixture over the base of the flan. Cut the breasts of the duck into even slices and put aside. Remove the rest of the duck meat and chop into bite-sized pieces. Spread these evenly over the apple and arrange the sliced breast meat on top. Sprinkle with the grated orange rind and coat with aspic, adding a second coat if necessary.

Coating with Aspic

The aspic should be liquid enough to coat the flan evenly. If it has set too firmly, heat gently until it liquefies. Stand the bowl containing the aspic in a dish with ice-cubes to cool the aspic again. The trick is to catch it at just the right temperature.

Duck and Apple Flan

The following three recipes form a group of Italian regional duck dishes. The Italians do marvellous things with ducks, often marinating them first in oil, which may seem a strange way to prepare an already oily bird, but the end result is added flavour rather than added fat.

Duck Italienne

Serve with Portuguese cucumber (page 181) and rice.

Serves 4

2 kg (4 lb) duck
2 tablespoons finely chopped parsley
2 large cloves of garlic, crushed
juice and finely grated rind of
*   2 oranges*
2 tablespoons olive oil
¾ cup (⅓ pt) dry Marsala
¾ cup (⅓ pt) duck giblet stock or
*   chicken stock*
salt
freshly ground black pepper

Pre-heat the oven to hot. Prick the duck skin all over. Fold the wings under the body and put the duck on a rack in a roasting dish. Cook for 15 to 20 minutes in the centre of the oven until the fat starts to run. In the meantime, put the parsley, garlic, orange juice and rind, oil, half of the Marsala, and the stock in a small pan and simmer.

Remove the duck from the oven, reduce the temperature to moderate, and drain the fat from the roasting dish, pour the hot sauce over the duck, season lightly with salt and black pepper, and roast in the centre of the oven for 1 to 1¼ hours, or until cooked. Baste occasionally with the pan-juices.

Place the duck on a heated serving dish, cover, and leave to stand in a warm place. Skim the excess fat from the surface of the sauce and add the remaining Marsala. Boil rapidly on top of the stove until the sauce is reduced by a quarter. Adjust the seasoning and serve with the duck.

Note: This is also a very good way to cook wild ducks.

Genoa Duck

Allow 3 or 4 hours to marinate the duck before roasting. Serve with roast potatoes and fennel peas (page 181).

Serves 4

2 kg (4 lb) duck
1 cup (9 fl oz) olive oil
6 parsley sprigs, chopped
2 bay-leaves, crumbled
duck giblets
2 cups (18 fl oz) water
salt
freshly ground black pepper
juice of 2 lemons

Put the duck in a plastic bag with the oil, parsley, and bay-leaves. Seal the bag and marinate for 3 or 4 hours, turning the bag occasionally.

Put the duck giblets in a small saucepan with the water and bring to the boil. Reduce the heat and simmer gently for 30 minutes. Discard the giblets and reduce the stock to 1 cup (9 fluid ounces) by boiling rapidly. Strain and reserve.

Pre-heat the oven to moderate. Remove the duck from the marinade. Pat the excess oil from the duck with paper towels, and prick the skin all over with a skewer. Fold the wings under the body and put the duck on a rack set over a roasting dish. Season with salt and black pepper and roast in the centre of the oven for 1 hour. Mix the reserved stock with the lemon juice, pour over the hot duck, and roast for 30 to 35 minutes, or until cooked. Baste two or three times with the stock.

Transfer the duck to a heated serving dish and leave to stand in a warm place. Skim excess fat from the dish and bring the pan-juices to the boil on top on the stove. Adjust the seasoning and serve separately.

Duck with Wine and Anchovies

This is hearty, informal, and perfect for a winter night. Serve with green beans and jacket-baked potatoes (page 186) or crusty bread.

Serves 4

duck giblets (not the liver)
2 cups (18 fl oz) water
3 salt-packed anchovies, soaked in 2 tablespoons milk, or 6 canned anchovy fillets, drained
1 tablespoon butter
1 tablespoon olive oil or vegetable oil
12 small pickling onions, peeled
2 kg (4 lb) duck, quartered
2 large cloves of garlic, crushed
½ teaspoon dried chervil
1¼ cups (11 fl oz) dry white wine
1 tablespoon tomato paste
freshly ground black pepper
juice of ½ lemon
3 teaspoons butter
3 teaspoons plain (all-purpose) flour
3 large tomatoes, peeled, seeded, and coarsely chopped
1 tablespoon finely chopped fresh coriander or parsley

Bring the duck giblets to the boil in the water. Reduce the heat and simmer until the liquid has reduced to 1¼ cups (11 fluid ounces). Strain and reserve the stock.

If using salt-packed anchovies, soak them in milk for 10 minutes; rinse, remove the bones, and chop finely. Melt the 1 tablespoon of butter with the oil in a heavy pan and quickly shake the whole onions in the hot fat until lightly browned on all sides. Remove and set aside. Add the duck quarters and sauté on all sides until brown. Drain all but 1 tablespoon of fat from the pan. Return the onions to the pan with the garlic, chopped anchovies, chervil, reserved giblet stock, wine, and tomato paste. Bring to the boil, season with black pepper to taste, more salt if necessary, and the lemon juice. Reduce the heat, cover, and simmer for 40 to 50 minutes, or until the duck is very tender.

Remove the duck to a heated serving dish and keep hot. Mix the 3 teaspoons of butter with the flour and whisk small pieces into the sauce until it has thickened to your liking. Add the tomatoes and simmer for 5 or 6 minutes. Pour the sauce around the duck and serve sprinkled with the coriander or parsley.

Duck with Wine and Anchovies

GOOSE

The goose's long history has attracted stories both factual and legendary, making it the most interesting of all the birds in this book. In Egyptian mythology the goose is associated with Geb, the earth god, who is sometimes depicted with his head surmounted by a goose. Some legends describe him as a gander whose mate laid the egg of the sun. Four thousand years ago geese were sacred to the Egyptians as one of the earthly representations of their god Ammon of Thebes. A thousand years later — and a little less sacred — they were trapped and fattened in Nile-side pens for mortal Egyptian feasts.

Skip another thousand years and there are records of geese all over Europe. Centuries before the French developed their famed Strasbourg geese, the Romans were already enjoying the delicacy of goose liver via the celebrated geese of Ferrara. In the fourth century St Martin of Italy killed a goose that had either teased or attacked him. On 11 November thereafter a goose was traditionally sacrificed in celebration of that saint.

In a small local battle in the thirteenth century the enemies of King Erik of Sweden flaunted a goose as a target. Although outnumbered the king successfully called their bluff. After his murder in 1208 the Swedes made King Erik their patron saint and adopted the feast of Martinmas at which goose was eaten. This also used to be the festive dish of France at Martinmas.

England also has a goose story to offer. On 29 September 1588 — Michaelmas Day — Queen Elizabeth I was eating goose when news of the defeat of the Spanish Armada was received. She decreed that goose should in future be eaten at Michaelmas in commemoration of the great victory of the English fleet. Another Michaelmas story just a shade more probable accounts for the belief that if you eat goose on Michaelmas Day you will not be short of money. Tenant farmers customarily gave their landlord a goose on this day, when their quarterly rent was due and the geese were fat and plentiful. Keeping on the right side of the lord might well have brightened their prospects.

Geese are regarded as intelligent birds and from ancient times have been used as 'watchdogs'. The largest commercial organisation using geese for this purpose today is Ballantyne's Scotch Whisky Distillers. The geese guard in excess of $980 000 000 worth of maturing liquor. How genuinely intelligent they are, or just how hissingly noisy when disturbed, is open to conjecture; it matters little if they do the job. With such a formidable reputation attaching to the goose it is curious that the expression 'a silly goose' has become commonplace in our language, that the word 'goose' alone denotes foolishness. But even the Egyptians in their hieroglyphics showed the same attitude by representing a silly man as a goose.

And so to cook our goose...

Roast Goose, page 75; with Apricot-Stuffed Apples, page 211

GENERAL INFORMATION

There are several recipes for roast goose in this chapter, but although they have some ingredients in common they are all quite different from each other. Like duck, the goose has dark, very succulent meat and a thick layer of fat under the skin. Because of this high fat content goose is generally roasted — by oven or spit — and served with a sharp sauce, traditionally apple, although redcurrant jelly and cranberry sauce are equally good. But whether you present it roast, braised or en cassoulet, few diners will need persuasion to enjoy this bird.

Roast Goose

A simply roasted goose is seasoned inside and out with salt and pepper. Prick the skin all over with a skewer to release the fat, then roast in a pre-heated very hot oven for 15 to 20 minutes until the fat starts to run. Reduce the temperature to moderate and roast an unstuffed bird for 30 minutes per kilogram (15 minutes per pound); a bird with stuffing needs to be cooked for 50 minutes per kilogram (25 minutes per pound).

Goose Fat

Collect the fat periodically as it drains into the roasting dish. Stored in a cool place it will keep indefinitely, and is marvellous for roasting, baking, and adding flavour to soup, casserole, and pâté. Canned goose fat can be bought in specialist poultry shops and delicatessens.

Carving, (see also page 15)

Geese and ducks are not the easiest birds to carve; the legs are set well under the back and the breast is broad and flat. The whole procedure is most easily done on a board in the kitchen. Cut the legs and wings off first. Make a cut along the top of the breast and with a sharp knife make a parallel cut down the breast and through to the bone. Finally release the slices by carving upwards, towards the original cut. This will give good long slices of meat with an even distribution of skin.

Trussing, (see also page 13)

The legs of geese are short for conventional trussing, but it is necessary to tie them loosely together to avoid losing the

Garlic Goose, page 80

stuffing during cooking. I prefer to leave the pinions on the wings and fold the whole wing under the body of the bird, thus making a natural rack which improves the drainage of fat. Alternatively, the pinions (that is, up to the first joint) can be removed and used in stock because there is little, if any, meat on them. The wings can then be pinned to the body before roasting.

Michaelmas Goose

It is said that 'Who eats goose on St Michael's Day, shan't want money his debts to pay'.

Serves 6

3.5–4 kg (7–8 lb) goose
1 lemon, halved
apple sauce (page 195)
giblet gravy (page 197)

Stuffing
60 g (2 oz) butter
2 large onions, finely chopped
2 celery stalks, finely chopped
3 teaspoons dried sage
250 g (8 oz) fresh breadcrumbs
1½ teaspoons salt
1 teaspoon freshly ground black pepper
2 large tart cooking apples, peeled, cored, and diced
2 eggs, well beaten

Pre-heat the oven to very hot. Prick the goose skin all over with a skewer and rub with half of the lemon. Squeeze the juice of the lemon into the goose cavity and put the bird, breast side down, on a rack set over a roasting dish. Cook in the centre of the oven for 15 to 20 minutes, until the fat starts to run. In the meantime, make the stuffing.

Remove the goose from the oven and drain the fat from the body and roasting dish. Spoon the stuffing loosely into the cavity and close the opening with poultry pins or coarse thread. Any excess stuffing can be used to fill the neck or be made into forcemeat balls (these can be cooked separately in a little goose fat shortly before serving).

Replace the goose in the oven, breast side down, and roast for 15 minutes. Reduce the oven temperature to moderate and cook for 2½ to 3 hours, turning the goose on to its back halfway through the cooking time. Prick the skin of the bird occasionally to let the fat run out. Remove the fat as it collects in the roasting dish.

Prepare the giblet gravy while the goose is cooking. Parboiled potatoes can be roasted in the goose fat underneath the bird. Serve with the apple sauce.

Stuffing

Melt the butter and quickly sauté the onions and celery until golden. Tip the vegetables and pan-juices into a bowl and add the sage, breadcrumbs, salt, black pepper, and apples. Mix with enough of the eggs to bind, without making the mixture too sticky.

Goose Caprice

This is a real extravaganza. The goose is crammed with a mixture of vegetables and olives, served with a brandy sauce, and needs little more than tiny new potatoes and crisp green beans to round it off.

Serves 4–6

3.5–4 kg (7–8 lb) goose
¾ cup (⅓ pt) brandy
½ cup (4 fl oz) chicken stock
salt and pepper
Stuffing
2 tablespoons butter
2 tablespoons olive oil
goose liver or 2 chicken livers, trimmed and chopped
3 medium onions, chopped
185 g (6 oz) mushrooms, sliced
2 large green (bell) peppers, seeded and chopped
2 celery stalks, sliced
185 g (6 oz) pimiento-stuffed olives, sliced
salt
freshly ground black pepper
½ cup (4 fl oz) dry Marsala

Make the stuffing and leave it to cool. Pre-heat the oven to very hot. Spoon the cooled stuffing into the cavity of the bird and close the opening with coarse thread or poultry pins. Fold the wings under the body and prick the goose skin all over with a fine skewer. Put the goose on a rack set over a roasting dish and cook in the centre of the oven for 15 minutes. Reduce the temperature to moderate and roast for 3 to 3½ hours, until the bird is cooked. Cover the breast of the goose loosely with foil if it browns too quickly, but remove the foil 1 hour before the end of the cooking time.

Carefully transfer the goose to a heated carving dish, discard the thread or pins, and leave to stand in a warm place before carving. Let the pan-juices settle in the roasting dish before skimming the fat from the surface. Bring the pan-juices rapidly to the boil and add the brandy and stock. Reduce the heat and simmer for 2 or 3 minutes. Adjust the seasoning and serve with the goose.

Stuffing

Melt the butter with the oil in a large pan and sauté the liver with the vegetables and olives for 2 or 3 minutes. Season lightly with salt and generously with black pepper. Stir the Marsala into the pan, cover, and cook over low heat for 10 minutes. Remove the lid and stir the vegetable mixture until most of the liquid has been absorbed. Remove from the heat and leave to cool.

Roast Goose with Baked Pears

The subtle flavour of pears is very good with goose. Serve with roast potatoes, broccoli, bacon rolls, and giblet gravy (page 197).

Serves 6

3–4 kg (6–8 lb) goose
juice of 1 lemon
1 teaspoon cracked black peppercorns
½ teaspoon salt
6 medium pears, peeled
6 bacon rashers, with rind removed
Stuffing
1 tablespoon vegetable oil
2 bacon rashers, chopped, with rind removed
1 large onion, chopped
1 goose liver, trimmed and chopped
2 medium pears, peeled, cored, and chopped
60 g (2 oz) fresh breadcrumbs
2 teaspoons dried chervil
salt
white pepper

Make the stuffing and pre-heat the oven to moderate. Spoon the stuffing loosely into the cavity of the bird and close the opening with poultry pins or thread. Any extra stuffing can be used at the neck end. Fold the wings under the body of the bird and loosely tie the legs together. Prick the skin all over with a skewer and put the goose on a rack set over a roasting dish. Cook in the centre of the oven for 20 minutes. Mix the lemon juice with the cracked peppercorns and salt and pour over the hot bird. Roast for 2 to 2½ hours longer, basting occasionally with the pan-juices and removing and reserving excess fat from the roasting dish when you do so.

About 50 minutes before the goose is ready, heat some of the reserved fat in a shallow ovenproof dish. Roll the pears in the fat and bake under the goose until tender. While the pears are cooking, roll the bacon rashers and secure with cocktail sticks. Grill (broil) for 5 or 6 minutes when needed.

Remove the poultry pins or thread and serve the cooked bird on a heated carving dish with the baked pears and the bacon rolls.

Stuffing

Heat the oil in a small pan and quickly sauté the bacon until lightly browned. Reduce the heat, add the onion, and cook until transparent. Add the liver and turn in the pan until sealed. Tip the contents of the pan into a bowl and mix with the pears, breadcrumbs, chervil, and salt and white pepper to taste. The stuffing will be crumbly but will absorb some of the fat from the goose.

Roast Goose with Baked Pears

St Martin's Goose

Serves 6−8

4−5 kg (8−10 lb) goose
salt
freshly ground black pepper
1 teaspoon poppy seeds
1 ⅓ cups (¾ pt) veal or chicken
  stock
1 tablespoon cornflour (cornstarch)
Stuffing
4 large tart cooking apples, peeled,
  cored, and quartered
375 g (12 oz) dessert prunes,
  stoned
250 g (8 oz) goose livers or chicken
  livers, skinned and halved
salt and pepper

This goose is stuffed with a mixture of fruit and goose livers. Serve with potatoes, roasted in goose fat, and red or green cabbage.

Pre-heat the oven to hot. Season the bird inside and out with salt and black pepper. Sprinkle the poppy seeds into the cavity of the bird and shake to distribute them evenly. Fill the bird with the stuffing and close the opening with poultry pins or thread. Fold the wings under the body of the bird, prick the skin all over with a fine skewer, and place on a rack set over a roasting dish. Roast in the centre of the oven for 30 minutes. Reduce the temperature to moderate. Remove the bird from the oven, drain the fat from the roasting dish, and put the goose directly into the dish, removing the rack. Add the stock and return to the oven. Cook for 3 hours, or until the juices run clear when a thigh is pierced with a skewer. Baste the bird occasionally with the stock.

Transfer the goose to a heated carving dish, discard the poultry pins or thread, and leave to stand in a warm place for 10 minutes. Skim the excess fat from the pan-juices. Mix the cornflour to a smooth paste with a little cold water and add to the pan. Stir over low heat on top of the stove until the sauce has thickened. Simmer for 2 or 3 minutes, adjust the seasoning, and serve separately.

Stuffing
Toss the apples with the prunes and livers. Season lightly with salt and pepper.

Austrian Roast Goose

Serves 6

3−4 kg (6−8 lb) goose
6 medium tart cooking apples,
  peeled and cored
2 tablespoons finely chopped fresh
  marjoram
salt
freshly ground black pepper
1 tablespoon drained and finely
  chopped capers
1 tablespoon Hungarian paprika
½ cup (4 fl oz) heavy sour cream
½ cup (4 fl oz) water

My visits to Austria have been happy times; the pretty country, the laughter, and the food all reflect the casual, light-hearted nature of the people. This goose is happy with apples and a superb sauce. Serve with roast potatoes and a green vegetable.

Pre-heat the oven to moderately hot. Prick the skin of the goose all over with a skewer. Coat the apples with the marjoram, season with salt and black pepper, and put inside the bird. Secure the cavity with coarse thread or poultry pins. Season the skin with salt and black pepper and put the bird on a rack set over a roasting dish. Cook just below the centre of the oven for 2½ to 3 hours, until the bird is cooked. Baste the bird occasionally, removing and reserving the excess fat from the dish. Potatoes can be roasted in some of the goose fat for the last 1 to 1½ hours of the cooking time.

Transfer the goose to a heated carving dish, remove the thread or pins, and keep hot. Drain the goose fat from the dish. Stir the capers and paprika into the pan-juices on top of the stove. Add the sour cream and water, simmer gently, and adjust the seasoning.

Hungarian Goose Loaf

Serves 4–6

2 tablespoons goose fat or butter
1 large onion, chopped
breasts from 1 goose, skinned and finely minced (ground)
250 g (8 oz) goose or chicken livers, trimmed and finely chopped
90 g (3 oz) sultanas (sultana raisins)
3 slices of bread, with crusts removed, soaked in 3 tablespoons milk
salt
freshly ground black pepper
½ teaspoon freshly grated nutmeg
2 teaspoons Hungarian paprika
1–2 teaspoons cracked black peppercorns

Only the goose breasts are used for this recipe, leaving the rest of the bird for one of the casseroles. Serve hot with potatoes rosemary (page 186) and fennel peas (page 181), or cold with salads.

Heat the fat or butter in a shallow pan and quickly fry the onion until softened and lightly browned. Mix the onion and pan-juices with the minced (ground) goose, livers, and sultanas (sultana raisins). Squeeze out the milk and mix the bread thoroughly with the goose mixture. Season with salt and black pepper to taste, the nutmeg, and the paprika.

Pre-heat the oven to moderate. Lightly oil a loaf tin and sprinkle the base with the cracked peppercorns. Spoon the goose mixture into the tin, pressing firmly into the corners. Level the top and cover loosely with foil. Bake in the centre of the oven for 50 to 60 minutes. Turn on to a heated serving dish and serve with the vegetables. To serve cold, cool the loaf in the tin before chilling.

Garlic Goose

Serves 6–8

3.5–4 kg (7–8 lb) goose
3 medium onions, halved
2 celery stalks, quartered
6 whole cloves
6 black peppercorns
salt
½ cup croûtons (page 210)
Sauce
1¾ cups (¾ pt) milk
4 cloves of garlic, peeled
3 egg-yolks
½ cup (4 fl oz) cream
salt and pepper

From Belgium comes the very best (I think) of the garlic goose recipes. The garlic sauce is not too overpowering, although very rich. Serve with braised chicory (page 181) and crisp green beans, lightly sprinkled with lemon juice.

Put the goose in a large pan with the onions, celery, cloves, and peppercorns. Add about 2 teaspoons of salt and enough cold water to cover the bird. Bring the water to simmering-point, cover, and simmer for 2 hours, or until the bird is tender. It must not be cooked until it is falling apart. In the meantime, make the sauce.

Carefully lift the cooked goose from the pan and cut into serving pieces. Arrange on a heated deep serving dish and keep hot. Stir the croûtons into the sauce and pour over the goose.

Sauce
Put the milk and garlic in the top of a double broiler and simmer for 30 minutes, with the pan half-covered. Strain 1½ cups (14 fluid ounces) of the garlic-flavoured milk into a heavy saucepan; discard the garlic. Whisk the egg-yolks into the milk and cook over very low heat, whisking all the time, until the milk begins to thicken. Add the cream and cook without boiling for 4 or 5 minutes. Season with salt and pepper to taste.

Goose Cassoulet

Serves 4–6

2·5–3 kg (5–6 lb) goose, cut into serving pieces
125 g (4 oz) smoked pork loin or spek, cut into small dice
1 medium onion, chopped
2 large cloves of garlic, crushed
2 bacon rashers, sliced, with rind removed
6 spring onions (scallions), sliced
2 cups (18 fl oz) goose stock or chicken stock
1 teaspoon Tabasco sauce
425 g (15 oz/No. 300) can chick peas (garbanzo beans), drained
12 small pickling onions, peeled
1 cabana sausage, cut into 1 cm (½ inch) slices
cherry tomatoes, whole, or 3 medium tomatoes, quartered

This is the way to cook an old goose. Since you are far more likely to have a delectable young goose, forget the age, just sit back and enjoy it. Served with crusty bread, it is complete.

Pre-heat the grill (broiler) and brown the goose, skin side up. When the fat starts to run, turn the goose and grill (broil) for 3 or 4 minutes. Set aside. Pre-heat the oven to moderately slow.

Lightly brown the pork loin or spek in a large, deep flameproof casserole. Add the onion, garlic, and bacon and cook gently until the onion is transparent. Put the goose in the casserole with the spring onions (scallions) and distribute the pork and vegetables around it. Add the stock and Tabasco and bring to the boil on top of the stove. Remove from the heat and check the seasoning — there should be enough from the smoked meats and Tabasco, but adjust if necessary. Cover and cook below the centre of the oven for 2 hours, skimming excess fat from the surface of the pan from time to time. Add the remaining ingredients. Re-cover the casserole and cook for 1 hour longer, until the goose is tender. Skim fat from the surface and adjust the seasoning before serving from the casserole.

Goose Cassoulet

Goose Liver Pilaff

This pilaff is easily and quickly made. Serve very hot, with a crisp green salad. If there is any left over, it can be frozen and used later as a stuffing for goose neck or roast chicken.

Goose Liver Pilaff

Serves 4

90 g (3 oz) butter
1 tablespoon olive oil or vegetable
    oil
1 large onion, halved and sliced
250 g (8 oz) goose livers, trimmed
    and cut into 1 cm (1/2 inch) slices
10 spring onions (scallions), white
    and green parts, cut into 1 cm
    (1/2 inch) lengths
60 g (2 oz) pinenuts
45 g (1 1/2 oz) seedless raisins
125 g (4 oz) dried apricots,
    chopped
approx. 1 1/2 teaspoons salt
1/2 teaspoon freshly ground black
    pepper
410 g (13 oz) long-grain rice
1 teaspoon sugar
2 teaspoons lemon juice
2 teaspoons tomato paste
1 teaspoon dried green dill tips
2 1/2 cups (1 1/8 pt) water or chicken
    stock

Melt one-third of the butter with the oil in a large frying pan (skillet). Add the onion and fry gently until transparent. Add the livers and turn in the fat until they are just sealed. Stir in the spring onions (scallions), half of the pinenuts, the raisins, apricots, salt, and black pepper, mixing thoroughly. Cook for 2 minutes longer and remove the pan from the heat.

Melt the remaining butter in a large flameproof casserole over moderate heat and add the rice, stirring until the grains are well coated. Cook until the rice changes colour and begins to look milky white. Stir in the liver mixture and all remaining ingredients except for the rest of the pinenuts. Bring to the boil, then reduce the heat until the stock is barely simmering. Cover and cook until the rice is tender and the liquid has been absorbed. Fork through the rice occasionally to keep the grains separated.

While the pilaff is cooking, sauté the remaining pinenuts in a little butter until golden. To serve, adjust the seasoning, pile the mixture on to a heated serving dish and garnish with the pinenuts.

Goose Liver Risotto

Serves 4

60 g (2 oz) butter
1 tablespoon vegetable oil
185 g (6 oz) goose livers, trimmed
1 medium onion, coarsely chopped
2 cloves of garlic, finely chopped
125 g (4 oz) mushrooms, chopped
250 g (8 oz) short-grain rice
1 tablespoon tomato paste
2 1/2 cups (1 1/8 pt) chicken stock
salt
white pepper
2 tablespoons grated Parmesan
    cheese

This is quite different in texture from a pilaff. Use short-grain rice, Italian if you can, and serve very hot, followed by a crisp green salad.

Melt half of the butter with the oil in a large shallow pan. When the fat is sizzling, add the whole livers and sauté quickly on all sides until lightly browned. Remove and set aside. Reduce the heat and add the remaining butter to the pan with the onion. Cook gently until the onion is transparent. Add the garlic and mushrooms and cook for 2 minutes. Stir the rice in, turning until the grains are coated with the pan-juices. Cook for a few minutes until the rice changes colour.

Cut the reserved livers into small slices and add to the rice mixture with the tomato paste and about one-third of the stock. Simmer, stirring occasionally until the mixture begins to thicken. Add 1 cup (9 fluid ounces) of the remaining stock and continue to cook, forking through the risotto until the stock has been absorbed. Season with salt and pepper, add the remaining stock, and cook, partly covered, until the rice is tender. Fork the mixture lightly to prevent it from sticking. The risotto should still be a little creamy when cooked; add a little more stock if necessary during the cooking time. Adjust the seasoning before transferring the risotto to a heated serving dish. Sprinkle with the Parmesan cheese and serve immediately.

TURKEY

The turkey, a native of the Americas, was first imported into northern Europe in the early sixteenth century and gradually became the festive bird of the leisured, ousting the once favoured peacocks and swans, which were then left to decorate the grounds. Turkey was still too expensive for the rest of society, who stayed faithful to goose. (In Central Europe goose has always remained everybody's all-round festive favourite, partly because turkey arrived in that area somewhat later, but mainly because of the massive goose liver industry.)

Intensive turkey farming — making hindquarters and specific portions readily available — is rapidly taking it from its eminence as the bird of special occasions to more commonplace uses. As with most changes there are good and bad aspects to this. The turkey has plenty of good meat and lends itself to a variety of cooking methods. It is good, too, that another flavour is so readily available to everyone.

But it is bad that we so quickly take turkey for granted and forget that it is another choice. I so frequently hear, 'Let's have a turkey to make a change from chicken!'. Turkey is a different bird, and although many chicken and turkey recipes are interchangeable, that just extends the range of each — they do not taste quite the same.

Herb-Roasted Turkey, page 86

Herb-Roasted Turkey

Cooked slowly, the herb butter used to baste this turkey imparts the most superb flavour. Serve with cross-hatched potatoes (page 185), simple crisp green vegetables, and giblet gravy (page 197).

Serves 8–10

5–6 kg (10–12 lb) turkey
stuffing (optional)
½ cup (4 fl oz) melted butter
2 cloves of garlic, crushed
1 teaspoon dried basil
1 teaspoon salt
½ teaspoon freshly ground black
*   pepper*
½ teaspoon dried thyme
1 teaspoon crushed rosemary needles
½ teaspoon dried marjoram
½ teaspoon Spanish paprika
rosemary sprigs

Pre-heat the oven to moderately slow. If stuffing the bird, fill the cavities loosely and close with poultry pins or coarse thread. Fold the neck skin over the stuffing and secure with pins. Tie the legs together and tuck the wings under the body. Put the bird on a rack in a roasting dish. Mix the butter with the garlic, basil, salt, black pepper, thyme, crushed rosemary, marjoram, and paprika. Pour the herbed butter over the turkey. Roast for 30 to 35 minutes per kilogram (15 minutes per pound), remembering to include the stuffing weight when calculating the cooking time. Cover the breast and legs of the bird loosely with foil for the first 2 hours of the cooking time and baste with the pan-juices every 30 minutes.

When the turkey is cooked, transfer it to a heated carving dish, cover, and leave to stand in a warm place for 10 minutes before carving. Garnish the dish lavishly with the rosemary sprigs and serve the vegetables and gravy separately.

Devilled Turkey

Coated with devilled butter, the turkey is then roasted and finished with a dusting of crisp crumbs. Serve hot with fried cauliflower (page 179) and peas or cold with assorted salads.

Serves 4–6

2.5–3 kg (5–6 lb) turkey
125 g (4 oz) butter
2 teaspoons dry English mustard
2 teaspoons Dijon mustard
125 g (4 oz) fried crumbs
*   (page 210)*
½ teaspoon cayenne or red pepper
½ cup (4 fl oz) light ale
salt

Fold the turkey wings neatly under the body, secure with string or poultry pins, and tie the legs together. Pre-heat the oven to hot. Melt the butter in a large shallow pan on top of the stove and stir the mustards in thoroughly. Turn the turkey in the hot butter until evenly browned on all sides. Remove from the pan and transfer to a casserole. Pour the pan-juices over the turkey, cover, and cook for 1½ hours.

Toss the fried crumbs with the cayenne or red pepper. Baste the bird with the pan-juices and immediately sprinkle with the crumbs. Roast, uncovered, for 25 to 30 minutes, until cooked.

Carefully transfer the turkey to a heated carving dish and leave to stand in a warm place. Remove as much of the fat as possible from the pan-juices and blot the surface with paper towels to clear any remaining fat. Bring the liquid rapidly to the boil, add the ale, and simmer for 2 or 3 minutes. Adjust the seasoning and serve with the turkey.

Roast Turkey with Cherry Stuffing

The Kirsch-flavoured stuffing is spiked with whole cherries, a special festive dish. Serve with glazed turnips (page 189), roast potatoes, and a green vegetable.

Serves 8–10

5–6 kg (10–12 lb) turkey, with
  giblets
salt
2½ cups (1⅛ pt) water
freshly ground black pepper
60 g (2 oz) butter
1½ tablespoons plain (all-purpose)
  flour

Stuffing

425 g (15 oz/No. 300) can stoned
  black cherries
1 egg
⅓ cup (3 fl oz) Kirsch
185 g (6 oz) soft breadcrumbs
2 teaspoons dried mixed herbs
60 g (2 oz) butter
1 large onion, finely chopped
turkey liver, trimmed and chopped
2 bacon rashers, chopped, with rind
  removed
500 g (1 lb) finely minced (ground)
  lean veal
500 g (1 lb) pork sausagemeat
salt and pepper

Put the turkey giblets (not the liver) in a saucepan with 1 teaspoon of salt and the water. Bring to the boil, reduce the heat, and simmer very gently for 30 minutes. Strain and reserve the stock. Season the turkey inside and out with salt and black pepper and set aside while you make the stuffing. Pre-heat the oven to moderately slow.

Spoon the stuffing and the reserved cherries loosely into the cavities of the bird. Fold the neck skin over the stuffing and secure with coarse thread. Close the vent with poultry pins or fine string. Fold the wings under the body, fasten with poultry pins, and tie the legs together. Put the bird on a rack in a roasting dish. Melt the butter and pour over the turkey. Cover the breast loosely with a piece of foil and cook just below the centre of the oven for 3½ hours, basting occasionally.

Increase the temperature to very hot, remove the foil, and roast for 30 to 40 minutes longer, until the bird is cooked and golden. Remove the thread and pins and transfer the bird to a heated carving dish. Leave to stand in a warm place for 10 minutes before carving.

Skim excess fat from the roasting dish, stir the flour into the pan, and cook over moderate heat until lightly browned. Gradually add the giblet stock, stirring between each addition, until the gravy reaches the consistency you prefer. Season to taste and simmer for 2 or 3 minutes. Serve separately.

Stuffing

Drain the juice from the cherries into a mixing bowl and reserve the fruit. Add the egg and Kirsch to the juice and mix together. Stir in the breadcrumbs and herbs and set aside. Melt the butter in a large pan, and cook the onion over low heat until softened. Stir in the liver and bacon and cook for 2 minutes. Crumble the veal into the pan and mix with the onion, using a fork to break up any lumps. Combine the onion mixture with the soaked crumbs and the sausagemeat, mixing thoroughly and seasoning well with salt and pepper.

Turkey Bubbly Jock

This is a lowlands Scottish recipe. The turkey is roasted with an oyster stuffing which is both delicious and very substantial. Serve with crisp roast potatoes and green vegetables.

Serves 6–8

4–5 kg (8–10 lb) turkey, with
  giblets
salt
2 cups (18 fl oz) water
1 medium onion, finely chopped
2 celery stalks, finely chopped
125 g (4 oz) fresh breadcrumbs
60 g (2 oz) ground almonds
1½ teaspoons dried mixed herbs
2 tablespoons finely chopped parsley
1 turkey liver, skinned and finely
  chopped
12 or more fresh oysters, quartered
3 tablespoons melted butter
freshly ground black pepper
2 tablespoons redcurrant jelly

Put the turkey giblets (not the liver) in a small pan with a little salt and the water. Bring to the boil, reduce the heat, and simmer for 30 minutes. Set aside and leave to cool.

In the meantime, combine the onion and celery with the breadcrumbs, ground almonds, herbs, liver, and oysters. Bind loosely with some of the melted butter and season with salt and black pepper to taste.

Spoon the stuffing into the turkey cavities. Secure the opening with thread or small poultry pins and tie the legs together. Fold the wings under the body and put the bird in a large roasting dish. Pre-heat the oven to hot. Brush the bird with the remaining butter and roast in the centre of the oven for 15 minutes. Reduce the temperature to moderately slow and cook the bird for 3 to 3½ hours, or until the juices run clear when a thigh is pierced with a fine skewer. Baste the bird with the pan-juices every 30 minutes and cover the breast with foil if it browns too quickly.

Strain the giblet stock and boil rapidly until reduced to 1¼ cups (11 fluid ounces). Stir in the redcurrant jelly and season with salt and pepper to taste. Simmer gently for a few minutes before serving.

Transfer the turkey to a heated carving dish and leave to stand in a warm place for 10 minutes before carving. Discard the thread or pins, surround with the vegetables, and serve the gravy separately.

Note: If you prefer a thicker gravy, the giblet stock can be thickened or gravy can be made in the roasting dish. Strain the excess fat from the dish, stir 2 tablespoons of plain (all-purpose) flour into the pan-juices, and cook until lightly browned. Gradually add the giblet stock to the pan, stirring constantly until the gravy is smooth and thickened. Thin with additional liquid from the vegetables if necessary. Season to taste and serve separately.

Cold Turkey Pilaff

The turkey is roasted and, when cold, filled with a savoury pilaff. It is ideal for a summer dinner party, smorgasbord, or a tropical Christmas dinner. Serve with assorted salads.

Pre-heat the oven to very hot. Season the turkey inside with salt, fold the wings neatly under the body, and tie the legs together. Put the bird on a rack set over a roasting dish. Brush liberally with goose fat or butter, season with pepper, and cook just below the centre of the

Serves 8—10

5—5.5 kg (10—11 lb) turkey
salt
goose fat or butter
white pepper
2 tomatoes, quartered (optional)
2 Kiwi fruit (Chinese gooseberries),
    sliced (optional)

Pilaff

3 tablespoons butter
2 medium onions, chopped
1 red (bell) pepper, seeded and diced
60 g (2 oz) pinenuts
1 tablespoon finely chopped
    coriander or parsley
425 g (13½ oz) cooked long-grain
    rice
salt and pepper

oven for 15 minutes.

Reduce the temperature to moderately slow, cover the thighs and breast loosely with foil, and cook for 2½ to 2¾ hours, until the juices run clear when a thigh is pierced with a skewer. Baste the bird every 20 minutes during the cooking time and remove the foil for the last 30 minutes. While the turkey is cooking, make the pilaff.

Remove the cooked turkey from the oven and leave to cool. Insert a sharp, pointed knife into the flesh at the end of the breastbone. Cut away the meat in a wide circle from the point of the breast to the front of the second wing joint; repeat on the other side of the bird (see the photograph below). Remove and discard the skin, chop the meat finely, and mix with the pilaff.

When the turkey is quite cold, put it on a large serving platter and spoon the pilaff into the cavity. Garnish with the tomatoes and Kiwi fruit (Chinese gooseberries).

Pilaff

Melt the butter in a saucepan and sauté the onions until golden. Add the pepper and nuts and cook over low heat until the pepper has softened. Stir in the coriander and rice, mix thoroughly, and season well with salt and pepper. Remove from the heat and cool before chilling.

Cold Turkey Pilaff

Turkey Parisienne

This is not an everyday recipe, although it does virtually cook itself. It is even better for a special dinner. The sauce is beautifully coloured and served with crisp green vegetables the whole dish looks very attractive.

Serves 6

2 tablespoons plain (all-purpose) flour
1 teaspoon salt
½ teaspoon white pepper
2–2·5 kg (4–5 lb) turkey, cut into serving pieces
3 tablespoons butter
1 tablespoon vegetable oil
10 spring onions (scallions), white parts finely chopped, green tops reserved
1¼ cups (11 fl oz) cream
1 cup (9 fl oz) port
4 egg-yolks

Season the flour with the salt and pepper. Dust the turkey with the seasoned flour. Melt the butter with the oil in a large, shallow, flameproof casserole and brown the turkey, a few pieces at a time. Add more butter and oil only if necessary. Arrange the turkey pieces in the casserole and sprinkle with the spring onions (scallions). Pour the cream and port over the turkey and bring just to simmering-point on top of the stove. Cover tightly and cook over very low heat for 1 to 1¼ hours, until the turkey is tender.

Lift the turkey from the pan with a slotted spoon, arrange on a heated serving dish, and keep hot. Bring the pan-juices to the boil and reduce by a quarter. Reduce the heat and simmer the sauce. Beat the egg-yolks in a small bowl with 2 or 3 tablespoons of the hot sauce and stir into the pan. Whisk over gentle heat until thickened, but do not let the sauce boil. Adjust the seasoning and spoon over the turkey. Garnish with the chopped, reserved spring onion (scallion) tops before serving.

Turkey with Cherry Sauce

Serves 6–8

1 large onion, studded with 6 cloves
3·5–4 kg (7–8 lb) turkey
turkey giblets (not the liver)
2 bay-leaves
1 carrot, sliced
2 sprays of celery leaves
1½ teaspoons salt
½ teaspoon white pepper
1 tablespoon arrowroot or cornflour (cornstarch)
Cherry Sauce
90 g (3 oz) seedless raisins
425 g (15 oz/No. 300) can stoned cherries
1 small clove of garlic
juice of 1 large lemon

I have included two recipes using cherries with turkey because they are completely different from each other. Here the turkey is simmered in stock and masked with the sauce. It can be served hot with potatoes rosemary (page 186) and a green salad. For turkey with cherry stuffing, see page 87.

Put the whole onion in the cavity of the bird. Fold the wings under the body and secure with poultry pins. Tie the legs together and put the turkey in a large saucepan. Add the giblets, bay-leaves, carrot, celery leaves, and just enough water to cover the bird. Season with the salt and pepper. Bring the liquid to the boil. Reduce the heat, cover, and simmer for 2 to 2½ hours, until the bird is tender, but not falling apart. While the turkey is cooking, prepare the cherry sauce.

Lift the turkey carefully from the stock, drain, and arrange on a heated serving dish. Stand in a warm place if it is to be served hot. Strain and reserve the stock, discarding the flavouring ingredients.

Mix the arrowroot to a smooth paste with a little of the cherry sauce mixture. Stir into the sauce with 1¼ cups (11 fluid ounces) of the reserved stock and simmer over low heat until the sauce has cleared and thickened. Adjust the seasoning, cook for 2 minutes, and spoon evenly over the turkey.

Cherry Sauce
Put the raisins in a small pan with the juice strained from the cherries. Simmer very gently for 15 to 20 minutes. Remove from the heat and leave to cool. Strain and reserve the liquid. Purée the cherries in a blender or food processor with the garlic and plumped raisins. Mix the purée in a saucepan with the lemon juice and ½ cup (4 fluid ounces) of the reserved raisin liquid. Stir well and set aside.

Turkey Provençal

There is nothing subtle about this traditional French dish. Pungent flavours are combined with meltingly tender turkey. Serve with pasta and a crisp salad.

Serves 6

2–2.5 kg (4–5 lb) turkey, skinned and jointed
⅓ cup (3 fl oz) olive oil
salt
freshly ground black pepper
4 large onions, halved and thickly sliced
3 cloves of garlic, crushed
6 medium tomatoes, peeled and sliced
2 large red (bell) peppers, skinned, seeded, and thickly sliced
1 small can anchovies, drained and chopped
1 teaspoon dried basil
1 cup (9 fl oz) dry white wine

Brush the turkey with some of the oil and season with salt and black pepper. Toss the onions, garlic, tomatoes, and peppers with the anchovies and basil. Spread a thick layer of the mixture over the base of a heavy flameproof casserole. Season and arrange the turkey in the pan. Pack the remaining vegetable mixture over the turkey, season again, and pour the remaining oil into the casserole with the wine.

Put the pan over moderate heat and bring the liquid to a very slow simmer. Cover tightly, using foil or paper to ensure a close seal. Reduce the heat even more and cook for 2 to 2½ hours. The turkey should be very tender.

Lift the turkey pieces from the pan, discarding the bones. Arrange on a heated serving dish and keep hot. Stir the vegetable residue together and beat lightly with a wooden spoon. Adjust the seasoning, reheat until the mixture bubbles, and spoon over the turkey.

Turkey Paprikash

Full of European flavour, this traditional dish can also be made with chicken. However, I think that the slightly stronger flavour of turkey remains apparent against the paprika and spek, and to support their separate entities even more I do not smother them with the sauce, but serve it separately, along with the vegetables. Brussels sprouts, lightly cooked and tossed with chestnuts (page 179), are a good accompaniment. Noodles also go well with this dish.

Turkey Paprikash

Serves 4–6

1 tablespoon vegetable oil
250 g (8 oz) smoked spek, cut into
  1 cm (½ inch) slices
1 large onion, coarsely chopped
2–2.5 kg (4–5 lb) turkey, cut into
  serving pieces
1–2 tablespoons Hungarian paprika
3 tablespoons water
1½ cups (14 fl oz) light sour cream
salt
freshly ground black pepper

Heat the oil in a heavy-based flameproof casserole until moderately hot. Add the spek and cook on both sides until lightly browned. Add the onion and cook for a few minutes until golden. Remove the spek and onion from the pan and set aside. Brown the turkey pieces in the flavoured oil, adding a little more if necessary. Sprinkle with the paprika, return the spek and onion to the pan, add the water, and cover very tightly. Simmer very gently for 1 to 1½ hours, until the turkey is tender. Add a little more water if necessary.

When the turkey is cooked, arrange it with the spek in a heated serving dish. Skim any excess fat from the pan-juices and stir in the sour cream. Simmer gently for 1 or 2 minutes, season to taste, and strain into a serving jug.

Turkey and Potato Goulash

This is a richly flavoured, all-in-together party dish. Serve with crisp green beans.

Serves 6–8

1 turkey hindquarter, skinned
salt
1 kg (2 lb) small new potatoes
2 tablespoons butter
1 tablespoon olive oil
1 large clove of garlic, crushed
2 large onions, halved and sliced
1 tablespoon Hungarian paprika
1 tablespoon plain (all-purpose)
   flour
2 tablespoons wine vinegar
freshly ground black pepper
1 large green (bell) pepper, seeded
   and chopped
2 large tomatoes, peeled, seeded, and
   chopped
3/4 teaspoon caraway seeds
3 tablespoons light sour cream
1 tablespoon coarsely chopped
   coriander

Cut the turkey meat into thick slices. Put the bones in a pan with a little salt and enough water to cover. Bring to the boil, reduce the heat, and simmer for 30 minutes. Strain the stock, discarding the bones, and return to the pan. Simmer the potatoes in the stock for 10 minutes. Strain the potatoes and reserve the stock.

Melt the butter with the oil in a heavy pan. Add the garlic and onions and cook over low heat until the onions are transparent. Turn the turkey slices with the onions until they are coated with the flavoured fat. Fry gently until turkey and onions are lightly browned. Sprinkle the paprika and flour into the pan, stir well, and cook for 1 minute. Gradually add 1½ cups (14 fluid ounces) of the reserved stock and the vinegar, stirring until the sauce is smooth and thickened. Simmer for 3 or 4 minutes and adjust the seasoning. Fold in the reserved potatoes with the green (bell) pepper, tomatoes, and caraway seeds. Cover and simmer gently until the potatoes are tender.

Just before serving, add the sour cream and adjust the seasoning. Simmer until hot and serve from the pan, garnished with the coriander.

Santa Eugenia Turkey

Jointed turkey is gently braised in port, with prosciutto and peas. Serve with tiny new potatoes or rice.

Serves 4–6

3–3.5 kg (6–7 lb) turkey, jointed
2 tablespoons olive oil
freshly ground black pepper
12 small slices of prosciutto
12 pickling onions, peeled
2 bay-leaves
1 kg (2 lb) fresh peas, shelled
1/2 cup (4 fl oz) turkey giblet stock
   or chicken stock
salt
1 cup (9 fl oz) port
2 teaspoons arrowroot or cornflour
   (cornstarch)

Pre-heat the grill (broiler). Brush the turkey joints with the oil and lay them in the grill (broiler) pan. Season with black pepper and cook for 8 minutes on each side until golden. Transfer the turkey to a wide, shallow, flameproof casserole. Roll the prosciutto and arrange with the turkey. Add the onions, bay-leaves, peas, and stock. Season lightly with salt, and bring to the boil on top of the stove. Add the port, reduce the heat, cover, and simmer the turkey for 1½ hours, or until tender.

Using a slotted spoon, transfer the turkey and ham to a heated serving bowl. Arrange the vegetables over the meat and keep hot. Mix the arrowroot or cornflour (cornstarch) to a smooth paste with a little water and stir into the sauce. Stir over moderate heat until thickened and clear. Simmer for 2 or 3 minutes. Adjust the seasoning and spoon over the turkey, discarding the bay-leaves as you find them.

Castilian Turkey

This recipe is from Mexico, where for centuries exciting things have been done with turkey. This dish must originally have been Spanish (probably for chicken) and the Mexicans have added chillies and some of their local spices. There is a distinct Middle Eastern touch with the pinenuts, uncommon in this region. They are, however, adapted to be used in the local nut purée fashion. This is a good recipe for turkey halves or pieces. I cook it in an attractive dish which can be taken straight to the table, and serve it simply with noodles or rice.

Serves 4–6

2–2.5 kg (4–5 lb) turkey, cut into
* serving pieces*
¼ teaspoon dried thyme
2 parsley sprigs
1 bay-leaf
2 cups (18 fl oz) chicken stock
salt
freshly ground black pepper
2 tablespoons sesame seeds
30 g (1 oz) blanched almonds
30 g (1 oz) pinenuts
30 g (1 oz) hazelnuts
30 g (1 oz) walnuts
6 sweet chilli peppers, seeded and
* coarsely chopped*
2 tomatoes, peeled, seeded, and
* chopped*
1 large clove of garlic
½ teaspoon ground coriander
2 tablespoons olive or vegetable oil
½ teaspoon sugar
extra 30 g (1 oz) pinenuts

Put the turkey pieces in a heavy flameproof casserole with the thyme, parsley, and bay-leaf. Add the stock and bring to the boil over moderate heat. Reduce the temperature until the stock is simmering. Season with salt and black pepper to taste. Cover and simmer for 1 to 1¼ hours, until the turkey is almost tender. Remove the pan from the heat and let the turkey cool, uncovered, in the stock.

Mix the sesame seeds in a bowl with the nuts, chillies, tomatoes, garlic, and coriander. Purée coarsely in a blender or food processor and set aside.

Using a slotted spoon, lift the turkey pieces from the stock and set aside. Strain the stock into a jug and discard the herbs. Skim any excess fat from the top of the stock with a skimming brush or kitchen towels.

Heat the oil in a frying pan (skillet) and cook the nut purée for 5 minutes, stirring constantly. Stir enough of the reserved stock into the nut mixture to bring it to a smooth sauce of coating consistency. Add the sugar, adjust the seasoning, and allow to simmer very gently for 2 or 3 minutes. Return the turkey to the casserole, pour the sauce over, and cook over low heat for 20 minutes. Sprinkle with the extra pinenuts before serving.

GUINEA FOWL

Originally a native of Africa, guinea fowl was introduced to other parts of the world largely as a by-product of the spice trade. In England, during the sixteenth century, they were called turkeys because of association with the spice merchants who traded with Turkey. It was some years later that these so-called 'turkeys' reverted to the original name they had been given by the Portuguese in the fourteenth century, during the discovery (or rather the rediscovery) and charting of the West African coast and the Gulf of Guinea. So guinea fowl they are to most of us, but guinea hen or Cornish rock hen in the U.S.A.

They are quite domesticated birds, which roost in rows, like plump little cushions, on farm sheds and barns. Perhaps it is because of this habit that I think of them as the bridge between poultry and game.

Similar to pheasant, guinea fowl has a strong, slightly gamy, flavour. The flesh is dark but less dry than that of pheasant, though they still, when roasted, need careful barding or basting to be enjoyed at their very best.

Salt-Baked Guinea Fowl, page 101

GENERAL INFORMATION

The preparation and thawing of guinea fowl is very much the same as for pheasant. Guinea fowl legs are, however, somewhat shorter and so can be tied together in the same way as chicken.

Roast Guinea Fowl

This is the basic way to roast these birds. Care must be taken not to overcook them, as, like most of the game birds, they have a natural tendency to dryness. They can be stuffed before roasting (see the recipes on page 206). Allow 20 minutes' cooking time for each 500 grams (1 pound) of unstuffed bird. Stuffed birds must have the total weight calculated for the cooking time. Serve carved or halved with game chips (page 184) and a creamed vegetable.

Serves 4

2 guinea fowl
1 tablespoon goose fat or butter
6 streaky bacon rashers or slices of ham fat
freshly ground black pepper
3 tablespoons dry red wine
juice of ½ lemon
salt
lemon twists (page 209)

Pre-heat the oven to very hot. Fold the wings of each bird under the body and tie the legs loosely together. Brush with the fat or butter, cover the breasts with bacon or ham fat, and place on a rack set over a roasting dish. Season with black pepper and roast in the centre of the oven for 20 minutes per 500 grams (1 pound). The birds will be cooked when the juices run clear from a thigh pierced with a fine skewer.

Transfer the birds to a heated serving dish, cover, and leave to stand in a warm place. Add the wine to the pan-juices with the lemon juice and boil rapidly for a moment or two. Adjust the seasoning and serve with the birds. Discard the bacon and garnish with lemon twists.

Roast Guinea Fowl with Brie

This uncomplicated recipe relies purely on the combination of port and Brie to provide both the superb flavour and the sauce for the guinea fowl. Serve with tiny Brussels sprouts or zucchini (courgettes).

Season the guinea fowl inside and out with pepper. Pre-heat the oven to hot. Melt the butter until sizzling and lightly brown the birds on all sides. Remove from the pan and set aside.

Mash the Brie with a fork and mix with the lemon juice and marjoram. Put half of the cheese mixture in the cavity of each bird. Fasten the wings to the body with poultry pins, but do not close the

2 guinea fowl
freshly ground black pepper
2 tablespoons butter
125 g (4 oz) Brie
juice of 1 lemon
1 teaspoon finely chopped fresh
    marjoram or 1/4 teaspoon dried
    marjoram
1/2 cup (4 fl oz) port
3 tablespoons cream
salt

cavity. Put the birds in a roasting dish, pour the pan-juices over, and cover loosely with foil. Roast in the centre of the oven for 35 to 40 minutes.

Remove the dish from the oven and halve the guinea fowl, discarding the spinal bones. Transfer to a heated serving dish. Stir the port into the pan-juices, on top of the stove, and simmer for 2 or 3 minutes. Add the cream and, stirring constantly, reheat without boiling until the sauce is smooth and well blended. Adjust the seasoning, adding salt if necessary. Spoon the sauce over the birds and serve immediately.

Roast Pheasant with Brie

Pheasant can be prepared in the same way. Roast for 45 to 50 minutes in a hot oven.

Guinea Fowl with Cornmeal Stuffing

This is an interesting stuffing for guinea fowl — substantial, but not too heavy. Serve with Portuguese cucumber (page 181) and cranberry sauce.

Serves 4

2 guinea fowl
2 tablespoons melted goose fat or
    butter
Cornmeal Stuffing
90 g (3 oz) cup cornmeal
1 teaspoon ground rosemary
1 cup (9 fl oz) chicken stock
60 g (2 oz) softened butter
1 celery stalk, finely chopped
1 medium onion, finely chopped
1 small green (bell) pepper, finely
    chopped
60 g (2 oz) mushrooms, chopped
salt
freshly ground black pepper
1 1/2 tablespoons Madeira or dry
    sherry

Pre-heat the oven to moderately hot. Make the stuffing and spoon it loosely into the birds. Secure the opening with small poultry pins or thread, and tie the legs together. Fold the wings under the body and place on a rack in a roasting dish. Pour the melted fat over the birds and roast in the oven for 40 to 50 minutes, basting frequently with the fat. As the stuffing is precooked the birds can be roasted quickly. Transfer the cooked guinea fowl to a heated dish, discard the pins or thread, and serve garnished with vegetables.

Cornmeal Stuffing

Stir the cornmeal, rosemary, and stock in a small pan. Cover and simmer for 8 or 9 minutes, stirring occasionally. Add the butter and vegetables, season to taste, and add the wine. Stir over low heat until all the liquid has been absorbed. Remove from the heat and leave to cool.

Guinea Fowl Curaçao

The guinea fowl are roasted on a bed of sliced apples, which forms a light, well-flavoured sauce. Serve with vine-leaf fritters (page 190) and a crisp green salad.

Serves 4

4 large tart cooking apples, peeled, cored, and sliced
½ teaspoon salt
¼ teaspoon white pepper
2 tablespoons curaçao
3 tablespoons butter
2 guinea fowl, halved

Pre-heat the oven to moderately slow. Spread the sliced apples in a casserole. Season with the salt and pepper and sprinkle the curaçao over. Cover and cook in the centre of the oven for about 15 minutes. Melt the butter in a heavy frying pan (skillet) and lightly brown the guinea fowl, seasoning with salt and pepper.

When the apples have started to soften, increase the temperature to moderately hot. Lay the birds on top of the apple mixture, pour the butter from the frying pan (skillet) over, and roast for 25 to 30 minutes, until tender.

Transfer the birds to a heated serving dish and leave to stand in a warm place. Beat the apple mixture until smooth, adding a little water or curaçao, if the purée is too thick. Adjust the seasoning and spoon a little of the sauce over each bird.

Roast Guinea Fowl Jerez

Guinea fowl cooked in Spanish style are served on a bed of ham and mushrooms with a sherry sauce. Serve with Seville potato cakes (page 186) and coffee pot asparagus (page 178) or braised chicory (page 181).

Serves 4

60 g (2 oz) chicken livers, trimmed
salt
2 guinea fowl
90 g (3 oz) butter
4 slices of ham
125 g (4 oz) mushrooms, sliced
1 tablespoon plain (all-purpose) flour
½ cup (4 fl oz) chicken stock
½ cup (4 fl oz) dry sherry
freshly ground black pepper

Pre-heat the oven to very hot. Season the chicken livers lightly with salt and divide between the cavities of the birds. Fold the wings under the body and tie the legs loosely together. Put the birds on a rack set over a roasting dish. Melt 60 grams (2 ounces) of the butter and pour over the birds. Roast in the centre of the oven for 25 to 30 minutes, until cooked.

Spread the slices of ham over the base of a grill (broiler) pan, cover with the sliced mushrooms, and dot with the remaining 30 grams (1 ounce) of butter, cut into tiny pieces. Shortly before the fowl are cooked, pre-heat the grill (broiler) and cook the ham and mushrooms for 5 or 6 minutes. Transfer the ham to a heated serving dish, arrange the guinea fowl on top, and surround with the mushrooms. Keep warm while you finish the sauce.

Stir the flour into the pan-juices in the roasting dish and cook on top of the stove until lightly browned. Gradually add the stock and sherry, stirring constantly until the sauce has thickened. Simmer for 2 minutes, adjust the seasoning, and spoon over the guinea fowl.

Spiced Guinea Fowl

This is a self-saucing dish. Blend the ingredients in the morning, or even the night before, pour over the guinea fowl, and cook them when you are ready. Serve with cracked wheat pilaff (page 190) or boiled rice.

Serves 4

2 guinea fowl, halved and trimmed
Sauce
1 clove of garlic, crushed
60 g (2 oz) butter, melted
3 tablespoons Worcestershire sauce
2 teaspoons Dijon mustard
2 teaspoons Tabasco sauce
½ teaspoon salt
½ cup (4 fl oz) redcurrant jelly
½ cup (4 fl oz) orange juice
½ teaspoon ground ginger
1 teaspoon vegetable oil

Prepare the sauce. Put the guinea fowl, skin side down, in a baking dish. Pour the sauce over the birds, cover with plastic-wrap, and leave in a cool place until you are ready to cook.

Pre-heat the oven to moderate. Discard the plastic-wrap and cover the dish with a lid or foil. Cook in the centre of the oven for 20 minutes. Turn the birds and remove the lid or foil. Cook for another 20 minutes, basting once or twice with the sauce.

Transfer the guinea fowl to a heated serving dish with the pilaff or rice. Adjust the seasoning of the sauce and spoon a little over each bird, serving the rest separately.

Sauce
Combine all the ingredients in a blender or food processor.

Spiced Pheasant
Prepare and cook in exactly the same way as for guinea fowl.

Spiced Chicken
Quarter a 1·5 kilogram (3 pound) chicken. Cook for 25 minutes, turn, and cook for 25 to 30 minutes longer.

Salt-Baked Guinea Fowl

Baking the guinea fowl completely buried in rock salt has the same effect as overwrapping food in clay. The birds brown beautifully but are moist, they are (surprisingly) not salty, and, unlike clay-wrapped food, you do not quite need a hammer to break them out of bondage. Serve with roast potatoes and buttery beans. The salt can be stored and used again.

Serves 4

2 guinea fowl
3–4 kg (6–7 lb) rock salt

Pre-heat the oven to moderately hot. Tie the legs of each bird loosely together and tuck the wings under the body. Spread about 2.5 centimetres (1 inch) of salt over the base of a flameproof casserole and heat on top of the stove for 4 or 5 minutes. Arrange the birds on the salt and firmly pack enough salt over and around them to bury them completely. Cover and bake for 50 minutes. Remove the guinea fowl from the casserole, scrape off any salt which clings to them, and halve or carve them before serving.

Salt-Baked Pheasant or Salt-Baked Chicken

Pheasant can be cooked in the same way for 45 minutes. Chickens weighing about 1.5 kilograms (3 pounds) take 1¼ hours.

Guinea Fowl en Papillote

Serves 4

salt
freshly ground black pepper
2 guinea fowl, halved and trimmed
1 egg-white, lightly beaten
Sauce
4 medium carrots, thinly sliced
1 cup (9 fl oz) veal stock or chicken stock
8 spring onions (scallions), chopped
125 g (4 oz) button mushrooms, halved
1 cup (9 fl oz) champagne or dry white wine
1 tablespoon butter
1 tablespoon plain (all-purpose) flour
½ cup (4 fl oz) cream
white pepper
2 tablespoons finely chopped parsley

Since cooking began, foods have been wrapped in a variety of coverings — clay, leaves, various pastries, and papers. This paper method is particularly simple and very good for any food tending to be dry. Serve with parsleyed potatoes and a crisp green vegetable.

Season the guinea fowl and steam over simmering water for 20 minutes, until just tender. In the meantime, make the sauce and prepare the paper. Pre-heat the oven to hot.

Cut four oval-shaped pieces of paper (any non-porous paper, except non-stick paper) large enough to contain the birds and to allow for securing the edges. Make a fold across the centre.

Remove the skin and bones from the guinea fowl. Brush the paper with oil and spread out on baking trays. Centre one portion of guinea fowl on one half of each piece of paper and divide the reserved vegetables from the sauce between the parcels. Brush the edges of the paper with the egg-white, spoon the sauce over the birds and sprinkle with a little of the parsley. Fold the top half of the paper loosely over the bird, matching the paper edges together. Prepare the parcels one by one or the egg-white will dry. Roll to seal, crimping or pleating where necessary. Bake for 10 to 15 minutes, until the paper is puffed and crisp.

Serve the parcels individually on hot plates.

Sauce
Poach the carrots in the stock for 4 or 5 minutes, until they begin to soften. Add the spring onions (scallions) and mushrooms and simmer for 1 minute. Strain the vegetables and reserve the stock.

Add the champagne to the stock and bring rapidly to the boil. Reduce the heat. Work the butter into the flour and whisk small pieces into the stock until it has a light coating consistency. Simmer for 2 or 3 minutes and remove from the heat. Add the cream, adjust the seasoning, and set aside.

Note: When sealing the parcels, any particularly stubborn spots can be 'fixed' with a paper-clip, peg, or pin. Remove the hardware before serving!

Guinea Fowl en Papillote

Guinea Fowl Royale

Serves 4

3 tablespoons butter
2 tablespoons vegetable oil
2 medium onions, halved and sliced
1 medium green (bell) pepper,
    seeded and sliced
1 medium red (bell) pepper, seeded
    and sliced
2 medium carrots, thinly sliced
2 celery stalks, sliced
2 guinea fowl, quartered
salt
freshly ground black pepper
juice and finely grated rind of
    1 lemon
½ cup (4 fl oz) dry white wine
½ cup (4 fl oz) port

Flavoured with mixed vegetables and braised in a sauce of lemon, port, and wine, these guinea fowl are tender and moist. Serve with creamy potatoes and, if you wish, a salad.

Melt the butter with the oil in a flameproof casserole. Mix the vegetables together and fry very gently in the fat until they begin to soften but are not browned. Lift the vegetables from the pan with a slotted spoon and set aside. Add the guinea fowl to the casserole and turn in the pan-juices, adding a little more butter if necessary. Cook gently until they begin to colour slightly. Season with salt and black pepper. Add the lemon juice and rind with the wine and port. Cover and simmer very gently for 35 to 40 minutes, until the birds are tender. Lift them from the casserole, arrange on a heated serving dish, and keep hot.

Sprinkle the reserved vegetables lightly with salt and pepper, return them to the casserole, and simmer for a few minutes until they are heated through but still crisp. Adjust the seasoning and spread the vegetables around the guinea fowl before spooning the sauce over the birds.

Guinea Fowl Aureole

Serves 4

2 guinea fowl, quartered
3 tablespoons plain (all-purpose)
    flour
salt
white pepper
3 tablespoons hot water
140 g (4½ oz) seedless raisins
2 tablespoons butter
2 tablespoons olive oil or vegetable
    oil
1 large onion, chopped
2 large tomatoes, peeled and
    chopped
60 g (2 oz) pimiento-stuffed olives,
    sliced

The guinea fowl are braised in a piquant mixture of vegetables and dried fruit that provides enough liquid to keep them moist. Serve with rice or buttered pasta.

Dust the guinea fowl with the flour and season with salt and pepper. Pour the hot water over the raisins and set aside.

Heat the butter with the oil in a heavy pan and brown the quartered birds on all sides. Add the onion and cook until transparent. Pour the liquid from the raisins into the pan and stir until it is well blended with the pan-juices. Add the remaining ingredients, including the raisins. Cover and simmer for 40 minutes, until the birds are tender. Adjust the seasoning and serve on a bed of rice or pasta.

Guinea Fowl Royale

PHEASANT

If guinea fowl are the bridge between poultry and game, the handsome pheasant is the perfect introduction to game itself. They have an almost worldwide distribution, having spread naturally from their native China and been artificially introduced into some countries as a sporting bird.

They were certainly in the British Isles during the Roman occupation and records confirm that the marching Roman legions supplemented their food supplies with pheasant and other wild game. Since a legion numbered somewhere between 4000 and 6000 men one could suppose that pheasants were already plentiful.

George Washington introduced these birds into the U.S.A. in the late eighteenth century, but it was not until 1880 that they were imported in great numbers from China. They have since made themselves very much at home.

Establishment of the pheasant in Australia in the nineteenth century was frustrated by the hold that the rabbit had already taken on their new habitat. The long-legged pheasant is both ground feeder and nester; attacked, they run like mad for cover or reluctantly take off vertically for the nearest tree. Ground-cover and young trees having been destroyed by rabbits, they rapidly fell prey to foxes, feral cats, and other ills. It has taken much care and time to raise them in the wild, largely by releasing them on offshore islands.

Pheasant Ballotine, page 114

GENERAL INFORMATION
(U.K. season: 1 October to 1 February)

Preparation

If you have to deal with a feathered pheasant, hang it according to the table on page 11. An older bird will improve with a longer hanging period. For plucking and drawing, see page 12. Leave the legs on for roasting, and tie them across at the knee (see page 13).

Farmed Pheasants

While we would all prefer a plump, wild pheasant, its commercially-raised sibling should not be completely written off. These farmed birds, albeit frozen, allow those of us who live in regions where wild pheasant are hard to come by, to enjoy this bird. They do, however, fall into two categories: those which are plucked, drawn, de-legged, and ready for cooking (somewhat erroneously called 'table ready', they look like small chickens); the others, produced by better farmers, are hung for four days, plucked, and then frozen intact. These are the ones to look for. Being young birds they need no further hanging than the thawing time in the refrigerator.

Recipe Note

The recipes offer a choice of one or two pheasants because there is a discrepancy in size between wild and farmed birds. The game laws which protect wild birds also allow them time to grow and become plump, while the farmed variety has its short life planned from hatch to finish. When using the recipes consideration must be give to the size of pheasant used. When you can shoot, buy, or otherwise acquire a good mid-season cock (a bird of glorious plumage) it will adequately serve four. A hen of similar vintage (recognised by more muted plumage) will serve three. The young, commercial pheasant will serve two. Whether you use one cock, or one hen, or two farmed birds the rest of the ingredients in these recipes remain the same.

Defrosting

Put the frozen bird on a plate, cover loosely with paper, and allow 12 to 14 hours to defrost completely. Do not wrap in plastic or foil.

The 'table-ready' birds will be improved if allowed to 'hang' for an additional three or four days in the refrigerator.

Pheasant with Peaches

Of all the pheasant and fruit combinations, this Rumanian version is my favourite. Fresh or canned peaches are equally good. If you use fresh peaches, poach them before roasting the pheasants. Serve with braised chicory (Belgian endive, page 181) or braised celery (page 180) and game chips (page 184).

Serves 3–4

1 or 2 pheasants
salt
freshly ground black pepper
60 g (2 oz) butter
2 tablespoons olive oil or vegetable oil
4 bacon rashers, halved, with rind removed
4 large fresh peaches or 2 × 425 g (15 oz/No. 300) cans peach halves, with juice reserved
2 tablespoons dry sherry or brandy
finely grated rind of 1 orange
juice of 1 lemon
1 bay-leaf
1½ teaspoons arrowroot or cornflour (cornstarch)

Pre-heat the oven to moderate. Lightly season the pheasants inside and out with salt and black pepper. Tuck the wings under the body, secure with poultry pins, and tie the legs together.

Melt the butter with the oil in a heavy, flameproof roasting dish. Brown one bird at a time, turning frequently until golden on all sides. Remove the pan from the heat, set the pheasants side by side, and lay the bacon over the breasts. Mix 1½ cups (14 fluid ounces) of the reserved peach juice with the sherry or brandy, orange rind, and lemon juice. Push the bay-leaf between the birds and pour the juices over. Roast the birds in the centre of the oven for 45 to 60 minutes or until the pheasants are cooked — when the juices run clear from a thigh pierced with a fine skewer. Take the pheasants from the dish and quarter them, removing and discarding the spine bones. Kitchen snips or shears make this an easy job. Arrange the pheasants on a heated serving dish and keep hot.

Add the peach halves to the pan, on top of the stove, and turn them in the pan-juices for a few minutes until they are very hot. Lift them carefully with a slotted spoon and arrange with the pheasants. Mix the arrowroot or cornflour (cornstarch) to a smooth paste with 2 tablespoons of water. Add to the pan-juices, stirring constantly until the sauce has thickened and cleared. Adjust the seasoning, discard the bay-leaf, and spoon the sauce over the pheasants.

Note: Poaching Fresh Peaches. Halve the peaches and discard the stones. Lay them in a shallow pan with 1¼ cups (11 fluid ounces) of water. Simmer for 2 minutes, turn the fruit, and simmer for another 2 minutes. Remove the pan from the heat, skin the peaches, and set them aside until ready to use.

Roast Pheasant

A carefully roasted pheasant can be one of the greatest joys. It can also be very dry. Ham, pork fat, or bacon tied over the breast helps to counteract the dryness of the bird, but the surest way to ruin is overcooking. Traditionally, roast pheasant is served with game chips (page 184), braised celery (page 180), redcurrant jelly, and garnished with watercress.

Serves 3–4

1 or 2 pheasants
salt
freshly ground black pepper
1 teaspoon Spanish paprika
4 slices of fat ham, pork, or bacon
2 tablespoons melted goose fat or
*   butter*
3 tablespoons dry red wine
redcurrant jelly

Pre-heat the oven to moderate. Season the pheasants inside and out with salt and black pepper and sprinkle the paprika over the skin. Cover the breasts with the fat ham. Fold the wings under the body and tie the legs together.

Put the birds in a roasting dish, pour the melted fat over, and cook in the centre of the oven for 45 to 60 minutes, basting every 15 minutes with the pan-juices. Remove the fat covering from the breasts 10 minutes before the end of the cooking time. The birds are cooked when the juices run clear from a thigh pierced with a fine skewer.

Transfer the pheasants to a heated serving dish, halve or carve as for chicken, and leave to stand in a warm place. Remove any excess fat from the roasting dish, add the wine, and boil for 1 or 2 minutes. Adjust the seasoning and serve with the pheasants. Serve the redcurrant jelly separately.

Roast Pheasant

Roast Pheasants with Wild Rice Stuffing

The nutty flavour of the stuffing makes a luxurious and very special combination with this delicate game bird. Serve with creamed cauliflower (page 180), potatoes rosemary (page 186), and redcurrant jelly.

Serves 3–4

1 or 2 pheasants
½ quantity of wild rice stuffing
(page 207), cooled
4 tablespoons butter
1 teaspoon Spanish paprika
salt
freshly ground black pepper
2 fat bacon rashers
⅓ cup (3 fl oz) dry red wine
redcurrant jelly (optional)

Pre-heat the oven to moderately hot. Stuff the birds loosely and close the cavity with small poultry pins or thread. Truss the pheasants and rub the skin liberally with the butter. Sprinkle with the paprika, salt, and black pepper. Put the birds side by side in a roasting dish. Cover the breasts with the bacon and roast in the centre of the oven for 45 to 60 minutes, or until cooked (when the juices run clear from a thigh pierced with a fine skewer).

Transfer the birds to a heated serving dish and leave to stand for a few minutes before carving. Remove excess fat from the roasting dish, add the wine, and boil rapidly for 2 minutes. Season to taste and serve with the pheasants. Accompany with redcurrant jelly, if you wish.

Note: While I think this is the ultimate choice of stuffing for pheasants, any of the stuffing mixtures (page 206), which are basically pre-cooked, can be used.

Pheasant Véronique

Superb ingredients put together in the simplest way produce this French dish which spells complete luxury. Serve with potato balls (page 185) and tiny Brussels sprouts or green beans.

Serves 3–4

1 or 2 pheasants, trussed
salt
white pepper
2 fat bacon rashers
4 spring onions (scallions), finely
chopped
½ cup (4 fl oz) brandy
½ cup (4 fl oz) cream
250 g (8 oz) seedless white grapes
½ cup (4 fl oz) port
2 teaspoons lemon juice
watercress sprigs

Pre-heat the oven to moderate. Season the pheasants with salt and pepper and put them in a buttered roasting dish. Cover the breasts with the bacon and roast in the centre of the oven for 40 to 55 minutes, depending on size. The birds must not be overcooked.

Transfer the pheasants to a heated dish, cover with foil, and leave to stand in a warm place. Add the spring onions (scallions) to the roasting dish and sauté on top of the stove for 2 minutes. Stir the brandy in, add the cream, and boil for 2 or 3 minutes, until the sauce is slightly thickened. Add the grapes and simmer gently for 2 minutes while you halve or quarter the pheasants and arrange them on a heated serving dish. Stir the port and lemon juice into the sauce and simmer until hot. Adjust the seasoning and pour over the pheasants. Garnish with the watercress before serving.

Squire's Pheasant

Serves 3–4

1 or 2 pheasants, quartered
2 tablespoons melted butter
salt
freshly ground pepper
orange twists (page 209)

Sauce
3 medium onions, quartered
juice of 2 medium oranges
finely grated rind of 1 lemon
3 slices of bread, with crusts
*   removed*
¹/₃–¹/₂ cup (3–4 fl oz) dry white
*   wine*
salt and pepper

This is a very early English recipe which in the original form lacked finesse. Prepared today, with the aid of a blender or food processor, the flavour is unimpaired and the finished dish looks very appetising. Serve with game chips (page 184).

Pre-heat the oven to moderately hot. Brush the pheasant pieces with the butter and season with salt and pepper. Put the pheasants, skin side up, in a roasting dish, and pour any remaining butter over. Roast for 15 to 25 minutes. While the pheasants are cooking, make the sauce.

   Pour the sauce over the pheasants and cook for 10 minutes longer. Transfer to a heated serving dish or serve from the roasting dish. Garnish with the orange twists.

Sauce
Put the onions in a blender or food processor and purée with half of the orange juice. Add the lemon rind and one of the slices of bread and blend with the onions. Add more orange juice, another slice of bread, and blend again until smooth. Repeat with the last slice of bread and the remaining orange juice. Transfer the mixture to a saucepan and bring to the boil. Reduce the heat and add enough of the wine to make a light consistency. Season to taste and simmer for 5 minutes.

Pheasant with Bacon and Sour Cream

Serves 3–4

1 or 2 pheasants
2 thick fat bacon rashers, halved,
*   with rind removed*
2 tablespoons melted butter
1 cup (9 fl oz) light sour cream
salt
freshly ground black pepper
¹/₂ cup (4 fl oz) cream
salt

This is a Swedish dish that almost guarantees the moistness of the pheasant. A little care is needed to lay the bacon under the breast skin of the birds. Serve with braised chicory (page 181) and potato balls (page 185).

Pre-heat the oven to moderate. Carefully loosen the skin over the breasts of the pheasants. Insert a piece of bacon under the skin over each breast. Pull the skin back into position and brush the birds liberally with the melted butter. Fold the wings under the body of the birds, tie the legs together, and put them in a casserole. Roast, uncovered, in the centre of the oven for 15 minutes, until the birds begin to brown. Pour the sour cream over the pheasants and season lightly with salt and black pepper. Cover and cook for 40 to 55 minutes longer.

   Transfer the birds to a heated serving dish and keep hot. Stir the cream into the pan-juices, on top of the stove. Simmer gently until the sauce has thickened, adjust the seasoning, and serve with the pheasants.

Pheasant with Bacon and Sour Cream

Pheasant Ballotine

Casseroled in a rich sauce, this dish counteracts any of the bird's tendency to dryness. The birds are boned before being filled with a delicious stuffing and this greatly extends their serving portions. The skin of the pheasants should not be broken, so take care if buying frozen birds that the packaging is not damaged. They are particularly good served with snow peas and carrots Vichy (page 179).

Cut through the backbone of the pheasants. Prise the cut open and trim the backbone away. Flatten the birds and with a very sharp knife remove the ribs and breastbone, saving the trimmings for stock. Place the birds on a board, cut side down, and flatten by pressing along the breast with the heel of your hand. Turn them and sprinkle with the black pepper and allspice. Set aside and make the stuffing.

Divide the stuffing between the birds. Sew the sides together with a poultry needle and coarse thread, pressing the pheasants back into shape by moulding them around the stuffing. Tie the legs together and pin the wings into position, using heavy cocktail sticks or poultry pins. Pre-heat the oven to moderate.

Melt the butter in a flameproof casserole large enough to hold both birds, and brown them, one at a time. Start with the breasts and turn until they are evenly browned on all sides. Put the birds side by side in the casserole over low heat. Warm the sherry and pour over the pheasants. Allow the sherry to simmer for 2 or 3 minutes until it begins to glaze in the pan. Crush the tomatoes and pour, with the liquid from the can, around the birds. Cover and cook in the centre of the oven for 45 to 60 minutes, depending on the size of the birds.

Carefully lift the pheasants from the casserole. Remove the thread and pins and cover the breast of each bird with a slice of prosciutto. Arrange on a heated serving dish and keep hot. Strain the juices from the casserole into a small pan. Bring to the boil, adding a little more sherry if the sauce is too thick. Adjust the seasoning and pour over the pheasants.

Stuffing

Melt the butter in a heavy pan and quickly sauté the onion until softened but not browned. Tip the contents of the pan into a mixing bowl. Add the veal, pistachios, breadcrumbs, marjoram, and chicken livers. Mix thoroughly, seasoning with salt and pepper to taste.

Note: As only wing and leg bones are left in the pheasants they can very easily be carved at the table. Alternatively, the birds can be sliced before coating with the sauce. If you use a very sharp knife, you can carve the birds on the serving dish without disturbing their shape, and then coat with the sauce.

Serves 6–8

2 young pheasants
freshly ground black pepper
¼ teaspoon ground allspice
3 tablespoons butter
¾ cup (⅓ pt) brown sherry
425 g (15 oz/No. 300) can peeled tomatoes
10 slices of prosciutto
Stuffing
2 tablespoons butter
1 large onion, finely chopped
250 g (8 oz) minced (ground) lean veal
30 g (1 oz) coarsely chopped pistachios
125 g (4 oz) soft fresh breadcrumbs
½ teaspoon dried marjoram
185 g (6 oz) chicken livers, skinned and coarsely chopped
salt and pepper

Sesame Pheasant

The pheasants are pan-fried in a flavoured butter sauce. Serve with potato cheese puff (page 185).

Serves 3–4

1 or 2 pheasants, quartered
freshly ground black pepper
125 g (4 oz) butter, melted
3 tablespoons finely chopped fresh
   coriander
1 small clove of garlic, crushed
a pinch of ground ginger
2 tablespoons sesame seeds
salt
juice of ½ lemon
lemon twists (page 209)
coriander sprigs

Put the pheasant pieces in a shallow dish and season generously with black pepper. Mix the butter with the chopped coriander, the garlic, and ginger. Pour over the pheasant, turning the pieces until well coated. Set aside for 30 minutes.

Heat a wide, shallow pan over moderate heat. Sprinkle the sesame seeds into the hot pan, cover, and shake over the heat until the seeds are lightly browned. Put the pheasants, skin side down, in the pan with the seeds. Scrape any butter remaining in the dish into the pan and fry the pheasants over moderately low heat, turning from time to time, for 20 minutes or until the juices run clear when a thick portion is pierced with a fine skewer.

Transfer the pheasants to a heated serving dish, sprinkle lightly with salt, and keep hot. Stir the lemon juice into the pan, heat with the butter, and pour over the pheasants. Just before serving, garnish with the lemon twists and coriander sprigs.

Pheasant in a Pot

Pot-roasting is a very good way to cook any elderly bird, pheasant or otherwise, and especially those which have a tendency to be dry. The vegetables cooked with the bird flavour the dish as well as providing enough liquid to keep it moist. Serve with buttered new potatoes.

Serves 3–4

2 tablespoons butter
1 or 2 pheasants, loosely trussed
4 fat bacon rashers
2 medium onions, halved and sliced
2 large carrots, sliced
2 leeks, split and sliced
4 celery stalks, sliced
4 parsley sprigs
salt
freshly ground black pepper
½ cup (4 fl oz) chicken stock
3 tablespoons dry sherry

Melt the butter in a flameproof casserole. Add the pheasants, covering the breasts with the bacon. Pack the vegetables and parsley around the sides and season lightly with salt and black pepper. Cover and cook over medium heat for a few minutes until the vegetables start to sweat. Reduce the heat and simmer gently for 40 to 50 minutes, until the pheasants are tender.

Remove and discard the bacon, arrange the pheasants on a heated serving dish, and keep hot. Pour the stock over the vegetables, bring to the boil, and stir in the sherry. Adjust the seasoning and serve the vegetables in a separate dish.

Pheasant Casserole with Chestnuts

This casserole, which makes use of dried chestnuts, can be enjoyed at any time of the year. Serve with potato cheese puff (page 185) and braised fennel (page 182).

Serves 3–4

2 fat bacon rashers
1 or 2 pheasants
salt
freshly ground black pepper
3 tablespoons butter
1 clove of garlic, peeled
1 small onion, sliced
*125 g (4 oz) tiny button
   mushrooms*
3 tablespoons port
2 teaspoons butter
2 teaspoons plain (all-purpose) flour

Chestnut Stock
185 g (6 oz) dried chestnuts
*juice and finely grated rind of
   1 orange*
1 ½ cups (14 fl oz) chicken stock
*1 small thyme sprig or 1 teaspoon
   dried thyme*
salt and pepper

Prepare the chestnut stock. Wrap the bacon over the pheasant breasts, securing it with small poultry pins or coarse thread. Season inside and out with salt and black pepper, tie the legs together, and pin the wings to the body.

Melt the 3 tablespoons of butter in a flameproof casserole and cook the garlic and onion for 2 minutes to flavour the fat. Discard the garlic and brown the pheasants on all sides. Pour the stock and chestnuts around the pheasants and bring to the boil. Reduce the heat, cover, and simmer very gently for 40 minutes. Simmer the mushrooms in the port for 2 or 3 minutes until they are just tender. Add the port and mushrooms to the casserole and cook for 15 to 20 minutes, until the pheasants are cooked.

Transfer the birds to a heated serving dish. Using a slotted spoon, remove the chestnuts and mushrooms from the pan, arrange around the pheasants, and keep hot. Strain the pan-juices into a small pan. Work the butter and flour together and whisk small pieces into the sauce until it is lightly thickened. Simmer for 2 or 3 minutes, adjust the seasoning, and serve with the pheasants.

Chestnut Stock
Put the chestnuts in a saucepan with the orange juice and rind, stock, and thyme. Bring to the boil, lower the heat, and simmer gently for 30 minutes. Season to taste and discard the thyme sprig.

Sharp Sauce Pheasant

Browned pheasants are poached in an unusual Danish sauce which is both tart and savoury, as opposed to sweet and sour. Serve with sautéed broccoli (page 178) or any crisp green vegetable.

Melt the butter with the oil in a deep, heavy, lidded pan. Brown the pheasants, one at a time, on all sides. Season lightly with salt and black pepper. Add the stock, vinegar, and cayenne or red pepper and bring to simmering-point. Cover and cook gently for 50 to 60 minutes, until tender.

2 tablespoons butter
1 tablespoon vegetable oil
1 or 2 pheasants, trussed
salt
freshly ground black pepper
1 1/2 cups (14 fl oz) chicken stock
1 1/2 tablespoons wine vinegar
1/4 teaspoon cayenne or red pepper
1 tablespoon butter
1 tablespoon plain (all-purpose)
  flour
2–3 tablespoons dry sherry
white pepper
watercress sprigs

Transfer the pheasants to a heated serving dish and keep hot while you finish the sauce. Work the butter and flour together and gradually whisk small pieces into the stock, stirring constantly until it has all been absorbed. Stir in the sherry to taste and adjust the seasoning. Simmer for 2 minutes and spoon the sauce over the pheasants. Garnish with the watercress.

Pheasant with Sauerkraut

This very Bavarian dish combines the luxury of the pheasant with simple ingredients and, of course, beer. The result is an understated and very appealing dish. Serve it as it is or just garnish it with cobbler crescents.

Serves 4

1 or 2 pheasants
10 fat bacon rashers, with rind
  removed
2 tablespoons butter
2 tablespoons vegetable oil
1 cup (9 fl oz) dry white wine
12 white peppercorns
2 bay-leaves
750 g (1 1/2 lb) sauerkraut, rinsed
  and drained
1 cup (9 fl oz) beer
250 g (8 oz) kransky or cabana
  sausage
cobbler crescents (page 203)

Wrap the pheasants with the bacon, securing it with coarse thread. Loosely tie the legs together. Melt the butter with the oil in a heavy pan over moderately high heat. Fry the pheasants on all sides until the bacon fat starts to run.

Drain the excess fat from the pan (this dripping is worth saving). Reduce the heat and pour the wine over the pheasants. I have not included salt in the ingredients because the bacon may provide enough, but this needs to be tested. Add the peppercorns and bay-leaves and bring the wine to simmering-point. Cover the pan tightly and cook for 30 to 40 minutes, or until the birds are almost tender. Pack the sauerkraut around the sides of the birds and pour the beer over. Cover and simmer for 10 minutes. Add the sausage, cover, and heat through.

To serve, carefully lift the pheasants from the pan. Snip the threads and remove them without disturbing the bacon. Arrange the birds on a heated serving dish and keep them hot.

Remove the sausage and set aside for a moment. Adjust the seasoning of the sauerkraut before arranging it around the pheasants. Discard the bay-leaves and peppercorns as you find them. Quickly cut the sausage into 1 centimetre (1/2 inch) slices and lay them over the sauerkraut. Garnish with cobbler crescents if you wish.

Note: If you prefer not to carve the pheasants at the table, remove the trussing strings and carefully divide into serving portions, using snips or poultry shears. Try not to dislodge the bacon and you can set the halves or quarters together on the serving dish.

Basque Pheasant

The Basque region is abundant in poultry, game, fruit, and vegetables as well as herbs, spices, nuts, wine, ... and the French savoir-faire. Add the influence of Spain and echoes of north Africa from the Moors and the result is one of the most extensive and exciting styles of cooking to be found anywhere. Not surprising then that this recipe is a feast to see as well as eat. The spicy, Spanish-style chorizo sausages are available in delicatessens. If you have trouble finding them, use any spicy sausage instead.

Serves 4–6

2 pheasants
salt
freshly ground black pepper
3 tablespoons goose fat or olive oil
1 large onion, finely chopped
2–3 small carrots, coarsely chopped
3–4 cups (1 1/3–1 3/4 pt) chicken
* stock*
2 parsley sprigs
2 bay-leaves
1 thyme sprig or celery leaves
1 large clove of garlic, peeled
4 chorizo sausages
8 bacon rashers, with rind removed
410 g (13 oz) long-grain rice
Tomato Sauce
2 tablespoons goose fat or olive oil
500 g (1 lb) tomatoes, peeled,
* seeded, and roughly chopped*
3 red (bell) peppers, seeded and cut
* into 1 cm (1/2 inch) strips*
2 teaspoons Spanish paprika
salt and pepper

Season the pheasants inside and out with salt and freshly ground black pepper and tie the legs together. Heat the goose fat or oil in a large heavy pan, and brown the onion and carrots lightly over moderate heat. Add the pheasants and brown on all sides, turning them frequently. Arrange the pheasants side by side in the pan and add just enough of the stock to cover them. Tie the herbs together to make a bouquet garni and add to the stock with the whole clove of garlic. Cover and simmer gently for 15 to 20 minutes, depending on the size of the birds. Add the sausages and bacon. Cover and simmer for 20 minutes, or until the birds are tender.

While the birds are cooking, bring a large pan of water to the boil, add 2 teaspoons of salt, and stir in the rice. Cook the rice for 10 minutes, strain, and add a little more salt if necessary. Spread in the top of a steamer set over 2 cups (18 fluid ounces) of simmering water. Lay a folded cloth on top of the rice, cover, and steam for 15 minutes. If you do not have a steamer, leave the rice in the colander and steam over a saucepan in the same way. Prepare the sauce.

Spread the rice over a heated serving dish. Lift the pheasants from the casserole and cut into serving pieces, discarding as many small bones as you can. Arrange the pheasants on the rice and keep hot. Cut the sausages and bacon into bite-sized pieces, arrange on the serving dish, and surround the pheasants with the tomato sauce. Serve immediately.

Tomato Sauce

Heat the goose fat or oil in a small pan. Add the tomatoes and peppers and cook over fairly high heat, stirring constantly until the sauce is thick. Season with paprika, salt, and pepper. Reduce the heat to very low and keep the sauce hot — it should not be mushy.

Pheasant with Almond Sauce

The ingredients used for this dish suggest an old Portuguese, or an even earlier Moorish, influence. Whatever its history, the result is rich, spicy, and delicious. Serve with broccoli and rice.

Serves 3–4

3 cups (1 ⅓ pt) chicken stock
2·5 cm (1 inch) piece of fresh
   ginger, peeled and finely grated
3 large cloves of garlic, quartered
1 large onion, quartered
3 cloves
1 bay-leaf
salt
1 or 2 pheasants
juice of 1 lemon
60 g (2 oz) butter
1 large onion, finely chopped
½ teaspoon cayenne or red pepper
1 teaspoon ground coriander
fresh coriander or watercress

Almond Sauce

2 tablespoons boiling water
¼ teaspoon saffron threads
1 cup (9 fl oz) milk
1 teaspoon cardamom seeds
125 g (4 oz) blanched and finely
   ground almonds
½ cup (4 fl oz) cream
salt and pepper

Put the chicken stock in a large saucepan with the ginger, garlic, quartered onion, cloves, and bay-leaf. Add a little salt if necessary, bearing in mind that the flavoured stock will be reduced later. Bring to the boil, then reduce the heat and simmer for 30 minutes. Strain the stock, discard the flavouring ingredients, and return to the pan. Boil rapidly to reduce to half the original quantity. Adjust the seasoning and set aside.

Brush the pheasant with the lemon juice, tuck the wings under the body, fasten with poultry pins, and tie the legs together. Melt the butter in a heavy-based pan, add the chopped onion and fry over gentle heat until straw-coloured. Sprinkle with the cayenne or red pepper and coriander, stirring in well. Push the onion to one side of the pan and lightly brown the pheasant on all sides. Redistribute the onion mixture over the base of the pan, add the pheasant, and pour 1¼ cups of the reserved stock over. Bring to the boil, reduce the heat immediately and cover. Simmer for 20 minutes. In the meantime, make the sauce.

Uncover the pan and simmer for 15 minutes longer, until the flesh is tender and all the cooking liquid has been absorbed. Add the remaining stock if the pan becomes too dry before the pheasant is cooked.

Remove the pheasant from the pan, discard the pins and string, and cut into serving pieces. Arrange on a heated serving dish on a bed of rice. Surround with broccoli, pour the almond sauce over, and garnish with the fresh coriander or watercress.

Almond Sauce

Pour the boiling water over the saffron and set aside. Put the milk and cardamom seeds in a small pan and simmer gently for 6 or 7 minutes. Remove from the heat and leave to stand. Put the ground almonds in the top of a double boiler or a small bowl over simmering water and strain the milk and saffron liquid over. Set aside until the birds are almost cooked. Heat the almond mixture, stir in the cream, and season to taste. The sauce should be of a thick coating consistency — add a little more milk or cream if necessary.

Note: Guinea fowl, pigeon, and partridge can be cooked in the same way. Adjust the cooking time for the smaller birds.

PARTRIDGE

The most common member of the partridge family is the grey partridge which is found in the British Isles, across Europe, and as far as Siberia. When partridge is referred to, usually the grey partridge is meant. However, in some parts of the United Kingdom — particularly Ireland and the counties of Essex and Hertfordshire — the red-legged or French partridge is more common. This bird was introduced from France some time during the seventeenth century and is often referred to as the 'Frenchman'. The flavour of the French bird is best as it matures.

The introduction of partridges to Australia began in the middle of the nineteenth century but the establishment of the birds has been a failure. Initially the released birds showed remarkable signs that they would acclimatise but eventually, like pheasants, they fell prey to the massed ills of foxes, lack of cover, and indiscriminate hunters who were ungoverned by any game laws. Similarly, the true partridge is not native to the United States although the name is given to the ruffed grouse and the massena quail, both of which can be cooked in all ways suitable for partridge, bearing in mind that the ruffed grouse or ruffed partridge is a bigger bird and needs a longer cooking period.

Partridges should be plucked in the usual way and, like most game, benefit from hanging. Young birds should be hung for three to four days, older birds for up to one week. A young partridge is easily recognisable by the pointed tip of the first flight feather and, with grey partridge, by the yellow-brown feet. The first flight feathers of all partridges become rounded with age.

Roast Partridge, page 122; with Game Chips, page 184

Roast Partridge

Butter-roasted young partridges are traditionally served with game chips, watercress, and tiny Brussels sprouts or braised celery.

Serves 4

4 young partridges, trussed
salt
freshly ground black pepper
8 streaky bacon rashers, with rind
*   removed*
125 g (4 oz) butter, melted
2 tablespoons redcurrant jelly
½ cup (4 fl oz) port
watercress

Pre-heat the oven to very hot. Season the partridges with salt and black pepper and secure two bacon rashers over each bird. Arrange the birds, breast uppermost, in a roasting dish. Roast in the centre of the oven for 25 to 30 minutes, basting the partridges two or three times. Discard the bacon for the last 5 minutes of the cooking time.

Turn the oven off, transfer the birds to a serving platter, and keep warm. Skim excess fat from the juices in the roasting dish. Stir in the redcurrant jelly and the port and boil rapidly for 2 or 3 minutes. Season to taste. Garnish the partridges lavishly with watercress and glaze with the sauce before serving.

Partridge Pie

This extravagant, special-occasion pie is superb with braised celery or braised chicory (Belgian endive page 181).

Serves 6

1 quantity of cream cheese pastry.
*   (page 201)*
3 roasted partridges
1½ tablespoons butter
1½ tablespoons vegetable oil
500 g lean stewing veal, cut into
*   small dice*
salt
freshly ground black pepper
125 g (4 oz) lean ham, cut into
*   chunky pieces*
125 g (4 oz) trimmed and sliced
*   button mushrooms*
2 tablespoons finely snipped chives
1½ tablespoons finely chopped
*   parsley*
2 teaspoons dry mustard
½ cup (4 fl oz) chicken stock
½ cup (4 fl oz) medium-dry sherry
1 small egg, lightly beaten

Prepare the pastry, wrap closely with plastic-wrap, and chill in the refrigerator while you make the filling. Slice the meat from the partridges and cut into bite-sized pieces. Put the meat in a mixing bowl and set aside.

Melt the butter with the oil in a shallow pan set over moderate heat. When the fat is sizzling, add the veal and fry, turning occasionally, for about 5 minutes, until the meat is lightly browned. Season the veal, then add the ham and mushrooms and cook for 1 minute.

Fork the veal mixture and the herbs through the partridge meat. Blend the mustard smoothly with the stock, pour over the partridge with the sherry, and mix well. Spoon the filling into a deep, medium-sized pie-dish and put to one side. Pre-heat the oven to moderate.

Roll the pastry to a circle about 2 centimetres (¾ inch) larger than the top of the pie-dish. Cut a 1-centimetre (½ inch) strip around the dough and press the strip on to the rim of the dish. Moisten the pastry strip with cold water, cover the dish with the pastry, and press firmly to form a good seal. Trim and crimp the edges. Decorate the top of the pie with leaves made from the pastry trimmings, make a small slit in the top with a sharp knife, and brush all the pastry with the beaten egg.

Bake the pie on a centre shelf of the oven for 50 minutes, until the pastry is crisp and golden.

Partridge Pudding

Use second-year, or older, partridges for this hearty winter pudding. Serve with a creamed vegetable and crisp salad.

Serves 6

750 g (1½ lb) plain (all-purpose)
    flour
250 g (8 oz) grated suet
1½ teaspoons dry mustard
½ teaspoon salt
½ teaspoon freshly ground black
    pepper
iced water
125 g (4 oz) rump steak, cut across
    the grain into very thin slices
2 old partridges
125 g (4 oz) sliced mushrooms
90 g (3 oz) chopped raisins
2 tablespoons finely snipped chives
1 tablespoon chopped parsley
1 teaspoon chopped fresh tarragon,
    or
¼ teaspoon dried tarragon
1 teaspoon chopped fresh thyme, or
    ¼ teaspoon dried thyme
1½ cups (14 fl oz) rich beef stock
3 tablespoons dark ale

Generously butter a 1-litre (2 pint) pudding basin. Mix the flour, suet, mustard, salt, and black pepper in a bowl. Mix to a soft but fairly dry dough with iced water. Cut off one-third of the dough and put to one side. Roll the large piece of dough to a circle and use to line the basin, leaving approximately 1 centimetre (½ inch) overlapping the rim.

Season the steak lightly with salt and black pepper and layer it in the lined basin. Using a sharp knife, slice the meat from the partridges. Discard the skin and cut the meat into bite-sized pieces. Mix the partridge meat with the mushrooms, raisins, and herbs, seasoning lightly with salt and black pepper. Pack the mixture into the basin and pour the stock and ale over.

Roll the remaining dough to fit the top of the basin and press over firmly, pinching the edges of the lining and top firmly together to form a good seal. Trim the eges of the pastry and cover with a circle of buttered greaseproof paper and a pudding cloth. Tie the cloth securely around the basin and knot the cloth ends over the top of the pudding. Lower the pudding into a pan containing enough gently boiling water to reach halfway up the sides of the basin. Cover the pan and boil the pudding for 3 hours, topping the water up with boiling water when necessary.

To serve, remove the pudding cloth and paper. Secure a napkin around the basin and serve at table.

Partridges Segovia

Serves 4

4 young partridges, trussed
45 g (1½ oz) plain (all-purpose)
    flour
¾ teaspoon ground cardamom
salt
freshly ground black pepper
3 medium onions, coarsely chopped
250 g (8 oz) carrots, coarsely
    chopped
2 white turnips, coarsely chopped
125 g (4 oz) chopped lean ham
½ cup (4 fl oz) olive oil or
    vegetable oil
1 cup (9 fl oz) dry white wine
½ cup (4 fl oz) cream sherry
1 cup (9 fl oz) unsweetened tomato
    juice

This is a dish with an unusual combination of flavours. Serve with game chips and a simple, crisp green vegetable.

Pre-heat the oven to hot. Roll the partridges in the flour which has been seasoned with the cardamom and a little salt and pepper, then put the birds in a large casserole.

Toss the vegetables and ham together, season lightly with salt and plenty of black pepper, and pack this mixture around the birds. Pour the oil over the partridges and vegetables, cover the casserole, and cook in the upper half of the oven for 30 minutes.

Pour the wine, sherry, and tomato juice over the partridges. Lower the oven temperature to moderately hot and cook the birds, uncovered, for 1¼ to 1½ hours, until tender.

Transfer the birds and vegetables to a deep serving dish and keep warm. Boil the sauce rapidly until reduced by one-third. Adjust the seasoning and spoon over the birds before serving.

Partridges in Chocolate Sauce

There is a true Aztec influence in this recipe where the sauce is enriched with bitter chocolate. Serve with tiny new potatoes and a crisp green vegetable or salad.

Serves 4–6

4 partridges, trussed
salt
freshly ground black pepper
1 medium onion, chopped
2 cloves of garlic, finely chopped
3 tablespoons chopped parsley
90 g (3 oz) butter
⅓ cup (3 fl oz) olive oil
3 tablespoons wine vinegar
1½ cups (14 fl oz) water
2 tablespoons grated bitter chocolate
2 tablespoons fine fresh breadcrumbs
watercress sprigs

Pre-heat the oven to hot. Season the partridges with salt and black pepper and arrange in a flameproof casserole. Sprinkle the onion, garlic, and parsley over. Melt the butter with the oil and when sizzling pour over the birds. Roast in the centre of the oven for 20 to 25 minutes, until the birds are lightly browned. Remove the casserole from the oven and lower the temperature to moderately slow.

Mix the vinegar with the water and carefully pour over the partridges. Cover the casserole, replace in the oven, and cook for 1¼ to 1½ hours, or until the birds are tender.

Lift the partridges from the sauce and discard the trussing string. If the birds are small, arrange them, whole, on a serving plate. Large birds can be quartered first, in which case they will feed six people. Put the partridges in the turned-off oven to keep hot.

Boil the sauce rapidly for a few minutes until reduced by about one-third. Lower the heat, then stir in the chocolate and crumbs. Simmer for 2 to 3 minutes and adjust the seasoning before spooning the sauce over the birds. Garnish lavishly with watercress before serving.

Partridges with Chestnuts and Red Cabbage

This recipe is suitable for both young and second-year partridges — simply lengthen the suggested cooking time by 30 to 40 minutes for the older birds. Serve with tiny parsleyed potatoes.

Serves 4

250 g (8 oz) chestnuts
salt
2 tablespoons butter
2 tablespoons vegetable oil
125 g (4 oz) pork spek, cut into
  small dice
4 partridges
freshly ground black pepper
approx. 750 g (1½ lb) shredded red
  cabbage
1 small onion, finely chopped
1½ tablespoons drained capers
1¾ cups (¾ pt) dry white wine

Carefully make small slits in the shells of the chestnuts, drop them into a pan of boiling salted water, and cook for 15 minutes. Drain the chestnuts and remove their shells and inner skins while they are still hot. Pre-heat the oven to moderately slow.

Melt the butter with the oil in a large frying pan (skillet) set over moderate heat and lightly brown the diced spek. Remove from the pan and reserve. Add the partridges to the pan and brown lightly on all sides. Remove from the pan and season with salt and black pepper.

Fork the cabbage with the onion and capers, add to the frying pan, and turn until lightly coated with the pan-juices. Season lightly and pack half the mixture over the base of a casserole large enough to hold the partridges in one layer. Arrange the partridges, breast uppermost, on the cabbage. Add the chestnuts and spek and cover with the remaining cabbage mixture. Pour the wine over, cover the casserole with a sheet of foil and the lid, and cook for 1½ to 2 hours, or until the birds are fork-tender.

Partridges with Chestnuts and Red Cabbage

PIGEON

I cannot help wondering why the pigeon, also known as 'squab', is such a neglected bird in our kitchens. The distribution of these small birds is worldwide, with the result that there is a vast range of recipes for them. Even so, many people have never even tried them. It may be the association of pigeon with park, square, and piazza that deters the cook from using them. But the dressed pigeons which we buy do not in any way resemble the park variety. The very best kind is the King Squab, which is carefully fed and bred for the table — young and delectable, it is a very far cry from the wild or park variety.

Choosing recipes for the converted, as well as some to entice the wary, has been difficult. With so many good recipes, which can be discarded? Certainly not the rustic raised pigeon pie or the very elegant, but simple, pigeon with cherries. And how could I choose between a hearty jugged pigeon or the aptly named trencherman roast? I couldn't and so they are all here, old favourites and new variations with unusual combinations of ingredients.

Pigeons with Cherries, page 135

GENERAL INFORMATION

The cooking times given are only intended as a guide. The time will vary because of the age and feeding of the bird. You can be fairly sure that if the pigeon is a darkish colour it will need a slightly longer cooking time than a plump pale model will call for. The point of a sharp knife, gently piercing the breast, should produce a clear juice when the pigeon is cooked. The pigeon quantities are mostly given with King Squab in mind. If the pigeons are very small, allow two per person.

Roast Pigeons

This is a basic roast pigeon method, useful for the occasions when you need cooked pigeon meat for pies or to serve simply with a favourite sauce or stuffing.

Allow one pigeon per person

fat bacon rashers or ham fat
melted butter

Pre-heat the oven to moderate. Truss the pigeons and place them in a roasting dish with one rasher of fat bacon or ham fat over the breast of each bird. Pour 2 tablespoons of melted butter over each pigeon and roast for 30 to 50 minutes, or until the birds are tender. Remove the bacon or ham fat for the last 15 minutes of the cooking time to allow the breasts to brown.

To truss a pigeon, tie the legs together and fold the wings under the body. Secure the wings firmly with cocktail sticks or tiny poultry pins.

Roast Pigeons Carynthia

The combination of pigeon stuffed with an unusual Austrian pâté and topped with sour cream is exceptionally good. Serve with braised celery (page 180) and tiny new potatoes.

Serves 4

4 pigeons
1 tablespoon butter
1 tablespoon vegetable oil
½ cup (4 fl oz) light sour cream
fried crumbs (page 210)

Make the stuffing and pre-heat the oven to moderate. Stuff the pigeons loosely with the pâté, securing the openings with string or poultry pins. Melt the butter with the oil in a roasting dish, coat the stuffed pigeons with the oil, and roast in the centre of the oven for 30 to 40 minutes, or until cooked, basting frequently with the pan-juices. The cooking time is flexible because of the heat lost from

Pâté Stuffing

3 tablespoons butter
6 juniper berries
1 clove of garlic, halved
1 large onion, finely chopped
4 anchovy fillets, finely chopped
125 g (4 oz) calf liver, trimmed
    and minced (ground) or finely
    chopped
1/2 teaspoon dried thyme
freshly ground black pepper
salt

the oven during basting.

To serve, arrange the pigeons on a heated platter, drizzling a little sour cream over each one. Garnish with the fried crumbs.

Pâté Stuffing

Melt the butter in a heavy-based pan over gentle heat. Add the juniper berries and garlic and fry for 3 or 4 minutes, without browning the garlic. Remove and discard the berries and garlic. Add the onion to the pan and cook for 3 or 4 minutes, or until pale golden. Add the anchovies and liver and cook gently, turning the mixture in the butter until the liver changes colour. This will take only a minute or so — the liver should just be sealed, not cooked through. Remove the pan from the heat, tip the mixture and all the pan-juices into a bowl, and leave to cool. Mash the cooled mixture thoroughly with a fork; it should have a fairly coarse texture. Season with the thyme and black pepper but be careful about adding salt, because of the saltiness of the anchovies.

Roast Pigeons Trencherman

Cooked on a bed of vegetables and herbs, basted with wine and butter, this is one of the best ways to roast pigeon. You need a blender or food processor for the sauce. Jacket-baked potatoes (page 186) and crisp green vegetables round this dish off perfectly.

Serves 4

2 tablespoons butter
2 tablespoons vegetable oil
4 pigeons, trussed
2 medium onions, coarsely chopped
2 medium carrots, sliced
2 large tomatoes, peeled, seeded, and
    quartered
2 celery stalks, cut into large chunks
1 small cucumber, peeled, seeded,
    and coarsely chopped
2 large cloves of garlic, halved
4 parsley sprigs
approx. 1 cup (9 fl oz) white wine
salt
freshly ground black pepper

Pre-heat the oven to moderate. Melt the butter with the oil in a roasting dish on top of the stove. Turn the pigeons in the hot oil for 2 minutes until they are lightly browned on all sides. Remove from the heat, lift the pigeons out, and set aside. Mix the onions with the carrots, tomatoes, celery, and cucumber and spread out in a layer in the roasting dish. Put a piece of garlic and a parsley sprig under each pigeon as you return them to the pan. Press the birds lightly down into the vegetables. Heat the wine in a small saucepan and pour over the birds. Season with salt and plenty of black pepper. Roast for 35 to 40 minutes, or until the birds are tender. Baste the pigeon breasts with the pan-juices three or four times during the cooking period, adding a little more wine if necessary.

When the pigeons are tender, remove them to a heated serving dish and keep hot while you finish the sauce. Put the vegetables and pan-juices through the blender or food processor in batches. If the purée is too thick, add a little more wine, water, chicken stock, or vegetable stock. If you are cooking a green vegetable, a little of the cooking water is perfect, but do not over-thin the purée — it should be quite substantial.

To serve, reheat the vegetable purée and adjust the seasoning. Lightly coat the breasts of the pigeons with a little of the sauce and serve the rest separately.

Roast Pigeons Wonga

There is a very beautiful Aboriginal story about the Waratah and a Wonga pigeon. Once, when all Waratahs were white, a hen pigeon became worried about her mate and went to search for him. Attacked by a hawk, she took shelter in the forest and as she settled on the Waratahs they were stained forever with her blood. This recipe is a simple variation of a very early Australian dish. Serve with wilted spinach (page 189) or creamed spinach (page 188) or peas.

Serves 4

4 pigeons
1 tablespoon plain (all-purpose) flour
salt and pepper
juice of 1 lemon
2 tablespoons butter
½ cup (4 fl oz) chicken stock or white wine
1 banana, sliced and brushed with lemon juice
12–14 walnut halves

Banana Stuffing

2 bananas, roughly chopped
60 g (2 oz) fresh breadcrumbs
30 g (1 oz) finely grated beef suet
30 g (1 oz) coarsely chopped walnuts
1 teaspoon dried mixed herbs
1 tablespoon finely chopped parsley
1 egg, lightly beaten
salt and pepper

Make the stuffing and pre-heat the oven to moderately hot. Lightly fill the pigeons with the stuffing, remembering that it will expand when cooked. Secure the opening with thread or poultry pins. Dredge the pigeons lightly with the flour seasoned with salt and pepper. Arrange the birds in a roasting dish with the lemon juice and butter. Cover the breasts with buttered paper and cook for 15 minutes. Remove the paper and cook for 15 to 20 minutes longer, or until the birds are tender, basting them occasionally with the pan-juices.

To serve, spread the accompanying vegetable on a heated serving dish and arrange the pigeons on top. Keep hot in a low oven while you finish the sauce. Mix the stock or wine into the pan-juices, stirring any sediment into the sauce. Adjust the seasoning, spoon a little sauce over each bird, and serve the rest separately. Garnish the dish with the sliced banana and the walnut halves.

Banana Stuffing

Mix the bananas in a bowl with the breadcrumbs, suet, walnuts, dried herbs, and parsley. Add only enough of the egg to bind the ingredients together — the mixture should be fairly dry but not too crumbly. Season with salt and black or white pepper to taste.

Variation

Increase the stock to 1½ cups (14 fluid ounces), substituting white wine for half the quantity if you wish. The rest of the ingredients remain the same. Wrap 3 tablespoons of the stuffing in foil. Divide the remaining stuffing between the pigeons and secure the openings. Roast the pigeons, cooking the foil-wrapped stuffing in the same dish. Arrange the cooked birds on the vegetable and keep hot.

Open the foil and turn the stuffing into the pan-juices, mixing to form a thick paste. Gradually add enough of the stock, or stock and wine, to form a sauce thick enough to coat the back of a spoon. Adjust the seasoning, spoon a little of the sauce over each bird, and serve the rest separately. Garnish with the sliced banana and the walnuts.

Pigeon Pie

This is a rich and substantial pie topped with cream cheese pastry. To cook the pigeons, brush lightly with butter and roast in a pre-heated hot oven for 30 minutes. It needs only the simplest vegetable dish to make it complete — buttered baby carrots, perhaps, or the tiniest Brussels sprouts. Use the meat of three cooked pigeons.

Serves 4–6

½ cup (4 fl oz) chicken stock
3 tablespoons dry sherry
1 tablespoon brandy
salt and pepper
1 quantity of cream cheese pastry
  (page 201)
egg glaze (page 205)
Pigeon Filling
60 g (2 oz) butter
500 g (1 lb) lean stewing veal, cut
  into bite-sized cubes
125 g (4 oz) mushrooms, sliced
125 g (4 oz) lean ham pieces,
  chopped
meat of 3 cooked pigeons, skinned
  and chopped
2 tablespoons finely chopped parsley
2 tablespoons Dijon mustard
salt
freshly ground black pepper

Prepare the filling and use to fill a medium-sized pie-dish. Pour the stock, sherry, and brandy into the dish and adjust the seasoning. Set aside while you roll out the pastry to the shape of the pie-dish and about 2.5 centimetres (1 inch) larger than the overall size. Trim a 1 centimetre (½ inch) strip from the sides of the rolled pastry. Moisten the rim of the pie-dish with water and press the ribbon of dough on to the rim. Pre-heat the oven to moderate.

Brush the pastry-covered rim lightly with water and lift the rolled pastry on to the pie. Trim the edges with a sharp knife and crimp or pinch to seal. Use the pastry trimmings to decorate the pie. Cut a slit in the centre and brush with the egg glaze. Bake the pie for 50 to 55 minutes, until the pastry is golden, and serve immediately.

Pigeon Filling

Melt the butter in a large frying pan (skillet) and lightly brown the veal on all sides. Reduce the heat a little, add the mushrooms and ham, and stir the ingredients together, cooking for 2 or 3 minutes until the juices start to run from the mushrooms. Remove the pan (skillet) from the heat and tip the contents into a bowl. Add the pigeon meat, parsley, mustard, and seasonings, mixing together thoroughly.

Raised Pigeon Pie

This old English pie is finely textured, gamy, and full of flavour. Serve it hot, forget the potatoes, and add an extra vegetable: Brussels sprouts with chestnuts (page 179) and carrots with cream make a great combination. Serve a hunk of it with salad and you have a feast. Prepare the filling before making the pastry, unless you are going to raise the pie by hand (the instructions are on page 205).

Make the filling. Pre-heat the oven to hot. Spoon the filling into the pastry case or mould, carefully packing the mixture into the sides. Roll the lid of the pie, cover, and seal. Cut a hole or slit in the top of

1 quantity of hot-water crust pastry
   (page 204)
egg glaze (page 205)
½ cup (4 fl oz) beef stock
3 tablespoons red wine

Pigeon Filling

2 tablespoons butter
breast meat of 4 pigeons, thinly
   sliced
1 small onion, finely chopped
125 g (4 oz) ham, finely chopped
250 g (8 oz) sausagemeat,
   preferably pork
250 g (8 oz) button mushrooms,
   finely chopped
2 hard-boiled eggs, coarsely chopped
1 teaspoon salt
white pepper
finely grated rind of 1 lemon
a generous pinch of cayenne or red
   pepper

the pie, decorate, and brush with the egg glaze. Put the pie on a baking tray and cook for 1 hour.

Remove the pie from the oven and set aside. Reduce the temperature to moderate. Rapidly bring the beef stock and wine to the boil. If the pie has been hand-raised, remove the foil while the stock is boiling. Carefully pour the hot stock into the pie, through the vent. Return the pie to the oven and cook for another hour. Serve immediately, or allow to cool at room temperature and then store.

Pigeon Filling

Melt the butter in a frying pan (skillet) over gentle heat. Add the sliced pigeon breasts and turn in the butter until they change colour slightly. Remove the meat to a large mixing bowl. Increase the heat and add the onion to the pan (skillet); stir into the pan-juices and cook for 1 or 2 minutes. The onion will absorb most of the liquid. Tip the contents of the pan into the bowl with the pigeon meat. Add the ham, sausagemeat, mushrooms, eggs, salt, pepper, lemon rind, and cayenne or red pepper. Combine all the ingredients — this is most easily done in a kneading fashion, by hand.

Note: You will have four pigeon carcasses left after this performance. Use one to make stock and the other three will make a very good game pâté (page 23). Extend the quantity of meat needed in that recipe by using chicken livers.

Raised Pigeon Pie

Pigeons with Port

This simple-to-cook French recipe is mildly extravagant and very delicious. Serve with Seville potato cakes (page 186) and whole French beans or snake beans.

Serves 4

90 g (3 oz) butter
4 pigeons, halved
250 g (8 oz) button mushrooms
salt
white pepper
3 tablespoons brandy
300 ml (½ pt) cream
1 tablespoon cornflour (cornstarch)
½ cup (4 fl oz) port
grated nutmeg

Melt the butter in a heavy, lidded pan large enough to hold all of the pigeons. Turn the pigeons until they are completely coated in butter and cook them over gentle heat with the butter just simmering, for 15 minutes. They should not be browned. Add the mushrooms and season with salt and pepper to taste. Cover and simmer for 20 to 30 minutes, until the pigeons are tender. Transfer the cooked birds to a heated serving dish, arrange the mushrooms around them, and keep hot while you finish the sauce.

Add the brandy to the pan-juices, mixing well to incorporate any sediment. Stir the cream in and allow it to simmer for 1 minute. Mix the cornflour (cornstarch) to a smooth paste with the port and add to the sauce, stirring constantly until it thickens. Raise the heat and cook for 2 minutes until the sauce is cooked and has reduced slightly. Add nutmeg to taste and adjust the seasoning before pouring the sauce over the pigeons.

Pigeons Catalan

These pigeons are braised in a rich and colourful sauce of the Catalan region, which combines the flavours of France and Spain. The sauce is cooked first and the longer it stands, the better the result will be. Serve with tiny new potatoes.

Serves 4

2–3 tablespoons olive oil or
*   vegetable oil*
4 pigeons, trussed
Sauce
1 tablespoon butter
1 tablespoon olive oil or vegetable
*   oil*
10 spring onions (scallions), green
*   and white parts, coarsely chopped*
425 g (15 oz/No. 300) can peeled
*   tomatoes*
4 cloves of garlic, finely chopped
125 g (4 oz) white button
*   mushrooms, finely chopped*
1 cup (9 fl oz) white wine
salt
freshly ground black pepper

Make the sauce and set it aside until you are ready to cook the pigeons. Heat the oil in a heavy, flameproof casserole and brown the pigeons on all sides, turning them frequently. Drain any excess oil from the casserole before pouring the sauce over the pigeons. Heat the sauce to a gentle simmer, cover, and cook on top of the stove for 1 to 1½ hours, or until the pigeons are tender. Serve straight from the casserole or transfer to a heated dish and serve the vegetables separately.

Sauce
Melt the butter with the oil in a heavy saucepan. Add the spring onions (scallions) and cook over gentle heat until they are transparent but not coloured. Add the tomatoes and garlic, crushing the tomatoes to a pulp with a fork, and bring slowly to simmering-point. Simmer for 15 minutes. Stir in the mushrooms and wine, cover, and cook for 20 minutes. Season generously with salt and plenty of black pepper.

Pigeons with Cherries

With such a variety of ways to cook pigeon it really is worth waiting to make this only when fresh, whiteheart (pale-coloured) cherries are in season. Serve with crisp French beans.

Serves 4

5 tablespoons butter
4 pigeons
1 medium onion, finely chopped
60 g (2 oz) pinenuts
1 tablespoon plain (all-purpose)
* flour*
2 cups (18 fl oz) chicken stock
1 bay-leaf
2 sprays of celery leaves
1 small celery stalk, quartered
3 parsley sprigs
salt
white pepper
500 g (1 lb) whiteheart cherries,
* stoned*
1/3 cup (3 fl oz) cream
4 croûtes (page 210)

Melt 3 tablespoons of the butter in a large pan, add the pigeons, and turn them in the butter until lightly browned. Remove and set aside. Add the onion to the pan and fry gently until transparent. Stir in the pinenuts and fry for 2 or 3 minutes until they are lightly coloured. Sprinkle the flour into the pan, stir, and cook for 2 minutes until straw coloured. Gradually add the stock, stirring constantly between each addition to form a smooth sauce. Simmer gently for 2 or 3 minutes.

Tie the bay-leaf, celery leaves or celery, and parsley together to make a bouquet garni and push deeply into the sauce. Season very lightly with salt and pepper and return the birds to the pan, spooning some sauce over each one. Cover and simmer for 35 to 40 minutes, until the pigeons are tender.

When the birds are cooked, lift them carefully from the sauce, arrange on a heated serving dish, and keep hot. Discard the bouquet garni and raise the heat to bring the sauce nearly to boiling-point. Allow the sauce to bubble and reduce by a quarter. In the meantime, melt the remaining butter in a shallow pan and fry the cherries for 3 or 4 minutes until they are very hot. Add the cherries with their pan-juices, and the cream, to the sauce. Bring back almost to boiling-point and adjust the seasoning before pouring over the pigeons. Serve garnished with the croûtes.

QUAIL

For such a small bird, the quail has managed to make quite an impact on our lives. Twice they supplied the food necessary for the Israelites in the wilderness, both occasions being the season when the birds migrate to the north and can be found in vast numbers on the coastal areas of the Red Sea and Mediterranean.

The Victorians dramatically 'quailed in fright'. This expression derived from the habit of migratory quails crashing with exhaustion at their destination (they are not birds of strong flight), only to be collected by the hands of waiting trappers.

And now, with domestication and commercial 'farming', we can readily enjoy these little game birds all year round.

Mango Quails, page 145

GENERAL INFORMATION

Unlike other game there is no advantage to be gained by hanging quails. They should be eaten within 24 hours of being killed.

If you have fresh quails to prepare, pluck them, singe away any light pin feathers, and remove the head before eviscerating them through the neck opening.

Since most of us buy frozen quails, cover them loosely, so that they do not dry out or absorb other flavours, and thaw them completely in the refrigerator before cooking. As they are so small this does not take very long.

Allow two quails per person for a main course.

Roast Quails

This is the simple way to roast these tiny birds. Bard them with rashers of fat bacon and serve with game chips (page 184) and a creamed vegetable.

Serves 4

8 quails
24 juniper berries, bruised
8 fat bacon rashers, with rind removed
3 tablespoons melted goose fat or butter
freshly ground black pepper
2 teaspoons plain (all-purpose) flour
3 tablespoons beef stock (from a cube)
3 tablespoons port
salt

Pre-heat the oven to hot. Put three juniper berries into the cavity of each bird. Fasten the wings to the body with poultry pins and wrap each bird with bacon. Put the quails compactly in a roasting dish, pour the melted fat over, and season with black pepper. Roast in the centre of the oven for 15 to 20 minutes.

Transfer the quails to a heated serving dish and leave to stand in a warm place. Pour off all but 1 tablespoon of the fat from the roasting dish. Stir the flour into the pan-juices and cook for 1 minute before adding the stock and wine. Stir constantly until the gravy is smooth. Adjust the seasoning and serve with the quail.

Variation

The quails can be flavoured in a variety of ways, rather than with the juniper berries. Roast them with a hot chilli in the cavity, a small bunch of fresh herbs, or a piece of peeled fresh ginger. Stuff them with 1 tablespoon of pâté and secure the opening before roasting.

Quails with Herb Sauce

Lightly browned and pot-roasted with stock and wine, the quails remain moist and delicious. Serve with stuffed pumpkin (page 188), crisp green beans, and the herb sauce.

Serves 4

2–3 tablespoons goose fat or butter
8 quails
salt
white pepper
1 thyme sprig
1 marjoram sprig
1 rosemary sprig
1 bay-leaf
3/4 cup (1/3 pt) dry white wine
*1/2 cup (4 fl oz) chicken stock or
   veal stock*
*1 tablespoon very finely chopped
   parsley*
1 tablespoon butter
*1 tablespoon plain (all-purpose)
   flour*

Pre-heat the oven to moderate. Heat the fat or butter in a flameproof casserole and quickly brown the quails on all sides. Season lightly with salt and pepper. Tie the thyme, marjoram, rosemary, and bay-leaf together to form a bouquet garni. Add the herbs to the pan with the wine and stock. Bring to the boil. Cover tightly, using foil or paper to make a good seal. Cook in the centre of the oven for 35 to 45 minutes.

Carefully lift the quails from the casserole, arrange on a heated serving dish, and keep hot. Discard the bouquet garni and stir the parsley into the liquid. Work the butter and flour together and add in small pieces to the pan, whisking between each addition, until the sauce has a light coating consistency. Adjust the seasoning and spoon over the birds.

Persimmon Quails

Marinated quails are lightly steamed and cooked on a bed of persimmons. Serve with sautéed broccoli (page 178) and game chips (page 184).

Serves 4

*1 quantity of spiced marinade
   (page 200)*
8 quails
2 tablespoons butter
4 large ripe persimmons, sliced
4 spring onions (scallions), chopped
1 large clove of garlic, crushed
1 teaspoon dry mustard
salt
light sour cream (optional)

Put the marinade in a plastic bag or lidded container large enough to hold the quails. Add the birds, seal the bag or container, and marinate for 1 hour, turning the bag or container once or twice.

Lift the quails from the marinade (reserving about 1/3 cup). Put the birds in a steamer set over simmering water. Cover and steam until just tender. Pre-heat the oven to moderate.

While the quails are steaming, spread the butter over the base of an ovenproof dish. Cover the butter with the sliced persimmons and sprinkle with the spring onions (scallions). Bake in the centre of the oven for 15 minutes. Mix the garlic and the mustard with the reserved marinade and set aside.

Lift the quails from the steamer and, when cool enough to handle, remove the meat from the bones. Spread the quails over the partly cooked persimmons, and pour the garlic mixture over. Cover and return to the oven for 15 minutes.

Serve the quails very hot, from the dish, accompanied by the vegetables and sour cream.

Marinated Roast Quails

If I could include only one quail roast in this book, this would be my choice. Use any of the pâtés in the first chapter (the goose liver pâté (page 21) is very good). Serve with a creamy vegetable.

Serves 4

small game marinade (page 198)
8 quails
250 g (8 oz) pâté
60 g (2 oz) butter
8 small slices of ham fat
1 ¼ cups (11 fl oz) dry white wine
2 tablespoons lemon juice
3 tablespoons redcurrant jelly
salt
white pepper
lightly fried quail eggs, or watercress

Put the quails in a dish, pour the marinade over, and leave to stand for 24 hours. Lift the quails from the marinade; drain and pat dry thoroughly. The marinade can be stored and used again. Pre-heat the oven to moderately hot. Stuff the birds with the pâté, about 2 tablespoons to each bird. Secure the openings with tiny poultry pins or cocktail sticks.

Melt the butter in a deep, heavy-based roasting dish until foaming. Add the quails, turning in the butter until they are browned on all sides. Arrange the quails, breast side up, compactly in the dish and cover each breast with a piece of ham fat. Add ¾ cup (⅓ pint) of the wine and the lemon juice to the pan. Roast the birds just above the centre of the oven for 15 to 20 minutes, or until tender. Baste the quails frequently with the pan-juices and discard the ham fat 5 minutes or so before the end of the roasting time. Remove the birds from the pan, discard the pins or sticks, and keep hot on a heated serving dish.

Skim any fat from the surface of the pan-juices. Add the remaining wine with the redcurrant jelly and bring to the boil on top of the stove. Gently boil until the sauce has reduced and thickened slightly. Adjust the seasoning and spoon a little of the sauce over each bird. Garnish with the quail eggs or watercress.

Gala Quails

These parcels of quail can be put together well in advance and quickly roasted when you are ready. Serve them 'en papillote' with vine-leaf fritters (page 190) and a crisp salad.

Serves 4

8 quails
goose fat or melted butter
salt
freshly ground black pepper
16 small button mushrooms, sliced
2 tablespoons butter
⅓ cup (3 fl oz) cream
⅓ cup (3 fl oz) Madeira

Pre-heat the oven to hot. Cut eight pieces of ovenproof plastic, large enough to enclose each bird loosely. Brush the quails lightly with fat or butter and season inside and out with salt and black pepper. Put some of the sliced mushrooms in each cavity with 1 teaspoon of butter and put each bird on a sheet of the plastic. Mix the cream with the Madeira and divide between the birds, folding each wrapper around them as you do so, to secure the sauce. Twist the ends of the parcels and roast for 15 to 20 minutes. Serve the quails in their parcels.

Marinated Roast Quails

Quails with Cherry Stuffing

The magnificent stuffing adds to the quails without detracting from their delicate gamy flavour. If you can acquire a fresh truffle so much the better but I think a canned one is a waste of money in this recipe. The quails take less than 30 minutes to cook, so make the cherry jelly beforehand to allow for setting. Serve with snake beans or French beans and roast potatoes.

Serves 4

8 quails
1 ½ teaspoons salt
freshly ground black pepper
60 g (2 oz) butter, melted
Cherry Jelly
425 g (15 oz/No. 300) can black
  cherries
juice of 1 lemon
1 ½ teaspoons powdered gelatine
Stuffing
30 g (1 oz) fresh breadcrumbs
⅛ teaspoon dried marjoram
1 pork sausage, skinned
1 truffle, finely chopped (optional)
1 egg, lightly beaten
salt and pepper

Make the jelly first, allowing a couple of hours for it to set.

Season the quails inside and out with the salt and black pepper. Set aside while you make the stuffing. Pre-heat the oven to very hot. Divide the stuffing between the quails and very loosely secure each cavity with small poultry pins or thread. Pin the wings to the sides of the bird and loosely tie the legs together. Arrange the birds, breast side up, in a roasting dish and pour the melted butter over them. Roast just above the centre of the oven for 15 to 20 minutes, or until the birds are tender.

To serve, remove the pins and trussing strings, arrange the quails on a hot serving platter, and surround with the vegetables. Serve the jelly separately, chopping it lightly before putting it in a serving bowl.

Cherry Jelly
Drain the syrup from the cherries into a measuring cup. Reserve twenty cherries for the stuffing. Add enough lemon juice to the cherry syrup to make 1 cup (9 fluid ounces) of liquid. Pour 2 tablespoons of the cherry juice into a small bowl and sprinkle the gelatine over the surface. Leave to stand for 2 or 3 minutes. Stand the bowl in a saucepan containing a little hot water. Heat gently until the gelatine has melted. Strain into the remaining cherry liquid, pour into a shallow dish, and cover. Refrigerate until set.

Stuffing
Mix the breadcrumbs with the marjoram and sausage until crumbly and well blended. Chop the twenty cherries reserved from the jelly and add with the truffle, mixing lightly together. Add only enough of the egg to bind the ingredients. The mixture should not be too wet.

Duck with Cherry Stuffing
Double the stuffing ingredients, making the cherry jelly in the same way. Pre-heat the oven to moderate. Spoon the cherry stuffing into a 2-kilogram (4 pound) duck. Prick the skin and close the cavity. Cook on a rack in a roasting dish for 1½ to 2 hours, until tender.

Serve with cross-hatched potatoes (page 185), crisp green beans, and the cherry jelly.

Quails with Cherry Stuffing

Wrapped Quails with Grapes

Wrapped Quails with Grapes

This is exotic but without any complicated techniques. It also incorporates that other quail favourite, grapes. Serve with game chips (page 184).

Serves 4

8 quails
salt
freshly ground black pepper
250 g (8 oz) seedless grapes
3 tablespoons butter
8 slices of prosciutto
1 pack or small can vine-leaves
1 cup (9 fl oz) veal or chicken stock
½ cup (4 fl oz) dry white wine
2–3 tablespoons coffee liqueur
1 tablespoon cream

Season the quails inside and out with salt and black pepper. Put five or six grapes in the cavity of each bird and tie the legs together. Melt the butter over moderate heat in a heavy, flameproof casserole. Brown the birds on all sides. As soon as they are browned, lift them carefully from the pan and leave until cool enough to handle. Pre-heat the oven to hot.

Lay a slice of prosciutto over the breast of each bird and completely overwrap with vine-leaves. Secure the leaves in position with a length of coarse thread, criss-crossing once over the breast before tying. Arrange the birds in the casserole and pour the stock and white wine over them. Cover and cook just above the centre of the oven for 15 minutes. Remove the lid and cook for 5 to 10 minutes longer, until the birds are tender. Remove the casserole from the oven and reduce the temperature to very slow. Arrange the quails on a heated serving platter and keep them hot in the oven while you finish the sauce.

Boil the pan-juices rapidly on top of the stove until reduced to half the original quantity. Lower the heat and add the remaining grapes to the pan with the coffee liqueur. Simmer gently for 2 minutes. Lift the grapes from the sauce with a slotted spoon and arrange over and around the quails. Stir the cream into the sauce and heat through briefly without boiling. Adjust the seasoning and pour the sauce over the birds.

Mango Quails

Mangoes, understated spicing, and the tang of lemon make a very tempting combination. If you use canned mangoes, drain and slice the fruit into thin strips. Use as directed but increase the amount of lemon juice if necessary. Do not serve this dish with carrots, as the colours clash horribly. Crisp vegetables and salad are far more appealing.

Serves 8

16 quails
salt
freshly ground black pepper
2 tablespoons butter
2 tablespoons vegetable oil
1 small clove of garlic, peeled
1 medium onion, finely chopped
1 large or 2 small fresh mangoes,
 stoned and sliced, or
 425 g (15 oz/No. 300) can
 sliced mangoes
1 ½ teaspoons very finely grated
 lemon rind
2 cloves
¼ teaspoon ground cinnamon
¼ teaspoon ground coriander
1 ½ teaspoons plain (all-purpose)
 flour
¾ cup (⅓ pt) chicken stock
2-3 tablespoons lemon juice
¾ cup (⅓ pt) cream
hard-boiled quail eggs or thin lemon
 slices

Season the quails inside and out with salt and black pepper. Secure the wings to the body with poultry pins or cocktail sticks. Pre-heat the oven to moderate.

Heat the butter with the oil in a frying pan (skillet) and sauté the garlic cloves without browning for 2 minutes, to flavour the fat. Discard the garlic and lightly brown the quails on all sides, cooking only a few at a time. Transfer to a casserole large enough to hold them upright without crowding.

Add the onion to the frying pan (skillet) and cook over low heat until transparent. Add the mangoes and fry with the onion for 2 minutes, turning once or twice. Using a slotted spoon, transfer the mangoes and onion to the casserole, spreading the mixture over and between the quails.

Add the lemon rind and cloves to the frying pan (skillet) and sprinkle with the cinnamon, coriander, and flour. Stir until blended into the pan-juices and cook for 1 minute. Gradually add the chicken stock and 2 tablespoons of the lemon juice, stirring constantly between each addition, until the sauce is smooth. Simmer for 1 minute, adjust the seasoning, and, if you like, add a little more lemon juice. Pour the sauce over the birds, cover, and cook for 30 to 35 minutes, until the quails are tender.

Carefully lift the birds from the casserole, arrange on a heated serving dish, and keep hot. Bring the sauce quickly to the boil on top of the stove. Reduce the heat, stir in the cream, and simmer for 1 or 2 minutes. Adjust the seasoning before pouring the sauce over the quails. Garnish with quail eggs or lemon slices.

WOODCOCK AND SNIPE

The woodcock is a migratory game bird and is a native of the northern hemisphere. It is fairly widespread throughout Europe, North America, and parts of Asia (the Asian woodcock migrates as far south as New Guinea).

These are meaty birds with darker flesh on the body than the legs. The taste is unusual — vaguely reminiscent, to me, of very good liver — and quite powerful. Anything cooked with woodcock is imbued with its flavour.

Woodcock are frequently eaten with the trail which is much prized in some circles and the recipes offer you this choice. The birds can be eaten freshly shot or hung for a few days (see page 11) — an advisable step to take as the season progresses. Like all game birds they need to be well barded with ham fat or bacon and should never be overcooked.

From the food writer's point of view these delicious birds present one problem: not only do they vary in size, as all game birds do, from start to end of season, but woodcock also differ in size, and quite markedly, from country to country. Thus, one mid-season woodcock will amply feed one person in England or France but a North American woodcock of similar vintage will leave you hungry indeed, being some 40 per cent smaller than its European counterpart. The answer to the problem of how many woodcocks to serve lies, as ever, in the judgment of the cook, but certainly North American readers must look towards almost doubling the quantity of birds used in these recipes.

The common snipe is found in many parts of the world but the snipe family also includes the great snipe, red-breasted snipe, and jack snipe. These small birds — they weigh between 90 grams (3 ounces) and 250 grams (8 ounces) — are highly prized and delicious to eat, although to make a decent main course you will need two birds for each serving.

The flesh of snipe is very delicate and needs quite careful handling. The feathers can almost be rubbed off with the skin and any stubborn ones lightly plucked. The birds are seldom drawn before cooking (not as grisly as it may sound because the birds are marsh-eaters and do not have a stomach in the usual sense), and so the tail is usually secured with small skewers. To truss snipe, make a small hole through the wings and breast of the bird, then twist the head around the body and push the long beak, skewer-fashion, through the hole, cross the legs, and tie together.

In the northern hemisphere snipe are at their best in October and November. The season, in the United Kingdom, is from 12 August to 31 January. Snipe can be eaten freshly shot but the flavour is improved if the birds are hung for two to four days.

Roast Snipe, page 152

Roast Woodcocks

Woodcocks are usually roasted with the trail, but this is very much a matter of personal taste. Whether the birds are drawn or undrawn, however, the cooking method remains the same. Serve with game chips (page 184), fried crumbs (page 210), and a green vegetable.

Serves 4

4 woodcocks
60 g (2 oz) butter, softened
salt
freshly ground black pepper
4 fat bacon rashers
4 slices of toast, with crusts removed
2 tablespoons plain (all-purpose) flour
1 cup (9 fl oz) rich beef stock
2 tablespoons port, or
* 1 tablespoon redcurrant jelly*
finely grated rind of ½ orange
watercress

Pre-heat the oven to very hot. Fold the wings of the birds under the breast and tuck the ends into the neck cavity. Tie the legs together. Reserve 2 tablespoons of the butter and spread the rest over the woodcocks. Season with salt and black pepper. Secure a bacon rasher over each bird.

Arrange the toast in a roasting dish (where it will catch the drippings from the birds, making a delicious accompaniment). Put the birds on a rack and set this over the toast. Cover the woodcocks with greaseproof paper and roast for about 15, and not more than 20, minutes, basting frequently. Remove the paper and bacon 3 or 4 minutes before the end of the cooking time and sprinkle ½ teaspoon of the flour over each bird. Baste the birds and return to the oven to brown.

Transfer the toast to a heated serving platter and arrange the birds on the toast raft. Discard the trussing string and keep the birds hot. Melt the remaining butter in the roasting dish, stir in the remaining flour, and brown over moderate heat for 2 minutes. Gradually add the stock, stirring constantly to form a smooth gravy. Add the port, or redcurrant jelly, and the orange rind. Simmer gently for 2 or 3 minutes and adjust the seasoning. Garnish the woodcock with watercress and surround with the vegetables of your choice before serving.

Woodcock Casserole

These migratory birds winter in the southern States of America, particularly Louisiana, source of the Creole influence in this recipe.

Halve the woodcocks through backbone and breast. Trim the backbone away and cut the wings to the first joint. Place the trimmings in a pan with 1¼ cups of cold water. Bring to the boil, then simmer for 15 minutes. Strain and set aside.

Melt 2 tablespoons of the butter in a large, shallow pan. Add the onions, red (bell) pepper, and garlic and stir until lightly coated with the butter. Cover and cook the vegetables over low heat for 10 minutes. Season the mixture lightly with salt and black pepper and spread over the base of a casserole. Pre-heat the oven to moderate.

Serves 4

4 woodcocks
60 g (2 oz) butter
2 medium onions, sliced
1 large red (bell) pepper, seeded and
    sliced
1 large clove of garlic, finely
    chopped
salt
freshly ground black pepper
1 1/2 tablespoons plain (all-purpose)
    flour
1/2 cup (4 fl oz) dry white wine
boiled rice

Add about 1/2 teaspoon of salt and pepper to the flour and dust over the woodcock. Melt the remaining butter in the pan in which the vegetables were cooked and briskly fry the bird until browned. Arrange, skin side up, on the vegetables. Add 1 cup (9 fluid ounces) of the strained stock to the pan drippings with the wine. Bring to the boil and season to taste before pouring over the woodcocks. Cover the casserole tightly and cook for 35 to 45 minutes, depending on the size of the birds.

Arrange the woodcocks on a serving dish with a border of rice and keep hot. Stir the liquid and vegetables remaining in the casserole until smooth. You can put the whole lot through a blender but I feel the sauce is better with some texture. Adjust the seasoning and reheat, if necessary, before spooning over the birds.

Roast Woodcocks with Orange Sauce

A fine marriage of flavours to serve with fried cauliflower (page 179) and a crisp green vegetable.

Serves 4

60 g (2 oz) butter, softened
4 woodcocks, trussed
salt
freshly ground black pepper
ham fat or fat bacon
4 slices of bread, with crusts
    removed, crisply fried in butter
juice and finely grated rind of
    1 large orange
1/2 cup (4 fl oz) dry white wine
1/2 cup (4 fl oz) rich game stock or
    chicken stock
2 extra teaspoons butter
1 large orange, peeled and thinly
    sliced

Pre-heat the oven to very hot. Spread the butter liberally over the woodcocks and season with salt and black pepper. Tie a piece of ham fat or bacon over each bird and place on a rack set over a roasting dish. Roast in the centre of the oven for 12 to 15 minutes, basting frequently.

While the birds are cooking, blanch the orange rind for a few minutes in a little boiling water. Prepare the fried bread and arrange over the base of an ovenproof serving dish. Remove the birds from the oven and reduce the temperature to moderate. Discard the fat or bacon, seat the birds on the prepared bread, and return them to the oven.

Add the wine and stock to the drippings in the roasting dish. Bring to the boil, then simmer for 2 or 3 minutes. Add the strained orange juice and season to taste. Stir the extra butter in and spoon the sauce over the birds. Garnish with the orange slices.

Woodcocks Flambée

The woodcock trail is considered by some a great delicacy, by others to have too strong a flavour. This accommodating recipe should please everyone as the trail is cooked and served separately.

Serves 4–6

8 woodcocks
salt
freshly ground black pepper
125 g (4 oz) butter
4–6 slices of bread, with crusts removed
1 teaspoon chopped fresh marjoram or ¼ teaspoon dried marjoram
3 tablespoons brandy
2 tablespoons red wine
juice of ½ lemon

Pre-heat the oven to very hot. Draw the woodcocks and reserve the trail. Season the birds inside and out with salt and black pepper, cross the legs, and tie together. Reserve 2 tablespoons of the butter and smear the rest liberally over the birds. Place the woodcocks on a rack set over a roasting dish and cook for 15 minutes, or until they are still pink but not bloody.

Quarter the birds, cutting them over a plate to catch any juices. Trim the quarters into neat cutlets, arrange on a serving dish, and keep hot. Quickly fry the bread in the buttery juices left in the roasting dish until crisp. Set aside. Add the remaining butter to the dish with the juices from the cooked birds. Cook the trail for 2 or 3 minutes, sprinkle with the marjoram, and season to taste. Mash the cooked trail and spread over the fried bread. Halve the slices diagonally and arrange around the woodcocks.

Pour the brandy into the roasting dish, flame, and add the wine and lemon juice. Boil briefly, season, and spoon over the birds.

Sautéed Woodcocks

Short, sweet, simple, and very delectable ... serve with braised celery (page 180).

Serves 4

4 woodcocks
2 tablespoons plain (all-purpose) flour
salt
1 teaspoon dried green peppercorns
90 g (3 oz) butter
1 tablespoon lemon juice
⅓ cup (3 fl oz) Madeira
2 tablespoons cream

Halve the woodcocks through backbone and breast. Trim the wing-tips, spine, and any loose bones. Dust the skin side of the birds with the flour and season with salt and the peppercorns, which have been lightly crushed (you can use green peppercorns pickled in brine but the flavour will be less subtle).

Melt the butter in a large shallow pan. Brown the woodcocks quickly on the skin side, reduce the heat a little, and fry for 2 or 3 minutes. Turn the birds and cook, still over moderate heat, for 5 minutes. Turn once again, reduce the heat, cover, and cook gently for 5 minutes longer.

Transfer the birds to a serving dish and keep hot. Add the lemon juice and Madeira to the pan, stirring well into the pan-juices. Stir the cream in and adjust the seasoning. Spoon over the birds and serve immediately.

Barbecued Woodcocks

Woodcocks can be eaten freshly shot ... and what better way than grilled (broiled) over a glowing open fire? Serve them with really well-done jacket-baked potatoes and crisp vegetables.

Serves 4

4 woodcocks
^{1}/$_3$ cup (3 fl oz) olive oil or vegetable oil
2 tablespoons gin
juice and finely grated rind of ^{1}/$_2$ lemon
salt
freshly ground black pepper
1 large clove of garlic

Halve the woodcocks, cutting through backbone and breast with kitchen scissors or snips. Trim away wing pinions and backbone. Mix the oil with the gin, lemon juice and rind, and about ½ teaspoon each of salt and black pepper. Make several small cuts in the clove of garlic, add to the oil mixture, and leave to soak for a few minutes.

Have the accompanying vegetables almost ready and the fire glowing, not blazing. Brush the woodcocks all over with the oil mixture and place, cut side down, on the grill (broiler). Cook for 3 to 5 minutes on each side, basting frequently with the oil mixture. The woodcocks should still be slightly pink when cooked. Season lightly and serve immediately.

Grilled (Broiled) Woodcocks

Serve simply grilled (broiled) woodcocks with a creamed vegetable and a fruit sauce — the musky flavour of lingonberry jelly is perfect but redcurrant jelly is also good.

Serves 4

4 woodcocks
125 g (4 oz) butter, melted
8 juniper berries, lightly bruised
^{1}/$_4$ teaspoon powdered bay-leaves
1 tablespoon chopped parsley
salt
freshly ground black pepper
4 slices of crisp toast
watercress
lemon wedges

Pre-heat the grill (broiler) to medium. Split each woodcock through the backbone, trim the spine, and press the bird flat with the palm of your hand. Trim away the wing pinions and reserve the trail if you wish.

Mix the butter with the juniper berries and the herbs. Season the birds lightly and place, skin side up, in a grill (broiler) pan. Pour half of the butter mixture over the birds. Set the pan about 15 centimetres (6 inches) from the heat and grill (broil) the birds for 3 or 4 minutes, basting every minute.

Turn the birds and, if using the trail, add it to the pan at this point. Pour the remaining butter over the birds and trail and cook for 3 or 4 minutes longer. To serve, dip the slices of toast into the buttery pan-juices and cut it into triangles. Mash the trail on to the toast, season lightly, and arrange around the birds on a hot serving platter. Garnish with watercress and lemon wedges.

Roast Snipe

Allow one bird per person as a savoury, two for a main course. Serve on crisp rafts of buttery, oven-fried bread with watercress and game chips

1 or 2 snipe per serving
2 tablespoons melted butter
salt
freshly ground black pepper
1 streaky bacon rasher, with rind removed, for each bird
1 slice of buttered bread, with crusts removed, for each bird

Pre-heat the oven to hot. Brush the snipe with the melted butter, season with salt and black pepper, and cover each bird with a bacon rasher. Lay the bread slices in a roasting dish to catch the drippings and set a rack over the top. Arrange the snipe on the rack and roast for 15 minutes. There is little virtue in a cool snipe — they need to be served straight from the oven, on top of the bread slices.

Compôte of Snipe

The initial roasting of the snipe can be completed well ahead of time then finished shortly before serving with a creamed potato dish.

Serves 4–6

6 snipe
6 streaky bacon rashers, with rind removed, or 6 ham fat slices
60 g (2 oz) butter, melted
2 medium carrots, sliced
90 g (3 oz) green beans, cut into small pieces
1 small turnip, diced
2 unpeeled zucchini, sliced
90 g (3 oz) fresh peas
salt
2 medium tomatoes, sliced
1/2 cup (4 fl oz) water
3/4 cup (1/3 pt) white wine
1/2 cup (4 fl oz) port
1 parsley sprig
1 thyme sprig
1 spray of celery leaves
1 bay-leaf
pepper
extra butter

Pre-heat the oven to hot. Truss the snipe and secure a bacon rasher or slice of ham fat over each bird. Put the snipe in a baking dish, pour a little of the melted butter over each, and roast for 10 minutes.

While the snipe are roasting, cook the carrots, beans, turnip, zucchini, and peas in boiling salted water until crisply tender. Strain the vegetables and reserve.

Remove the snipe from the oven and cool them enough to handle. Slice the meat from the carcasses, toss with the mushrooms, and reserve.

Pack the carcasses into a saucepan and crush with the back of a spoon. Add the tomatoes, water, wine, port, and herbs. Bring to the boil, season lightly with salt and pepper, then simmer very gently for 20 minutes. Strain through a fine sieve.

When you are ready to finish cooking, put the snipe and mushrooms in a shallow pan and pour the sieved stock over the pan and simmer the birds gently for 10 minutes. Toss the reserved vegetables in a little butter until hot, pile them in a mound on a serving dish, and keep warm in a low oven.

When the snipe is cooked, adjust the seasoning and spoon around the vegetables.

Grilled (Broiled) Snipe with Juniper Butter

When grilling (broiling) snipe the timing depends very much on personal taste. For those who enjoy these tender birds merely 'passed through a flame', and for very tiny snipe, grill them for the shorter suggested time. Certainly the birds should never be overcooked for, like most game, they can easily become very dry. Serve with a crisp potato dish, watercress, and a sharp jelly.

Serves 4, or 8 as an entrée

8 snipe, trussed
10 juniper berries
125 g (4 oz) unsalted butter
salt
freshly ground black pepper
8 croûtes (page 210)

Pre-heat the grill (broiler) on low setting and arrange the snipe on their sides, well spaced, in the grill (broiler) pan.

Put the juniper berries in a small pan with the butter and stab them a few times with a fork. Melt the butter over low heat and simmer for 3 to 4 minutes, until the butter is imbued with the flavour of the berries. Pour the butter over the snipe, season with salt and black pepper and set the pan at the lowest point from the heat. Grill (broil) for 3 to 7 minutes on each side, basting frequently. Serve the snipe very hot on the croûtes (fried bread) and glazed with the juices from the pan.

Alternatively, the snipe can be grilled (broiled), barbecue-fashion, over glowing coals and basted with the juniper butter.

Sautéed Snipe with Madeira Glaze

As the snipe are sautéed in next to no time you will need to have accompanying vegetables ready before you start cooking the birds. Creamed cauliflower and a crisp salad are complementary to this dish.

Serves 4–6

8–12 snipe
3–4 tablespoons plain (all-purpose) flour
125 g (4 oz) butter
salt
freshly ground black pepper
³/₄ cup (¹/₃ pt) Madeira

Halve the snipe through backbone and breast and dust lightly with the flour. Melt the butter in a shallow pan set over moderate heat. When the foam subsides, add the birds to the pan and brown them evenly on the skin side. Keep moving the snipe in the hot butter as they scorch easily; the browning will take about 3 to 4 minutes. Lower the heat a little, turn the snipe, and season the browned sides with salt and black pepper. Cook for 3 to 4 minutes, then turn the birds again and shake the pan over the heat for 3 to 4 minutes longer.

Lift the birds from the pan and arrange on a serving platter. Keep them warm in a low oven. Pour the Madeira into the pan, stirring and scraping up all the crusty bits. Boil rapidly for 3 to 4 minutes, until well reduced and glossy. Spoon the glaze over the birds before serving.

GROUSE

(U.K. season: 12 August to 10 December)

The red or Scotch grouse of the British Isles is considered to be the most delicious of all game birds, the very finest being those shot from mid-August to mid-October of the year in which they have been bred.

The bird feeds mostly on heather and berries and has a mild, gamy flavour which develops on hanging (see page 11) although many birds are eaten unhung, particularly those comprising the traditional grouse dinner on the opening of the grouse season, known as the 'Glorious Twelfth'.

Grouse are usually bought in brace (pair), one hen, one cock. The hen is considered the better of the two. Early in the season a whole bird is the usual serving for each person. These tender young grouse need no special sauce to enhance them — simple roasting is enough. As the birds become plump they will serve two or more, and as they grow old are better made into casseroles, pies, and puddings.

Although there are several varieties of the grouse family in Europe — blackcock or black grouse, capercaillie, and ptarmigan — the true grouse does not exist in North America although, to confuse matters, many birds there are called grouse. The larger American prairie chicken, sage grouse, and ruffed grouse can all be prepared and cooked using the grouse recipes but more time must be allowed for cooking. As far as I can discover no one has even attempted to introduce grouse into Australia but it is interesting to note that despite this the terms 'grouse' and 'extra grouse' are used colloquially in Australia to describe something very good or excellent!

Salmis of Grouse, page 158

Roast Grouse

This is probably the best way to enjoy plump, young grouse. To be really traditional, serve with game chips (page 184), fried crumbs (page 210), and redcurrant jelly.

Serves 4

*4 young grouse, each weighing
    about 375 g (12 oz)*
salt
freshly ground black pepper
4 tablespoons butter
4 fat bacon rashers
2 teaspoons plain (all-purpose) flour
*1 cup (9 fl oz) rich game stock or
    beef stock*
1 tablespoon brandy
watercress

Pre-heat the oven to hot. Reserve the livers and dry the grouse thoroughly with paper towels. Season inside and out with salt and black pepper and place a tablespoon of butter inside each bird. Fasten a bacon rasher securely over each grouse, fold the wings close to the body, and tie the legs loosely together.

Place the birds on a rack set over a roasting dish and cook in the centre of the oven for 25 to 30 minutes, a little longer if the birds are large. Baste frequently. Drop the livers into the roasting dish 10 minutes before the end of the cooking time and discard the bacon.

Arrange the grouse on a heated serving dish, removing the trussing string, and keep them hot. Mash the livers into the pan-juices in the roasting dish. Stir in the flour and cook over low heat for 1 minute. Gradually add the stock and stir constantly until the gravy is lightly thickened. Add the brandy, adjust the seasoning, and simmer for 2 or 3 minutes. Garnish the grouse with watercress and strain the gravy into a sauceboat.

Roast Grouse

August Grouse

To celebrate the 'Glorious Twelfth', roast very young grouse quite simply filled with buttered raspberries. The grouse takes less than 30 minutes to cook, so prepare the vegetables in advance. Serve with game chips (page 184) and a crisp green vegetable.

Serves 4

4 young grouse
90 g (3 oz) butter, melted
salt
freshly ground black pepper
185 g (6 oz) raspberries
¼ teaspoon freshly grated nutmeg
watercress

Pre-heat the oven to hot and lightly oil a roasting dish. Brush the grouse inside and out with a little of the butter, then sprinkle with salt and black pepper. Fold the wings under the birds and tuck the ends into the neck cavity.

Combine the raspberries with the remaining butter and the nutmeg. Spoon a quarter of the mixture into the cavity of each grouse. Tie the legs loosely and place the birds in the roasting dish. Cover loosely with buttered greaseproof paper and roast in the centre of the oven for 25 to 30 minutes. If the grouse weigh more than 375 grams (12 ounces), allow a little longer, but be careful not to overcook. Remove greaseproof paper for the last few minutes.

Transfer the birds to a heated serving dish, discarding the trussing string, and keep them hot. Stir the pan-juices over low heat until smooth. Season to taste and strain. Spoon the sauce over the grouse and garnish with watercress.

Grouse Pie

This is a melt-in-the-mouth way to use a mature bird. Although the grouse is cooked on the bone in the pie many of the small bones can be removed before baking. Serve with carrots Vichy (page 179) and a crisp green vegetable.

Serves 4–6

½ quantity of swag pastry (page 205)
1 mature grouse
250 g (8 oz) stewing steak, cut into 2-cm (¾ inch) cubes
2 tablespoons plain (all-purpose) flour
salt
freshly ground black pepper
2 bacon rashers, with rind removed, cut into strips
2–3 hard-boiled eggs, quartered
1 medium onion, chopped
125 g (4 oz) mushrooms, sliced
½ cup (4 fl oz) beef stock
2 teaspoons tomato paste

Prepare the pastry and chill for 30 minutes before rolling. Pre-heat the oven to very hot.

Cut the grouse into eight pieces, trimming away the backbones and wing pinions and removing as many small bones as possible. Dust the grouse and steak with the flour, season generously with salt and black pepper, and arrange in a deep pie-dish with the bacon, eggs, onion, and mushrooms. Mix the stock with the tomato paste and pour into the dish.

Roll the pastry to cover the pie-dish and trim the edges. Cut a vent in the top of the pie and decorate with pastry leaves. Bake the pie in the centre of the oven for 20 minutes. Reduce the oven temperature to moderately hot, cover the pastry with foil or greaseproof paper, and bake for 1¼ hours longer.

Salmis of Grouse

The salmis — part roast part braise — is a traditional method of cooking game birds. The roasted birds can be 'finished' or chafed at the table or just as easily be completely cooked in the kitchen, and with the advantage of being partially boned.

Serves 4

90 g (3 oz) butter
2 × 500 g (1 lb) grouse
salt
freshly ground black pepper
2 slices of ham fat or fat bacon
1 medium onion, finely chopped
1 clove of garlic, finely chopped
3 small carrots, finely chopped
1 ½ tablespoons plain (all-purpose) flour
1 cup (9 fl oz) chicken stock
1 cup (9 fl oz) red wine
2 parsley sprigs
1 bay-leaf
1 thyme sprig
185 g (6 oz) mushrooms, thinly sliced
3 tablespoons port
triangular fried croûtes (page 210)

Pre-heat the oven to very hot. Place 1 tablespoon of the butter inside each bird and season, inside and out, with salt and black pepper. Fold the wings close to the breast and tie the legs together. Drape the ham fat or bacon over the birds and place them on a rack set over a roasting dish. Roast the birds for 15 minutes and baste frequently, using a little extra butter if necessary.

While the birds are roasting, melt the remaining butter in a saucepan and fry the onion, garlic, and carrots until just softened. Sprinkle the flour over the vegetables and cook over low heat for a minute or so, stirring occasionally. Add the stock and wine, stirring constantly to form a smooth sauce. Bring almost to the boil, then simmer for 3 or 4 minutes. Tie the herbs together to form a bouquet, add to the sauce, and season lightly. Simmer for a few minutes more.

Remove the grouse from the oven and discard the fat or bacon and the trussing string. Quarter the birds, trim away the backbone and wing pinions, and remove the skin. Many of the small bones can also be discarded at this point. Arrange the grouse in a heatproof dish and scatter the mushrooms over.

Add the port to the simmering sauce, discard the bouquet, and adjust the seasoning. Strain the sauce over the grouse and mushrooms and simmer over low heat for 10 minutes, or until the birds are just cooked through. Arrange the croûtes around the salmis.

Grouse Casserole with Dumplings

This layered grouse and beefsteak casserole is a fine way to use older grouse. Use the grouse livers to make liver dumplings and serve with a creamy potato dish and redcurrant jelly.

Serves 6

2 old grouse
1 ¼ cups (11 fl oz) chicken stock (page 194)
375 g (12 oz) lean chuck steak or round steak
2 tablespoons vegetable oil
1 large onion, thinly sliced
salt

Quarter the grouse, trim away the wing pinions and backbones, and reserve the livers. Simmer the bones in the chicken stock for 30 minutes.

Cut the steak across the grain into 1-centimetre (½ inch) slices. Heat the oil and brown the steak quickly. Remove the steak from the pan, add the grouse, and lightly brown the meaty side of the quarters. Add the onion and turn until lightly coated with the pan-juices.

freshly ground black pepper
3 parsley sprigs
1 bay-leaf
1 thyme sprig
½ cup (4 fl oz) port or red wine
freshly grated nutmeg
liver dumplings (page 211)

Pre-heat the oven to moderately slow. Layer the grouse, steak, and onion in a casserole, seasoning each layer lightly with salt and black pepper. Tie the herbs together to form a bouquet and bury it in the casserole. Strain the stock, season to taste, and pour a scant cup (9 fluid ounces) over the grouse. Add the port or wine and a light sprinkling of nutmeg. Cover tightly and cook for 1 hour.

Prepare the dumplings and chill for 30 minutes. After the initial cooking time, place the dumplings in the casserole, replace the lid, and cook for another hour. Remove the lid for the last 10 minutes to allow the top to brown. Discard the bouquet before serving.

Grouse Pudding

Here is a hearty pudding to make towards the end of the grouse season when the weather is cold and the grouse old. Brussels sprouts, at their best in winter, make the perfect accompaniment.

Serves 6

2 mature grouse
1 small onion, quartered
½ bay-leaf
2 cloves
salt
freshly ground black pepper
2 tablespoons butter
1 tablespoon vegetable oil
500 g (1 lb) lean stewing steak,
 cut into 2·5-cm (1 inch cubes)
1 medium onion, coarsely chopped
1 large tomato, peeled and chopped
250 g (8 oz) plain (all-purpose)
 flour
1 teaspoon baking powder
125 g (4 oz) grated suet
2 tablespoons port

Using a very sharp knife, cut the grouse flesh from the bones. Trim the meat into bite-sized pieces and set aside. Put the carcass in a saucepan with the quartered onion, bay-leaf, cloves, and a little salt and black pepper. Cover with cold water, bring to the boil, then simmer for 45 minutes. Strain the stock, season to taste, and cool.

Melt the butter with the oil in a large shallow pan and brown the grouse and steak cubes lightly. Toss the meats with the onion and tomato, season lightly, and leave to cool.

Sift together the flour, baking powder, and ½ teaspoon of salt. Stir in the grated suet and mix to a soft (but not sticky) dough with cold water. Reserve one-third of the dough and use the rest to line a pudding basin of 4-cup (1¾ pints) capacity. Pack the grouse mixture into the lined basin and add ¾ cup (1/3 pint) of the stock and the port. Roll the remaining dough to form a lid and press over the top. Cover the crust with buttered greaseproof paper and tie a cloth over that.

Have ready a large saucepan containing enough simmering water to reach three-quarters of the way up the sides of the basin. Boil the pudding for 3 hours (the pudding will come to no harm if boiled for half an hour or so longer). Use boiling water to top the water-level up when necessary. To serve, discard the paper and cloth and wrap a folded napkin around the basin.

Note: Additional gravy can be made by thickening the remaining stock with a little beurre manié — equal quantities of butter and plain (all-purpose) flour worked together smoothly and whisked in a little at a time.

FURRED GAME

Man has hunted for thousands of years, and eaten just about everything that moves, from armadillo to zebra.

The game included in this chapter is that which is most readily hunted in shops or donated by huntin'-'n'-shootin' friends.

*Top: Rabbit with Maple Sauce, page 169; **foreground:** Roast Saddle of Hare, page 162*

Hare

The hare — quite my favourite game animal — is not just a very big rabbit as most people seem to imagine. It is a different species and quite unlike rabbit in texture and flavour, having very dark flesh and a rich gamy taste. Like rabbit, however, it is widely distributed and there are many ways of dealing with it.

The forequarters of hare are most suitable for casseroling or potting, the saddle and hind legs for roasting. The body is covered with a thick, rather shiny membrane which must be removed before cooking; this is not difficult as it can be released with a sharp knife and peeled off.

Hares freeze well. Defrost them in the refrigerator for 12 to 16 hours, depending on size.

Roast Saddle of Hare

Use just the back and hind legs and serve with crisp French beans or snake beans and almost any potato dish or noodles.

Serves 4–6

saddle and hind legs of hare
salt
freshly ground black pepper
4 thin slices of pork or ham fat
2 tablespoons melted goose fat or
* vegetable oil*
1/2 cup (4 fl oz) game stock or beef
* stock*
1/2 cup (4 fl oz) port
watercress
Cumberland sauce (page 196)

Pre-heat the oven to moderately hot. Using a sharp knife, carefully remove any shiny membrane from the hare. Position the legs close to the body and season lightly with salt and black pepper. Put the hare in a roasting dish, cover with the pork fat, and pour the melted fat or oil over. Roast in the centre of the oven for 30 minutes.

Mix the stock with the port and bring to the boil in a small pan. Remove the fat from the hare and discard. Pour the port mixture over and cook for 15 minutes longer.

Transfer the hare to a heated serving dish and keep hot. Reduce the pan-juices rapidly, on top of the stove, over high heat until syrupy. Glaze the hare with the sauce and garnish with watercress before serving with the Cumberland sauce.

Roast Saddle of Hare with Chestnut Sauce

This has a very rich sauce, but the hare carries it well. Serve with tiny new potatoes and Brussels sprouts or zucchini, lightly sprinkled with lemon juice.

Serves 4–6

saddle and hind legs of 1 hare
3 tablespoons melted goose fat or
butter
freshly ground black pepper
8 juniper berries, bruised
1 small can unsweetened chestnut
purée
½ cup (4 fl oz) cream
salt

Pre-heat the oven to hot. Using a sharp knife, carefully remove any shiny membrane from the hare. Put the saddle in a roasting dish and pour the melted fat or butter over. Season lightly with black pepper, put the juniper berries in the dish, and roast in the centre of the oven for 45 to 50 minutes, basting frequently with the fat.

Transfer the saddle to a heated serving dish and keep hot. Discard all but 1 tablespoon of fat from the roasting dish. Stir the chestnut purée into the pan-juices and simmer for 1 or 2 minutes, until reduced to a smooth paste. Add the cream, heat through without boiling, and season with salt and pepper to taste. Spoon a little of the sauce over the hare and serve the rest separately.

Hare Fillets Duxelles

The meat is cut from the hare in strips, leaving the fore legs and carcass to be used for soup, potted hare, or game pie. Serve with Seville potato cakes (page 186) and a crisp green salad or vegetable.

Serves 4–6

saddle and hind legs of 1 hare
juice of 1 lemon
4 juniper berries
freshly ground black pepper
90 g (3 oz) butter
8 spring onions (scallions), chopped
1 teaspoon dried mixed herbs
250 g (8 oz) button mushrooms,
left whole if small, otherwise
halved
salt
2 tablespoons plain (all-purpose)
flour
½ cup (4 fl oz) beef stock
½ cup (4 fl oz) dry white wine
3 tablespoons cream
60 g (2 oz) fried or dry
breadcrumbs
1 teaspoon Spanish paprika

Remove the shiny membrane from the hare and cut the meat thinly from the saddle and hind legs. Lay the fillets in a shallow dish. Pour the lemon juice over the juniper berries and pound together. Pour the mixture over the hare and season with black pepper.

Melt half the butter in a small flameproof casserole and cook the spring onions (scallions) until softened. Sprinkle with the herbs, add the mushrooms, and cook for 2 minutes. Season lightly and remove from the heat.

Pre-heat the oven to moderate. Remove the hare from the lemon juice, pat dry, and dust with the flour. Melt the remaining butter in a shallow pan and brown the fillets, cooking the meat from the legs for a few minutes longer than the saddle fillets. Add the stock and wine, season to taste, and simmer gently for 10 to 15 minutes. Lift the fillets from the pan and arrange over the vegetable mixture. Boil the wine mixture for 3 or 4 minutes, remove from the heat, and add the cream. Adjust the seasoning and pour over the hare. Mix the crumbs with the paprika, sprinkle over the hare, and bake for 15 to 20 minutes, until the top is browned and bubbling. Serve from the casserole.

Hare with Prune Sauce

Serves 4–6

1 hare, jointed
60 g (2 oz) butter, melted
60 g (2 oz) fresh breadcrumbs
salt
freshly ground black pepper
Sauce
250 g (8 oz) dessert prunes, stoned
60 g (2 oz) ground almonds
1½ cups (14 fl oz) dry red wine
½ cup (4 fl oz) beef stock
2 tablespoons wine vinegar
¼ teaspoon cinnamon
1 teaspoon sugar
salt and pepper

This is a traditional hare casserole. Whereas the Central Europeans counteract the richness of hare with sour cream, the English fashion, as achieved here, is to add prunes. If you are using dried prunes, soak them in cold water overnight. Simmer until tender, discard the stones, and use as directed. Serve with braised fennel (page 182) and glazed turnips (page 189).

Pre-heat the oven to moderate. Brush the joints of hare liberally with the butter and roll in the breadcrumbs. Season with salt and black pepper and put the joints in a casserole. Cook in the centre of the oven, uncovered, for 20 minutes while you prepare the sauce.

Pour the sauce over the hare. Cover and cook for 1 to 1¼ hours, until the hare is tender. Serve from the casserole or transfer to a heated serving dish.

Sauce

Purée the prunes in a blender or food processor. Add the ground almonds and 1 cup (9 fluid ounces) of the wine, blend thoroughly, and pour into a saucepan. Simmer over gentle heat, gradually adding the remaining ingredients. Season with salt and pepper to taste.

Hunter's Hare

Serves 4–6

750 g (1½ lb) hare
6 juniper berries
4 cloves
1 small clove of garlic, unpeeled
salt
freshly ground black pepper
1 cup (9 fl oz) red wine
185 g (6 oz) spek
1 tablespoon oil
2 large onions, coarsely chopped
1 tablespoon Hungarian paprika
1½ teaspoons dried mixed herbs
12 small pickling onions
sour cream (optional)

Top: *Hunter's Hare;*
 foreground: *Cabbage Medley,*
 page 179

This dish is of Polish origin. Use the legs and trimmings of the hare after the saddle has been removed. Serve with creamy potatoes and red cabbage or cabbage medley (page 179).

Put the hare in a saucepan with the juniper berries, cloves, garlic, and ½ teaspoon each of salt and black pepper. Add the wine and just enough cold water to cover the meat. Simmer the hare gently for 30 to 40 minutes, then remove from the heat, and cool slightly in the cooking liquid. Remove the hare from the pan and reserve the stock. Cut the meat into cubes and set aside. Pre-heat the oven to moderate.

Fry the spek in a pan over moderate heat until the fat starts to run. Adding a little oil if there is insufficient fat from the spek, fry the chopped onions until golden. Reduce the heat a little and stir in the hare. Sprinkle with the paprika and herbs and transfer to a casserole. Set aside.

Bring the reserved liquid to the boil, adjust the seasoning, and strain into the casserole. Cover and cook in the centre of the oven for 30 minutes. Add the pickling onions and cook for 30 to 40 minutes longer, until the hare is tender. Adjust the seasoning and serve very hot. Offer the sour cream separately.

Paprika Hare

This Hungarian dish is really delicious. The meat is cut in thick slices from the saddle and hind legs, and simply cooked with the traditional paprika and sour cream. Serve with tiny forcemeat dumplings (page 210) and buttered noodles.

Serves 4
1 ½ teaspoons salt
3–4 teaspoons Hungarian paprika
meat of 1 hare, sliced
2 tablespoons goose fat or butter
2 large onions, coarsely chopped
1–1 ½ cups (9–13 fl oz) water
500g (1lb) noodles
1 tablespoon vegetable oil
1 tablespoon butter or olive oil
1 cup (9 fl oz) sour cream

Mix the salt with the paprika in a large paper bag. Shake the slices of hare in the bag until coated on all sides with the seasoning.

Melt the fat or butter in a heavy pan and quickly sauté the onions until golden. Reduce the heat a little and brown the hare slices on all sides. Add 1 cup (9 fluid ounces) of the water, shake the pan, and cover tightly. Simmer gently for 40 to 50 minutes, adding a little more water from time to time if the hare looks dry. Towards the end of the hare's cooking time, cook the noodles until tender, in boiling, salted water with the oil added. Strain and toss with the butter or oil. Keep hot while you finish the sauce.

When the hare is cooked, pour the sour cream into the pan. Stir the ingredients together and adjust the seasoning. Serve very hot on the bed of noodles.

Paprika Hare

Rabbit

Rabbits have a worldwide distribution (there are even arctic species) and this has led to the creation of a vast variety of cooking methods. The beauty of rabbit is that it is available all year round and is inexpensive yet makes fine eating. The flesh is pale, not unlike chicken in appearance, and the flavour just hints of the wild.

Rabbits are not governed by any game laws, and, strictly speaking, are rough shooting rather than game. Indeed, many rabbits available to us have never seen the 'great outdoors' but have been specially bred in hutches for the table. However, all rabbit is cooked as game and needs the same larding or barding or basting to prevent the lean flesh from becoming dry.

Rabbits freeze well and should be thawed, in the refrigerator, for 12 to 14 hours.

Honeyed Rabbit

This rabbit is marinated in a mixture of honey and lemon. Although this marinade is used in the dish, the honey flavour does not dominate. Serve with creamed spinach (page 188) and potato cheese puff (page 185).

Serves 4

1 rabbit, cut into serving pieces
juice of 2 lemons
3 tablespoons honey
45 g (1 ½ oz) plain (all-purpose) flour
½ teaspoon white pepper
1 teaspoon salt
30 g (1 oz) sesame seeds
1 teaspoon dried tarragon
3 tablespoons butter
3 tablespoons olive oil
watercress or spring onion (scallion) bon-bons (page 209)

Put the rabbit in a shallow dish. Mix the lemon juice and honey together in a small pan, heating gently until the honey has dissolved. Pour the mixture over the rabbit, turning each piece until well coated. Marinate for 1 or 2 hours, turning the rabbit occasionally.

Mix the flour with the pepper, salt, sesame seeds, and tarragon. Spread over a sheet of paper. Lift each rabbit piece from the marinade, allowing any excess liquid to drain back into the dish, and coat with the seasoned flour. Pre-heat the oven to moderate.

Melt the butter with the oil in a heavy-based, flameproof casserole. Fry the rabbit, turning each piece until evenly browned. Drizzle the remaining marinade over the rabbit, cover, and bake for 30 minutes. Remove the lid and cook for 30 minutes longer, until tender, basting occasionally with the pan-juices.

Transfer to a heated dish and garnish with the watercress or spring onion (scallion) bon-bons before serving.

Devilled Rabbit

Lightly seasoned rabbit is roasted in butter and finally topped with a devilled sauce. Serve with buttery creamed potatoes, peas, or carrots.

Serves 4

1 rabbit, cut into serving pieces
60 g (2 oz) butter, melted
salt
freshly ground black pepper
1 teaspoon Dijon mustard
1 teaspoon English mustard
1 cup (9 fl oz) cream

Pre-heat the oven to moderate. Brush the rabbit liberally with the butter and sprinkle with salt and black pepper. Put the pieces in a roasting dish, and cook in the centre of the oven for 50 minutes, basting frequently with the pan-juices.

Lift the rabbit from the roasting dish, arrange in an ovenproof serving dish, and return to the oven. Mix the mustards with the cream, pour over the rabbit, and cook for 10 minutes. Serve immediately.

Rabbit with Sour Cream Sauce

This recipe more than any other brings out the gamy quality of the rabbit. The rabbit is marinated for three days before being roasted. Either the herb and milk marinade (page 199) or game marinade (page 198) is suitable. Serve with creamy potatoes and a crisp green vegetable — whole French beans or Brussels sprouts are particularly good.

Serves 4

1 rabbit, marinated
90 g (3 oz) butter
6 lean bacon rashers, with rind removed
3 tablespoons brandy
freshly ground black pepper
2 cups (18 fl oz) light sour cream
salt
1 tablespoon finely chopped parsley
a pinch of cayenne or red pepper

Lift the rabbit from the marinade and dry thoroughly. Separate the front and hind legs and cut the back into two, possibly three, pieces, depending on the size of the rabbit. Discard the herb and milk marinade; strain and store the game marinade for further use. Pre-heat the oven to moderately slow.

Divide the butter into pats and put one on each piece of rabbit. Overwrap the pieces with the bacon and secure with cocktail sticks or fine string. Put the rabbit in a roasting dish with the brandy and season generously with black pepper. Cover and cook for 1 to 1¼ hours. Discard the bacon, baste the rabbit with the pan-juices, and roast uncovered for 15 to 20 minutes longer.

Mix the sour cream with 3 tablespoons of the pan-juices and set aside. Arrange the rabbit on a heated serving dish and keep hot while you finish the sauce. Drain the excess fat from the pan and stir in the sour cream. Simmer for 2 or 3 minutes, adjust the seasoning, and pour over the rabbit. Sprinkle with the parsley and a little cayenne or red pepper and serve immediately.

Rabbit with Maple Sauce

Deliciously tender, the light rabbit meat is glazed with a sweet, tangy sauce. Serve with new potatoes and a mixed green salad.

Serves 4

2 tablespoons butter or goose fat
1 tablespoon vegetable oil
6 spring onions (scallions), sliced
4 bacon rashers, sliced, with rind removed
1 rabbit, cut into serving pieces
1 tablespoon plain (all-purpose) flour
salt
freshly ground black pepper
1 teaspoon cayenne or red pepper
1 clove of garlic, crushed
2 tablespoons lemon juice
3 tablespoons water
3 tablespoons maple syrup
3 tablespoons cream

Heat the butter or goose fat with the oil in a flameproof casserole. Toss the spring onions (scallions) with the bacon in the hot fat until lightly browned. Push the mixture to one side of the pan and lightly brown the rabbit pieces on all sides. Distribute the spring onions (scallions) and bacon evenly between the rabbit pieces and sprinkle with the flour. Turn the rabbit in the pan-juices until the flour has been absorbed. Season with the salt, black pepper, and cayenne or red pepper. Add the garlic, lemon juice, and water. Stir together and trickle the maple syrup over the rabbit. Cover and cook over low heat for 1 to 1¼ hours, until the rabbit is tender.

Transfer the rabbit to a heated serving dish and keep hot. Stir the cream into the pan and heat through without boiling. Adjust the seasoning and spoon the sauce over the rabbit.

Creole Rabbit

The full flavours of Louisiana are well matched with the pale rabbit. Serve with boiled rice or noodles and a green salad.

Serves 4

2 tablespoons butter
2 tablespoons olive oil
1 rabbit, cut into serving pieces
2 medium onions, chopped
3 tablespoons chopped parsley
2 cloves of garlic, crushed
3 large tomatoes, peeled and chopped
1 cup (9 fl oz) beef stock, from cubes
½ cup (4 fl oz) dry sherry
2 tablespoons rum
1 teaspoon ground bird's eye chilli
salt
freshly ground black pepper
1 tablespoon lemon juice
90 g (3 oz) ground hazelnuts

Melt the butter with the oil in a heavy, flameproof casserole and brown the rabbit pieces on all sides. Lift the browned rabbit from the pan and set aside. Add the onions, parsley, and garlic to the casserole and cook over low heat until the onions are transparent. Stir in the tomatoes, stock, sherry, and rum. Bring to the boil, then reduce the heat and simmer gently for 3 or 4 minutes.

Sprinkle the chilli, salt, and black pepper over the rabbit and return it to the casserole. Spoon the sauce over the rabbit, cover, and cook over low heat for 2 hours, until tender.

Stir the lemon juice into the sauce with the hazelnuts. Simmer uncovered for 4 or 5 minutes, adjust the seasoning, and serve from the casserole or transfer to a heated serving dish.

Casserole of Rabbit with Lentils

The French combine game and lentils in a variety of ways. This recipe is from Normandy, and traditionally the cooked rabbit is reheated with boiled lentils. I prefer to cook the lentils in the Italian style and then combine them. Lentils cooked in this way can also be served as a cold salad with a vinaigrette dressing. Serve with a crisp salad or green vegetable.

Serves 4

3 tablespoons olive oil
220 g (7 oz) lentils
1 small onion, sliced
2 tablespoons goose fat or butter
3 bacon rashers, sliced, with rind removed
1 rabbit, cut into serving pieces
freshly ground black pepper
1 thyme sprig
1 spray of celery leaves
1 bay-leaf
3/4 cup (1/3 pt) cider
1 teaspoon dried mint
1 clove of garlic, unpeeled
salt

Heat the olive oil in a heavy pan, add the lentils and onion, and simmer over gentle heat until most of the oil has been absorbed. In another pan, melt the goose fat or butter and sauté the bacon until lightly browned. Add the rabbit and brown lightly. Season with black pepper and add the herbs tied together to form a bouquet garni. Pour the cider over, cover, and simmer for 40 to 50 minutes, until tender.

In the meantime, add the mint, garlic, salt, and black pepper to the lentils, with enough water to cover. When the water is simmering, cover, and cook until the lentils are tender. Strain and add to the rabbit. Adjust the seasoning before serving.

Tamarillo Rabbit

The bitter-sweet tamarillos imbue the rabbit with a superb and most unusual flavour. Serve with peas and a crisp salad.

Serves 4

1 rabbit, cut into serving pieces
2 tablespoons plain (all-purpose) flour
1/2 teaspoon salt
1/2 teaspoon white pepper
2–3 tablespoons butter
1 tablespoon olive oil or vegetable oil
1 large onion, chopped
2 medium carrots, thinly sliced
4 tamarillos, quartered
1 cup (9 fl oz) chicken stock
1 tablespoon honey
1 tablespoon finely snipped chives

Dust the rabbit pieces with the flour seasoned with the salt and pepper. Melt the butter in a shallow pan and lightly brown the rabbit on all sides. Transfer the pieces to a flameproof casserole. Add the oil to the butter and sauté the onion and carrots until golden. Reduce the heat and add the tamarillos, chicken stock, and honey. Simmer gently for 2 or 3 minutes. Adjust the seasoning and pour the mixture over the rabbit. Cover and simmer on top of the stove for 1 hour, until the rabbit is tender. Remove and discard the tamarillo skins as they loosen.

Serve from the casserole or transfer to a heated serving dish. Sprinkle with the chives.

Rabbit Pudding

Surprisingly, the light rabbit meat is in harmony with this hearty pastry, providing at once a sophisticated and rustic dish. Serve with fennel peas (page 181) and redcurrant jelly.

Serves 4–6

1 quantity of suet crust pastry (page 203)
2 tablespoons plain (all-purpose) flour
½ teaspoon cayenne or red pepper
750 g (1½ lb) cubed boneless rabbit
250 g (8 oz) cubed ham pieces
1 large tart cooking apple, peeled, cored, and diced
2 leeks, split and thinly sliced
200 g (6½ oz) apple sauce
1 teaspoon dried thyme
6 dried figs, coarsely chopped
3 tablespoons dry white wine
1½ teaspoons salt
½ teaspoon white pepper

Prepare the pastry and use to line a 1.5-litre (3 pint) pudding basin, reserving enough pastry for the lid.

Put the flour in a bag with the cayenne or red pepper. Add the rabbit meat and shake until evenly coated. Mix the rabbit with the remaining ingredients and pack the mixture into the lined basin.

Roll the reserved pastry to a circle large enough to cover the basin, brushing the edge with water before covering the pudding. Pinch the pastry together to seal. Cut a large circle of foil, oil it lightly, and make a pleat across the centre. Put the oiled side of the foil over the pastry, secure with string, and stand the basin in a large saucepan. Add enough boiling water to reach halfway up the sides of the basin, cover, and cook for 3½ hours, topping up the water-level with boiling water when necessary.

To serve, discard the foil and wrap the basin with an attractive napkin.

Venison

Venison is the meat of deer. Rich and dark with little fat, it should have been hung by the butcher for at least four to five days, although some prefer their meat hung for a longer period, depending on the climate (see the table on page 11).

Generally it should be marinated and the individual recipes indicate which marinade to use. In some recipes, smaller cuts of the meat are cooked unmarinated.

The prime roasting cuts are from the haunch or fillet. The meat should be trimmed of fat before marinating and can be deep-frozen afterwards. To defrost venison allow 10 hours per kilogram (2 pounds) in the refrigerator.

Roast Venison

Venison trimmed of all fat and marinated for five or six days in game marinade results in this superb brown roast which is a joy to see. The apparent simplicity belies the careful preparation, so keep it understated and serve with tiny new potatoes and a crisp green vegetable. Redcurrant jelly is a good extra if you want one.

Serves 4–6

1 quantity of game marinade (page 198)
1.5–2 kg (3–4 lb) venison fillet
3–4 tablespoons melted goose fat or butter
1½ tablespoons plain (all-purpose) flour
½ cup (4 fl oz) water
3 tablespoons port
salt
white pepper

Put the venison in a plastic bag or bowl, pour the marinade in, and leave for five or six days, turning occasionally.

Pre-heat the oven to moderate. Remove the venison from the marinade and dry thoroughly. Strain the marinade and reserve ½ cup (4 fluid ounces) for the gravy, discarding the flavouring ingredients. Stand the venison on a rack set over a roasting dish, pour the melted fat or butter over, and roast in the centre of the oven for 50 minutes per kilogram (25 minutes per pound). Cover the meat loosely with foil after the first 30 minutes of the cooking time. Baste the meat occasionally with the pan-juices.

Transfer the cooked venison to a heated serving dish and leave to stand in a warm place while you prepare the gravy. Pour off all but 3 tablespoons of the pan-juices. Stir the flour into the dish until well incorporated with the juices and sediment. Gradually add equal quantities of the reserved marinade and water to the pan, stirring constantly until the gravy is smooth. Add the port and season with salt and pepper to taste. Simmer for 3 or 4 minutes, adding more marinade and water if the gravy is too thick. Strain, spoon a little over the venison, and serve the rest separately.

Australian Venison Roast

As a child I read of distant places, and countless names caught my imagination. Some I still have to look forward to, some I have caught up with — the magical bougainvillaea and whispering oleander, custard apples and mangoes. Not one has been a disappointment but for me the jewel of them all is the passionfruit. Forget the pavlova and ice-cream and marry that distinctive and pungent flavour with venison. Marinate for two days and serve with roast potatoes and braised chicory (Belgian endive, page 181).

Using a larding needle, 'sew' the ham strips all over the surface of the venison. Put the venison in a plastic bag or large lidded bowl with the onion, juniper berries, pepper, and salt. Shake the gin in a screwtop jar with the oil and passionfruit juice and pour into the bag or bowl. Seal and marinate for two days, turning the container occasionally.

Roast Venison

90 g (3 oz) ham fat, chilled and cut into 5-mm (¼ inch) strips
2 kg (4 lb) venison cut from the rump or fillet, trimmed of fat
1 large onion, halved and sliced
12 juniper berries, bruised
¼ teaspoon white pepper
1½ teaspoons salt
3 tablespoons gin
3 tablespoons olive oil
1½ cups (14 fl oz) passionfruit juice, sieved of pips (about 12 passionfruit)
1 tablespoon butter
1 tablespoon plain (all-purpose) flour

Pre-heat the oven to very hot. Lift the venison from the marinade and put it in a roasting dish. Pour the marinade over and roast in the centre of the oven for 20 minutes. Reduce the temperature to moderately slow and cook for 2 hours, basting the meat frequently with the pan-juices.

Transfer the venison to a heated dish, cover, and leave to stand in a warm place for 10 minutes before carving. Strain the pan-juices into a saucepan. Work the butter and flour together and add, in small pieces, to the sauce. Whisk each addition until the sauce is thickened and smooth. Adjust the seasoning and simmer for 2 or 3 minutes. Carve the venison thinly and serve the sauce separately.

Note: Larding needles are readily available at kitchenware shops. Their barbed hinge allows a lardon to be easily pulled through the surface of the meat. Chilling the larding fat before slicing makes the job easier.

Venison Steak Hussar

Venison fillet is roasted with a delicious stuffing. Serve with game chips (page 184) and a creamed vegetable.

Serves 4

1 kg (2 lb) thick venison fillet
2 egg-yolks
60 g (2 oz) butter
freshly ground black pepper
3 tablespoons red wine
Stuffing
125 g (4 oz) mushrooms
125 g (4 oz) chicken livers, trimmed and finely chopped
8 spring onions (scallions), chopped
60 g (2 oz) fresh breadcrumbs
2 teaspoons chopped fresh chervil or ½ teaspoon dried chervil
60 g (2 oz) butter
salt and pepper

Make the stuffing. Pre-heat the oven to moderately hot. Cut a deep pocket through the centre of the fillet. Beat the egg-yolks into the cooled stuffing mixture and spoon into the venison. Secure with string and stand the fillet on a rack set over a roasting dish. Spread with the butter, season with black pepper, and roast for 40 minutes, basting occasionally. Add the mushroom caps reserved from the stuffing to the dish, turn in the butter, and cook for 5 minutes.

Transfer the fillet to a heated serving dish, surround with the mushrooms, and keep hot. Pour off most of the fat from the dish and add the wine. Adjust the seasoning and bring rapidly to the boil. Carve the fillet into thick slices and spoon a little of the sauce over.

Stuffing

Separate the mushroom caps from the stems and reserve the caps. Chop the stems finely and mix with the livers, spring onions (scallions), breadcrumbs, and chervil. Melt the butter in a saucepan and add the stuffing mixture. Stir, cooking for 3 or 4 minutes. Season to taste and set aside to cool.

Venison Braise

This joint of venison, marinated for three days and slowly cooked on a bed of vegetables, has quite a different texture from that of a roasted joint. Serve with braised celery (page 180) and jacket-baked potatoes (page 186).

Serves 4–6

1 quantity of game marinade
   (page 198)
1.5–2 kg (3–4 lb) venison haunch
2 celery stalks
1 thyme sprig
2 parsley sprigs
1 bay-leaf
3 tablespoons goose fat or
   vegetable oil
2 medium carrots, sliced
2 medium onions, sliced
³/₄ cup (¹/₃ pt) beef stock
salt
freshly ground black pepper
1 tablespoon tomato paste
redcurrant jelly or Cumberland sauce
   (page 196)
1 tablespoon butter
1 tablespoon plain (all-purpose)
   flour

Trim all fat from the venison, put it in a plastic bag or a bowl, and add the marinade. Leave to marinate for three days.

Remove the meat and dry thoroughly. Strain and reserve the marinade. Cut the leaves from the celery and tie with the thyme, parsley, and bay-leaf into a bouquet garni. Heat the fat or oil in a deep flameproof casserole and brown the venison on all sides. Remove and add the carrots, onions, and celery cut into thick chunks. Reduce the heat, cover, and cook gently until the vegetables begin to sweat. Pre-heat the oven to moderately hot.

Put the venison on top of the vegetables with the bouquet garni. Pour ½ cup (4 fluid ounces) of the reserved marinade and the stock over. Season to taste and bring the liquid to the boil. Cover with foil and the lid. Braise just below the centre of the oven for 2½ to 3 hours, until the meat is very tender.

Lift the venison from the pan, transfer to a heated carving dish, and keep hot. Strain the cooking liquid into a saucepan and leave to stand for 1 or 2 minutes for the fat to rise. Skim the surface or blot with paper towels. Add the tomato paste and 1 tablespoon of redcurrant jelly or Cumberland sauce and simmer the gravy for 2 or 3 minutes. Work the butter and flour together and add in small pieces, whisking thoroughly between each addition. Adjust the seasoning and simmer for 2 minutes. Carve the venison and arrange on a heated serving dish. Spoon a little of the gravy over the meat and serve the rest separately.

VEGETABLES

Vegetables can make or mar a meal. They add colour, texture, and when carefully chosen enhance the flavour of the main attraction, at the same time supplying nutrients essential to our diet.

Selection of fresh vegetables

GENERAL INFORMATION

The vegetable recipes chosen fall into five main groups: creamed, root, crisp green, and stuffed — the classic and traditional accompaniments of poultry and game — and an odd little miscellany of salads and misfits. They are arranged alphabetically by the name of the vegetables, with a final section of recipes for grains.

Coffee Pot Asparagus

Cooked in an old-fashioned, narrow-necked coffee pot, the asparagus tips can be steamed while the stalks cook in the boiling water. They are also easily drained without damaging the tips. Choose young asparagus spears of even thickness. The most usual sauces served with asparagus are hollandaise and mousseline. I still think, though, that it is hard to improve on the simple butter, or lemon butter, sauce.

Serves 4

500 g (1 lb) asparagus
salt
60 g (2 oz) butter, melted
freshly ground black pepper
juice of ½ lemon (optional)

Snap or cut the tough ends from the asparagus stalks, making the spears more or less of even length. Tie loosely into bundles and stand upright in an enamelled coffee pot or asparagus pan. Add about 1 teaspoon of salt to the pot and pour in enough boiling water to cover the thickest part of the stems, leaving the tips to steam. Bring the water back to the boil, then reduce the heat until the water is just rolling. Cover and cook until the stalks are barely tender (this depends very much on their thickness and could vary between 10 and 20 minutes).

Pour the cooking liquid off (save it because it makes the foundation for a superb soup). Arrange the asparagus on a heated serving dish, pour the melted butter over, and season with black pepper. Use the lemon juice if it fits in with the main dish.

Sautéed Broccoli

This can be half cooked in advance and finished just before serving.

Serves 4–6

1 kg (2 lb) broccoli
salt
60 g (2 oz) butter
freshly ground black pepper

Trim the larger leaves from the broccoli stalks (if they are really fresh they can be cooked as you would spinach). Cut the tough ends from the stems and discard them. Bring a pan of water to the boil, add 1 teaspoon of salt, and plunge the broccoli in. Cook for 7 minutes, slightly less if the stalks are very thin. Drain the broccoli and cool slightly before slicing into 2.5-centimetre (1 inch) lengths. They can be refrigerated until you are ready to finish cooking them.

Melt the butter in a large shallow pan, until foaming. Add the sliced broccoli and sauté quickly for 3 or 4 minutes. Adjust the seasoning and serve very hot.

Brussels Sprouts with Chestnuts

Serves 4–6

12 dried chestnuts, soaked in cold water for 1 hour
salt
24 small Brussels sprouts
2 teaspoons butter
freshly ground black pepper

Drain the chestnuts and cook in lightly salted water until tender; drain. Steam or boil the sprouts until just tender; drain. Shake the chestnuts and sprouts with the butter in a saucepan, season to taste, and serve very hot.

Variation
Cook the sprouts and sauté 3 tablespoons of slivered almonds in butter. Toss the drained sprouts and almonds together and season with a little freshly grated nutmeg.

Cabbage Medley

Serves 4–6

2 tablespoons butter
1 tablespoon vegetable oil
1 large onion, thinly sliced
2 medium tart cooking apples, peeled, cored, and diced
½ teaspoon celery seed
2 medium tomatoes, peeled, seeded, and sliced
1 medium firm white cabbage (not Savoy), thickly shredded
salt
freshly ground black pepper
½ cup (4 fl oz) natural yogurt or light sour cream

Melt the butter with the oil in a large saucepan. When the fat is just sizzling, add the onion and cook until transparent. Stir the apples, celery seed, tomatoes, and cabbage into the pan and mix thoroughly until all the ingredients are lightly coated with the fat. Season lightly with salt and black pepper. Cover and cook over moderate heat for 10 minutes, stirring from time to time.

Remove the lid and turn the mixture with a fork until most of the liquid has evaporated and the cabbage is just tender. Add the yogurt or sour cream, stir into the cabbage, and adjust the seasoning before transferring to a heated serving dish.

Carrots Vichy

Serves 4–6

500 g (1 lb) young carrots, trimmed and thinly sliced
2 tablespoons butter
½ teaspoon salt
3 teaspoons brown sugar

Peel the carrots, if you must, with a vegetable peeler or give them a good scrub to remove any grit. Put the sliced carrots in a saucepan with the butter, salt, and brown sugar. Cook over very low heat, stirring occasionally, until the carrots are tender and glazed. Adjust the seasoning and serve very hot.

Fried Cauliflower

Serves 4

1 small cauliflower
salt
oil for deep-frying
30 g (1oz) plain (all-purpose) flour
2 eggs, beaten
125 g (4 oz) dry breadcrumbs
freshly ground black pepper

Break the cauliflower into small sprigs and trim away the tough stalks. Bring quickly to the boil in lightly salted water, then simmer for 5 minutes. Drain, refresh under cold running water, and drain thoroughly. Pre-heat the oil to 160°C (325°F). Dust the cauliflower with the flour, dip in the egg, and roll lightly in the breadcrumbs.

Deep-fry until crisp and golden. Drain on paper towels and sprinkle with salt and black pepper before serving.

Creamed Cauliflower

This is one of my favourite ways to cook cauliflower. It is essential to buy the cauliflower with the green leaves left on. If possible, choose a small one with tight flowers. It is delicious with roast game, particularly the small game birds.

Serves 4–6

1 cauliflower
salt
1 egg-yolk
3 tablespoons cream
white pepper

Separate the leaves from the cauliflower, trim away the tough stalks, and chop the leaves coarsely. Set aside. Divide the cauliflower into small sprigs, discarding the thickest parts of the stems. Boil with a little salt and barely enough water to cover until they are very tender but not falling apart. Drain and set aside.

Wash the leaves thoroughly and put in a saucepan with a little salt and about ¾ cup (⅓ pint) of boiling water. Cook until the leaves are just tender. While they are cooking, mash the sprigs until quite smooth. Over gentle heat, beat the egg-yolk into the purée. Add the cream and season with salt and pepper to taste. Keep hot.

Drain the leaves, chop lightly, and adjust the seasoning. To serve, arrange the creamed cauliflower in the centre of a heated dish and surround with the leaves.

Braised Celery

Serves 4

1 large or 2 small heads of celery
½ cup (4 fl oz) beef stock, from a cube
2 tablespoons butter
freshly ground black pepper
salt (if necessary)
2 teaspoons cornflour (cornstarch)
1 tablespoon finely snipped chives

Trim the heads of celery to 20-centimetre (8 inch) lengths. Quarter or halve the heads and reserve the trimmed stalks and leaves for other uses. Pre-heat the oven to moderate.

Lay the celery in a casserole. Pour the stock over, add the butter, and season with black pepper to taste. Cover and bake in the centre of the oven for 30 to 35 minutes, or until the celery is just tender. Transfer the celery to a heated serving dish.

Mix the cornflour (cornstarch) to a smooth paste with a little water and stir into the pan-juices. Stir over gentle heat until the sauce thickens, then simmer for 2 or 3 minutes. Adjust the seasoning and pour the sauce over the celery. Garnish with the chives and serve hot or chilled.

Note: The cooking liquid does not necessarily have to be thickened — it depends on personal taste and the particular dish that the celery is to be served with. Omit the cornflour (cornstarch) for a thin sauce and correct the seasoning before garnishing with chives.

Braised Chicory (Belgian Endive)

Serves 4

2 teaspoons butter
4 medium heads of chicory (Belgian endive), trimmed
juice of 1 small lemon
2 tablespoons dry white wine
½ teaspoon salt
freshly ground black pepper

There is occasionally a case for standardisation. This versatile vegetable is variously called chicory, Belgian endive, and witloof. Call it what you may, it is very good with poultry and game, either cooked or as a salad.

Pre-heat the oven to moderate. Spread the butter over the base of a shallow roasting dish. Arrange the chicory (Belgian endive) in the dish and pour the lemon juice and wine over. Sprinkle with the salt and black pepper to taste. Cover the dish with foil. Bake for 35 to 40 minutes, until just tender.

Portuguese Cucumber

Serves 4–6

4 small cucumbers, peeled and quartered lengthwise
2 tablespoons butter
2 tablespoons vegetable oil
2 medium onions, finely chopped
1 clove of garlic, crushed
2 tomatoes, peeled, seeded, and coarsely chopped
2 teaspoons tomato paste
juice of ½ lemon
salt
freshly ground black pepper
½ teaspoon dried oregano

Restricting the use of cucumber largely to salads, sandwiches, and pickles is a shame when they are so good lightly cooked as a vegetable. This recipe can be served hot or chilled rather as you would use ratatouille.

Remove the seeds and cut the cucumbers into 2.5-centimetre (1 inch) lengths. Cover with boiling water and leave to blanch for 5 minutes. Drain and refresh under cold running water. Set aside.

Melt the butter with the oil in a frying pan (skillet) and sauté the onions over a fairly high heat until lightly browned but still crisp. Reduce the heat and add the garlic, tomatoes, and tomato paste. Cook for 2 or 3 minutes, until the vegetables are hot but not mushy. Stir in the lemon juice and cucumbers, cook gently for 1 or 2 minutes, and season with salt and black pepper to taste, and the oregano.

Fennel Peas

Serves 4-6

3 tablespoons butter
2 large bulbs of fennel, trimmed and thickly sliced
375 g (12 oz) shelled peas
2 tablespoons white wine or water
salt
freshly ground black pepper

This twin-textured vegetable is delicious with poultry and game. Add a cup of chopped ham to the mixture and you have a super first course.

Melt the butter in a saucepan and cook the fennel over moderate heat, until lightly browned but still crisp. Reduce the heat, add the peas and wine, and cover. Simmer for 10 minutes. Season with salt to taste and with a generous amount of pepper. Serve hot or chilled.

Note: If using fresh peas, as opposed to frozen, blanch them in boiling water for 3 or 4 minutes, strain, and add to the fennel. Frozen peas, if very hard, should be dipped into cold water to separate them.

Braised Fennel

Serves 4

60 g (2 oz) butter
2 large or 4 small bulbs of fennel,
*   trimmed and quartered*
1/3 cup (3 fl oz) water
salt and pepper

Melt the butter and sauté the fennel quickly until it is lightly browned on all sides. Lower the heat, add the water, and cover. Simmer until the fennel is just tender. Season to taste and serve hot or chilled.

Stuffed Onions

These are particularly good with rabbit, and chicken.

Serves 4

4 medium onions, peeled
salt
1 tablespoon butter
60 g (2 oz) fresh breadcrumbs
1 teaspoon dried mixed herbs
2 teaspoons currants
freshly ground black pepper

Cut a slice from the base of the onions so that they will stand evenly. Put them in a saucepan with a little salt and add just enough water to cover. Bring to the boil, reduce the heat, and simmer for 10 minutes. Drain and leave to cool. Pre-heat the oven to hot.

Scoop out the centres of the parboiled onions, leaving about a 5-millimetre (1/4 inch) shell. Set aside. Chop the onion centres finely. Melt the butter in a shallow pan over low heat and cook the onions for 1 or 2 minutes. Add the breadcrumbs, herbs, and currants. Season with salt and black pepper to taste, and mix together thoroughly. Divide the stuffing between the onion shells and bake in a lightly oiled dish for 25 to 30 minutes.

Parsnips in Orange Sauce

I find the flavour of parsnips so dominant that a little goes a long way. Cooked this way the flavour becomes more subtle and is an excellent accompaniment to poultry and game.

Serves 4–6

2 tablespoons butter
1 teaspoon honey
1/4 teaspoon cinnamon
2 teaspoons finely grated orange
*   rind*
1 1/2 cups (14 fl oz) orange juice
500 g (1 lb) young parsnips, peeled
*   and cut into small wedges*
1 tablespoon plain (all-purpose)
*   flour*
salt
1 orange, thinly sliced

Melt 1 tablespoon of the butter with the honey in a saucepan set over low heat. Add the cinnamon and the orange rind. Stir well and add the orange juice. Raise the heat and bring the mixture to the boil. Add the parsnips, reduce the heat, and cover. Simmer for 25 to 30 minutes, until the parsnips are just tender. Lift the parsnips from the pan with a slotted spoon and set aside.

Work the flour into the remaining tablespoon of butter and add in small pieces to the sauce, whisking between each addition, until the sauce has thickened enough to coat the parsnips lightly. Adjust the seasoning and return the parsnips to the pan, turning in the sauce until hot. Serve in a heated dish, garnished with the sliced orange.

Stuffed Pumpkin, page 188; surrounded by Stuffed Peppers, page 184; and Stuffed Onions

Stuffed Peppers

These make a very good accompaniment to roast poultry and game. Conveniently, the main preparation can be done well in advance of the cooking time.

Serves 4

4 medium red or green (bell) peppers
3 tablespoons butter
2 tablespoons olive oil or vegetable oil
1 medium onion, chopped
2 small cloves of garlic, crushed
3 tomatoes, peeled, seeded, and coarsely chopped
2 tablespoons tomato paste
2 teaspoons finely chopped fresh basil or ½ teaspoon dried basil
½ teaspoon dried oregano
1 tablespoon finely chopped fresh parsley
salt
freshly ground black pepper
155 g (5 oz) cooked long-grain rice
2 anchovy fillets, very finely chopped
4 black olives, finely chopped
30 g (1 oz) grated Parmesan cheese

Cut about 2 centimetres (¾ inch) from the top of each pepper. Discard the stems and chop the pepper lids very finely. Set aside. Scoop out the pith and seeds (sponge) from each pepper and discard.

Melt 2 tablespoons of the butter with the oil in a frying pan (skillet) and gently cook the onion, garlic, and the chopped pepper lids until soft but not browned. Add the tomatoes, tomato paste, and herbs, seasoning lightly with salt and black pepper. Cover and simmer gently until the sauce is cooked and has thickened, stirring occasionally to prevent it from sticking. Stir in the rice, anchovies, and olives. Adjust the seasoning and set aside. When ready to cook the peppers, pre-heat the oven to moderately slow.

Divide the rice mixture between the peppers and put them in a lightly oiled baking dish. Divide the remaining tablespoon of butter into four pats and put one on top of each pepper. Bake for 15 minutes. Sprinkle the cheese over the peppers and bake for 15 minutes longer, until the cheese is lightly browned.

Variation

Fill the prepared peppers with 2 to 2½ cups of any of the stuffing mixtures on page 206, adding ½ cup of cooked rice or fried crumbs (page 210) to lighten the density of the filling.

Game Chips

This is one of the best potato dishes to serve with poultry and game. They have just a little more body than potato crisps and by using a food processor to slice them they can be prepared very easily.

Serves 4–6

4–6 medium potatoes, peeled and thinly sliced
oil for deep-frying
salt

Cover the sliced potatoes with iced water and soak for 20 to 30 minutes before deep-frying.

Pre-heat the oil to 190°C (375°F). Dry the potatoes and fry, a few at a time, for 2 to 3 minutes. Drain on paper towels.

Shortly before serving, fry the chips again until crisp and golden. Drain and sprinkle lightly with salt. Serve in a shallow dish or basket.

Note: Double-frying the chips means that you can do the first cooking early in the day and finish them when needed. However, having prepared and cooked so many during the past few months, we found that they are just as good cooked once, for about 4 to 5 minutes. They also retain their crispness just as well.

Potato Balls

These take a little trouble but the result is worth the effort. The trimmings can be kept in the refrigerator, in water, for a few days and used in other recipes. I usually add a few potatoes to the trimmings and cream them. Use the smallest side of a potato baller and soak the potatoes in iced water for the best result.

Serves 4–6

6 large potatoes, peeled
salt
90 g (3 oz) of butter
2 tablespoons vegetable oil

Cut balls out of each potato using the smaller side of the cutter. Cover with iced water and leave for 20 to 30 minutes.

Drain the potatoes and put them in a small pan with a little salt. Add enough boiling water to cover. Set the pan over high heat, bring the water back to the boil, and cook the potatoes for 4 minutes. Drain immediately.

Melt the butter with the oil in a large, heavy-based frying pan (skillet). When the fat is hot add the potatoes and cook over moderate heat for 6 to 8 minutes. Shake the pan occasionally until the potatoes are evenly browned. Drain on paper towels, sprinkle with a little salt, and serve immediately.

Variation
When tiny new potatoes are unavailable, substitute potato balls. Boil until just tender and at the last moment toss in a little butter and finely chopped parsley or dill.

Potato Cheese Puff

Serves 4–6

750 g (1½ lb) potatoes, peeled and
*   cut into small chunks*
½ teaspoon salt
3 eggs, separated
1–2 tablespoons butter
125 g (4 oz) grated Cheddar cheese
1 small onion, very finely chopped
1 small green (bell) pepper, very
*   finely chopped*
½ teaspoon celery salt
white pepper
½ teaspoon Hungarian paprika

Cover the potatoes with water, add the salt, and boil until tender. Drain and transfer to a mixing bowl. Pre-heat the oven to moderately hot.

Mash the potatoes and beat the egg-yolks in, one at a time, until thoroughly combined. Beat in 1 tablespoon of the butter with the cheese, onion, green (bell) pepper, celery salt, and white pepper to taste. Add the remaining butter only if the mixture is very stiff.

Beat the egg-whites until stiff and fold into the potato mixture. Spoon carefully into an oiled baking dish. Sprinkle with the paprika and bake for 25 to 30 minutes, or until golden.

Cross-Hatched Potatoes

Allow two or three medium-sized potatoes per person. Before roasting, peel the potatoes and parboil in salted water for 6 or 7 minutes. Strain and run briefly under cold water. With a sharp knife, score diagonal lines across the potatoes. Repeat the scoring at right-angles to the original lines. When roasted, the potatoes will be crisp and attractive.

Jacket-Baked Potatoes

Scrubbed and baked without the oiling, salting, or foil-wrapping performance (soggy skins are not the aim), these potatoes can happily be served with most poultry and game. Allow one medium potato per person.

Pre-heat the oven to hot. Put the dried potatoes on a baking tray and cook just above the centre of the oven for 45 to 60 minutes, until the skin is crisp but the potato yields to the touch.

Cut a cross on top, squeeze open, and serve with any of the following dressings: butter and seasoning; sour cream and chopped herbs; finely grated cheese; equal quantities of cream cheese and chopped raisins, mixed.

Potatoes Rosemary

Serves 4–6

1 kg (2 lb) potatoes, peeled and cut into small chunks
2 rosemary sprigs
½ teaspoon salt
2–3 tablespoons butter
½ cup (4 fl oz) hot milk
salt
white pepper

Boil the potatoes in water with the rosemary and salt. Drain, discard the rosemary, and return the potatoes to the pan. Shake over low heat until they are dry. Mash the potatoes until they are fluffy. Add the butter and enough hot milk to whip to a creamy consistency. Season with more salt, if necessary, and white pepper.

Potato Patties

Left-over potatoes rosemary are delicious made into patties and fried in goose fat. Moisten the cold potatoes with a little beaten egg-yolk, shape into patties, dust lightly with flour, and fry until golden on each side.

Seville Potato Cakes

Serves 4

1 medium orange, unpeeled
3 large potatoes, peeled and cut into small chunks
90 g (3 oz) butter
1 small onion, very finely chopped
1 egg-yolk
salt
white pepper

Put the orange in a saucepan, cover with water, and boil gently until it is very soft, about 45 minutes. Boil the potatoes in salted water until tender. Drain, mash, and put aside.

Halve the soft orange, discard any pips, and chop the whole thing, peel and flesh, coarsely. Melt half of the butter in a large frying pan (skillet) and cook the onion until just golden. Add the chopped orange and simmer together for 2 or 3 minutes before adding the mashed potatoes. Mix the ingredients together over gentle heat, stir in the egg-yolk, and season with salt and pepper. Pre-heat the oven to moderately hot.

Lightly brush a baking tray with oil or butter and space generous tablespoonfuls of the mixture over it. Flatten each into a patty with a fork and bake for 15 to 20 minutes, until crisp on the bottom and golden on top.

***Clockwise from top:** Turnips with Pimiento Cream Sauce, page 189; sour cream with chives to serve with potato; Jacket-Baked Potato; Parsnips in Orange Sauce, page 182*

Pumpkin Sauté

This is a real winner with roast or fried chicken and game birds.

Serves 4

*500 g (1 lb) pumpkin, peeled,
  seeded, and cut into 1 cm
  (¹/₂ inch) slices*
*2 tablespoons castor (superfine)
  sugar*
2–3 tablespoons butter

Sprinkle each side of the pumpkin slices with castor (superfine) sugar and put aside for 10 to 15 minutes before cooking. Melt the butter in a pan large enough to hold the pumpkin in one layer. Gently fry the pumpkin for 3 or 4 minutes on each side, until golden. Serve immediately.

Stuffed Pumpkin

Shell-baked, the flavour of the pumpkin is intensified. Mix the scooped-out pumpkin with rice and seasoning and serve from the shell.

Serves 4–6

1 butternut pumpkin
250 g (8 oz) cooked long-grain rice
2–3 tablespoons butter
salt
freshly ground black pepper

Pre-heat the oven to moderate. Stand the whole pumpkin on a shelf rack (if it will not stand upright, lay it on one side and turn halfway through the cooking time). Bake for 30 to 45 minutes until the pumpkin yields slightly when squeezed.

Cut a good 2.5-centimetre (1 inch) slice from the top and scoop out the flesh. The seeds of these pumpkins are at the base, so there is no problem of sorting them out. Chop the pumpkin and mix with the rice. Melt the butter in a shallow pan. Stir in the pumpkin and rice. When very hot, season with salt and black pepper to taste and pile back into the shell. Replace the lid and keep hot in the oven until you are ready to serve.

Creamed Spinach

Serves 4–6

*approx. 1 kg (2 lb) bunch of
  spinach or silverbeet*
2 tablespoons butter
salt
approx. 3 tablespoons cream
white pepper

Wash the whole spinach or silverbeet leaves in several changes of water. Strip away and discard any coarse stalks. Chop the leaves roughly. Put the leaves in a large pan with only the water that clings to the leaves. Add the butter and sprinkle very lightly with salt. Cover and cook over gentle heat for 7 to 10 minutes, until the spinach is wilted and soft. Strain out any excess liquid.

Purée the spinach in a blender or food processor. Add enough cream to bring the spinach to a rich consistency. Season with more salt, if necessary, and pepper to taste. Reheat just before serving.

Wilted Spinach

This is a piquant cross between a cooked vegetable and a salad. It is an excellent accompaniment to some of the more bland dishes and very good with cold poultry and game.

Serves 4

500 g (1 lb) spinach or silverbeet
5 bacon rashers, diced, with rind removed
1 large onion, finely sliced
2 tablespoons white wine vinegar
juice of ½ lemon
1 teaspoon sugar
salt
freshly ground black pepper
1 hard-boiled egg, chopped

Wash the spinach or silverbeet and then strip the leaves from the coarse stalks. Pat dry on paper towels and tear the spinach rather than chopping it. Fry the bacon until the fat starts to run. Add the onion and cook until the bacon is crisp and the onion lightly browned. Add the torn spinach, vinegar, lemon juice, and sugar, mixing the ingredients together. Cover and simmer for 3 to 4 minutes, until the spinach has wilted but is not too soft. Adjust the seasoning and arrange on a heated serving dish. Sprinkle with the chopped egg.

Glazed Turnips

A long-time favourite with duck, glazed turnips also marry well with other roast poultry and are particularly good with goose. Choose the smallest turnips available.

Serves 4

4–8 turnips, peeled
½ teaspoon salt
30 g (1 oz) butter
30 g (1 oz) brown sugar, mixed with ¼ teaspoon ground nutmeg

Quarter or halve the turnips according to size. Cover with water, add the salt, and bring to the boil. Cook for 5 minutes and drain. Pre-heat the oven to hot.

Melt the butter in a baking dish, add the parboiled turnips, and turn until lightly coated with the butter. Sprinkle evenly with the brown sugar and nutmeg and cook just below the centre of the oven for 25 to 30 minutes.

Turnips with Pimiento Cream Sauce

Turnips are complementary both to duck and goose. Choose the smallest you can find and, if the green tops are fresh, they can also be cooked, in the same way as spinach or silverbeet.

Serves 4

8 small or 4 medium turnips, trimmed and peeled
1 tablespoon butter
1 quantity of pimiento cream sauce (page 196)

Rub the turnips lightly with the butter and steam over simmering water until tender. Prepare the sauce while the turnips are cooking and season it well.

Arrange the cooked turnips in a heated serving dish and coat with the sauce.

Vine-Leaf Fritters

These crisply coated and very pretty fritters can be served as a first course, topped with a little sour cream, or as a vegetable dish. Allow at least three for each person.

Serves 4–6

fresh young vine-leaves or
vacuum-packed vine-leaves
juice and finely grated rind of
1 lemon
1 teaspoon dried oregano
1 teaspoon salt
3 tablespoons dry white wine
1 quantity of savoury coating batter
(page 200)
oil for deep-frying
cayenne or red pepper

Lay the vine-leaves in a shallow dish. Mix the lemon juice and rind with the oregano, salt, and wine; pour over the leaves. Marinate for 2 or 3 hours.

Prepare the batter and leave to stand before using. Pre-heat the oil to 185°C (365°F). A small teaspoon of the finished batter dropped into the fat should sizzle and crisp in 45 seconds when the fat is at the correct temperature.

Drain the vine-leaves, pat dry on paper towels, and dip in the batter. Deep-fry until crisp and golden, drain on paper towels and sprinkle lightly with cayenne or red pepper before serving.

Vine Prosciutto Fritters

Marinate the leaves, drain, and pat dry. Sandwich a thin slice of prosciutto between two leaves before coating with the batter. Deep-fry until crisp and drain on paper towels before serving.

Cracked Wheat Pilaff

This can be served as you would any rice pilaff. Good with most poultry and game, it also doubles as a very interesting stuffing. If you do use it as a stuffing, make the full quantity and serve any that is left over as a side dish.

Serves 4–6

30 g (1 oz) butter
1 large celery stalk, finely chopped
1 medium onion, finely chopped
90 g (3 oz) sultanas (sultana
raisins)
220 g (7 oz) cracked wheat
(bulgar)
2 cups (18 fl oz) chicken stock
salt
freshly ground black pepper
30 g (1 oz) coarsely chopped
pistachios

Melt the butter in a flameproof casserole set over moderate heat. Add the celery, onion, and sultanas (sultana raisins) and cook until the onion is transparent. Mix the cracked wheat (bulgar) into the pan and stir until the grains are coated with the butter and very lightly browned. Add the chicken stock, stir, and bring to the boil. Reduce the heat, season with salt and black pepper, and cover. Simmer very gently for 20 to 30 minutes, until most of the liquid has been absorbed, stirring occasionally.

Remove the lid to finish cooking the pilaff and fork through the mixture once or twice, to prevent it from sticking and to keep it fluffy. Adjust the seasoning and sprinkle with the pistachios before serving.

Wild Rice

This rice-related grain comes from an annual water grass that grows mainly in North America. It is harvested once a year, almost solely by the Chippewa Indians who travel long distances to gather it in their time-honoured way. The gathering is a delicate process and much of the grain can be lost to wind and rain, making it a scarce, and therefore expensive, commodity. To compensate, a small quantity will serve several people and occasionally 'hang the expense' must surely be the order of the day. It can be served as a side dish or as wild rice stuffing (page 207).

Serves 4

140 g (4½ oz) wild rice
3 cups (1⅓ pt) hot chicken stock
2 tablespoons butter
1 tablespoon vegetable oil
1 large onion, chopped
1 small clove of garlic, crushed
1 medium bulb of fennel, trimmed and chopped, or 2 celery stalks, thinly sliced
185 g (6 oz) mushrooms, sliced
½ teaspoon dried mixed herbs
salt
freshly ground black pepper

Wash the rice thoroughly under cold running water. Drain and stir into the hot chicken stock. When the stock boils, reduce the heat and cover. Simmer until the grains are tender and most of the stock has been absorbed. This will take about 30 minutes.

While the rice is cooking, melt the butter with the oil and fry the onion, garlic, and fennel or celery until softened, but not browned. Add the mushrooms and cook for 1 or 2 minutes, until they begin to soften. Sprinkle with the herbs and season with salt and black pepper. to taste.

Strain the rice and fork together with the vegetables. Adjust the seasoning and serve hot or chilled.

STOCKS, SAUCES, AND SUNDRIES

This is the chapter that fills in the gaps, but very important gaps. It is a bit like the house that Jack built. If the stock is good, the sauce is better and the better the sauce, the more nearly perfect the finished dish will be (not for nothing is the sauce chef a restaurant's most valuable asset).

Like the foundations of Jack's house, if the pastry is ill-constructed, the end result will suffer no matter how good the filling may be.

Clockwise from top: *Shortcrust Pastry, page 201; Béchamel Sauce, page 196; Veal Stock, page 194*

Stocks

Chicken Stock

1·5–2 kg (3–4 lb) boiling fowl or
    soup pack; giblets, backs, necks
    (not the liver)
6–8 cups (2¾–3½ pt) water
salt
2 medium onions, peeled and
    quartered
2 medium carrots, quartered
1 leek, split and halved
4 cloves
6 peppercorns
1 spray of celery leaves
1 bay-leaf
2 parsley sprigs

Put the fowl or chicken pieces in a large saucepan with enough of the water to cover completely. Add about 1½ teaspoons of salt and bring slowly to the boil. Remove any scum that rises to the surface. A tablespoon of cold water added from time to time will increase the rate at which the scum is released. When the liquid has boiled add the vegetables, cloves, and peppercorns. Tie the celery leaves, bay-leaf, and parsley together to form a bouquet garni and push well down into the water. Bring the liquid back to boiling-point, lower the heat, and simmer gently for 1½ to 2 hours. Skim froth and fat from the surface occasionally.

Strain the stock, discard the chicken and flavouring ingredients, and chill thoroughly. Remove any fat from the surface of the cold stock. Freeze in measured quantities and use as needed.

Note: All poultry stocks can be prepared in this way.

Veal Stock

This is another white stock worth making and freezing in the same way as chicken stock.

1 meaty veal knuckle, sawn into 3
    or 4 pieces
6–8 cups (2¾–3½ pt) cold water
3 cloves
2 medium onions, peeled
2 large carrots, quartered
6 cloves of garlic, unpeeled
1 celery stalk, roughly chopped
1 leek, split and halved
2 sprays of celery leaves
2 parsley sprigs
1 rosemary sprig
salt

Put the veal knuckle in a large pan with the water (it must be well covered). Bring slowly to the boil, skimming the surface as the scum rises. A tablespoon of cold water added from time to time will increase the rate at which the scum is released. When the liquid reaches boiling-point, add the cloves and vegetables carefully — it is not good to shake the sediment about too much. Tie the celery leaves, parsley, and rosemary together to form a bouquet garni and add to the pan with 1 teaspoon of salt. Do not over-season as you may want to reduce the liquid. Bring the water almost back to boiling-point, reduce the heat, and simmer very gently for 3 to 4 hours. Skim the surface of froth and fat occasionally.

Strain the stock, discard the knuckle and flavouring ingredients, and cool before chilling in the refrigerator. Remove any fat from the surface of the cold stock. Finally, strain the stock through a double layer of scalded linen to remove any sediment. Freeze in measured quantities and use as needed.

Aspic Jelly

1 veal knuckle
1 pig's trotter
1 large onion, halved and sliced
2 medium carrots, sliced
1 leek, split and sliced
2 celery stalks, quartered
5 cups (2¼ pt) water
1 thyme sprig
1 parsley sprig
1 bay-leaf
salt
white pepper
1 egg-white and egg-shell

Put all the ingredients, except for the salt, pepper, and egg-white and shell, in a heavy pan. Bring slowly to the boil, removing scum from the surface as necessary. Reduce the heat, season with salt and pepper, and simmer very gently for 3½ to 4 hours. Strain the stock and leave to cool.

Remove all particles of fat from the cooled stock. Lightly beat the egg-white, crush the shell, and put them in a saucepan. Add the stock and bring slowly to boiling-point, whisking constantly. Reduce the heat when the stock has boiled and simmer for 20 minutes. Strain the aspic through a double layer of scalded linen and leave to cool.

The aspic can be additionally flavoured with 3 tablespoons of Madeira, sherry, or port, or as suggested in any individual recipe.

Sauces

Apple Sauce

Serves 4–6

2 tablespoons butter
1 small clove of garlic, crushed
3 large tart cooking apples, peeled, cored, and chopped
3 tablespoons dry cider
a pinch of sugar

Melt the butter in a saucepan, add the garlic and apples, and cover. Simmer over very low heat until the apples are almost tender. Add the cider and simmer until the apples are very soft. Beat until smooth and season with sugar to taste. Serve hot or cold.

Sauce Béarnaise

This is particularly good with hare, rabbit, and chicken and just as complementary to a venison steak as to beef.

Serves 4

4 tablespoons tarragon vinegar
4 black peppercorns, crushed
2 spring onions (scallions), very finely chopped
125 g (4 oz) softened butter
2 egg-yolks, beaten
1 teaspoon finely chopped fresh tarragon or ¼ teaspoon dried tarragon
1 teaspoon finely chopped parsley

Put the vinegar, peppercorns, and spring onions (scallions) in a small pan and simmer over low heat until the liquid is reduced to 1 tablespoon. Strain the liquid into the top of a double boiler set over warm water. Over gentle heat add 1 teaspoon of the butter to the reduced vinegar. Add the egg-yolks and, using a small wire or birch whisk, beat until the sauce thickens. As soon as the sauce has thickened, add the remaining butter, 2 teaspoons at a time, whisking thoroughly between each addition. When all the butter has been added and the sauce is creamy, remove the pan from the heat. Stir in the herbs and adjust the seasoning.

Note: If you have used dried tarragon, the nicest form is dried leaves, which need to be crushed a little by rubbing before they are added to the sauce.

Béchamel Sauce

1¼ cups (11 fl oz) milk
1 small onion
1 small bay-leaf
6 peppercorns
a few celery leaves
1 blade of mace
2 tablespoons butter
2 tablespoons plain (all-purpose)
    flour
salt
white pepper
3 tablespoons cream

Put the milk in the top of a double boiler with the onion, bay-leaf, peppercorns, celery leaves, and mace. Simmer very gently for 20 to 30 minutes. Strain and reserve the milk.

Melt the butter, stir in the flour, and cook without browning for 2 or 3 minutes. Gradually add the milk to the pan, stirring constantly between each addition until the sauce is smooth and thickened. Simmer very slowly for 10 to 15 minutes. Season to taste and add the cream. Heat through without boiling.

Pimiento Cream Sauce

Purée one drained, canned pimiento in a blender or food processor until smooth. Stir into the béchamel sauce with 1 teaspoon of tomato paste and 2 tablespoons of cream. Adjust the seasoning and serve hot with vegetables or chilled with cold, sliced poultry.

Bread Sauce

Serves 4–6

1½ cups (14 fl oz) milk
1 small onion, peeled
3 cloves
6 black or white peppercorns
1 small bay-leaf
approx. 90 g (3 oz) fresh white
    breadcrumbs
2 tablespoons cream
salt

I see no advantage in making this traditional sauce traditionally. With this method you save at least 15 minutes and the end result is just as good.

Put the milk in the top of a double boiler with the onion, cloves, peppercorns, and bay-leaf. Simmer for 15 minutes, then strain the flavoured milk into a saucepan. Add enough breadcrumbs to bring the sauce to the consistency you prefer. Beat with a wooden spoon until smooth and simmer until hot. Just before serving, add the cream and season with salt to taste.

Cumberland Sauce

This admirable sauce accompanies all game very well. It is sometimes made with the addition of chopped glacé (candied) cherries — quite awful!

Serves 6

1 medium orange
½ cup (4 fl oz) boiling water
½ cup (4 fl oz) redcurrant jelly
juice of ½ lemon
1 teaspoon Dijon mustard
⅓ cup (3 fl oz) port

Remove the rind from the orange with a vegetable peeler. Squeeze the juice from the orange, measuring 3 tablespoons. Cut the rind into very fine julienne (matchstick) strips, cover with the boiling water, and simmer for about 15 minutes until soft. Strain and refresh under cold water.

Melt the redcurrant jelly in a small pan and stir in the orange and lemon juices, mustard, and port. Bring rapidly to the boil, reduce the heat, and simmer for 5 minutes. Cool before adding the orange rind.

Giblet Gravy

This is made with the neck, giblets, and wing pinions (not the liver) of the poultry and game birds. If you have a deep-freeze it is worth making the stock with any given set of giblets for use when needed. The stock must be strained before freezing.

1 set of giblets
1 medium onion, quartered
1 small clove of garlic, unpeeled
1 celery stalk, roughly chopped
1 small carrot, roughly chopped
1/2 teaspoon salt
1/2 teaspoon freshly ground black
    pepper
2–2 1/2 cups (1–1 1/8 pt) water
1 cup (9 fl oz) dry white wine
1–1 1/2 tablespoons plain
    (all-purpose) flour
water or vegetable stock

Put the giblets, vegetables, and seasonings in a saucepan. Add the water and wine and bring to the boil. Reduce the heat and simmer gently until the liquid is reduced by half. Strain the stock and discard the vegetables.

To make the gravy, transfer the bird to a heated serving dish and keep hot. Strain all but 2 tablespoons of the pan-juices from the roasting dish and stir the flour into the remaining sediment. Add the giblet stock to the pan, on top of the stove, stirring constantly to form a smooth sauce. Add enough water or vegetable stock to bring the gravy to the consistency you prefer, and simmer gently for 3 to 4 minutes. Adjust the seasoning before serving.

Mushroom Sauce

Serves 4–6

2 tablespoons butter
125 g (4 oz) mushrooms, finely
    sliced
1 tablespoon vegetable oil
1 small onion, finely chopped
1 small carrot, finely chopped
1 1/2 tablespoons plain (all-purpose)
    flour
1/2 cup (4 fl oz) chicken stock
3 tablespoons red wine
1 tablespoon tomato paste
salt
white pepper

Melt the butter and simmer the mushrooms until softened. Lift from the pan with a slotted spoon and reserve. Add the oil to the pan and fry the onion and carrot until golden. Sprinkle the flour over the vegetables and cook for 1 minute, stirring the flour into the pan-juices. Gradually add the stock and wine to the sauce, stirring between each addition, until smooth. Simmer very gently for 3 or 4 minutes. Strain the sauce, discarding the vegetables.

Stir the tomato paste into the sauce and season with salt and pepper to taste. Fold in the reserved mushrooms and heat through before serving.

Sour Plum Sauce

Serves 6

1 large can red plums or 250 g
    (8 oz) fresh plums
3 tablespoons fresh coriander
1 large clove of garlic, crushed
juice of 1/2 lemon
1/4 teaspoon cayenne or red pepper
salt

This is a piquant sour-sweet sauce which can be used in place of any of the fruit-based sauces. It is particularly good with fried chicken and roast game.

Drain the canned plums and reserve the syrup. Simmer fresh plums in 1 cup (9 fluid ounces) of water until they are tender. Remove and discard the stones and sieve the flesh. Put the plum purée in a blender or food processor with the coriander, garlic, lemon juice, and cayenne or red pepper and mix until smooth. Add enough of the reserved juice to bring the sauce to a light creamy consistency. Season with salt and serve hot or cold.

Velouté Sauce

2 tablespoons butter
2 tablespoons plain (all-purpose)
   flour
2 cups (18 fl oz) well-flavoured
   chicken stock or veal stock
salt
white pepper

This is a simple sauce, perfect for coating a poached fowl, or for adding to crisply cooked Brussels sprouts or broad beans.

Melt the butter in a saucepan, stir in the flour, and cook gently until it is the colour of pale straw. Heat the stock and add gradually to the pan, stirring constantly between each addition, until the sauce is smooth and thickened. Simmer, while stirring, until the sauce has reduced by one-third and then season to taste.

Why Marinate?

The whole point of marinating food is to tenderise and add flavour to it.

Individual recipes indicate which is the most suitable of the various marinades included.

The easiest way to marinate is to seal the food and marinade into plastic bags so that the meat may be turned at regular intervals and evenly marinated.

Game Marinade

This quantity is sufficient for 4
   kilograms (8 pounds) of meat

2 large carrots, sliced
3 medium onions, sliced
6 black peppercorns, crushed
3 whole cloves
3 juniper berries, bruised
2 bay-leaves, crumbled
2 cloves of garlic, quartered
4 parsley sprigs, stems particularly,
   crushed
4 cups (1 3/4 pt) red wine
1 1/2 cups (14 fl oz) olive oil
1 1/2 cups (14 fl oz) wine vinegar

As a basic marinade for the more robust game this is full flavoured but not too strong to overpower the natural flavour of the meat.

Put the game in a large plastic bag or glass or enamelled container. Add the vegetables, spices, and herbs. Shake the wine, oil, and vinegar together and pour over the meat. Seal the bag or container and marinate for three to five days, or as directed by the particular recipe. Turn the bag occasionally to distribute the marinade, or turn the meat in the container.

Game Marinade

Herb and Milk Marinade

This is suitable for all furred game, particularly rabbit and dishes that contain fresh or sour cream.

This quantity is sufficient for 1.5 kilograms (3 pounds) of game

¹/₂ teaspoon salt
¹/₄ teaspoon white pepper
3 bay-leaves
6 parsley sprigs
2 thyme sprigs
1 rosemary sprig
2¹/₂ cups (1¹/₈ pt) milk

Mix the ingredients together and allow to stand while you prepare the meat. Remember to trim all fat from venison before marinating it. Use a narrow container or plastic bag to allow the marinade to cover the meat. Cover the dish or seal the bag and store in the refrigerator for two days. Turn the meat in the marinade two or three times during the marinating period. It is much more convenient to seal the meat in a bag and simply turn the bag. Use as directed by the individual recipe and discard any left-over marinade.

Pigeon Marinade

This quantity is sufficient for four to six birds

1 cup (9 fl oz) dry sherry
¹/₂ cup (4 fl oz) brandy
1 medium onion, coarsely chopped
1 medium carrot, coarsely chopped
¹/₂ cup chopped parsley stems
4 cloves
1 bay-leaf, crumbled
2 teaspoons chopped fresh thyme or
  ¹/₂ teaspoon dried thyme

Put the birds in a plastic bag. Combine all the marinade ingredients, pour into the bag, and seal. Marinate the birds for 24 hours, turning the bag once or twice during that time.

Note: The marinating should be done in a cool place, but not the refrigerator. Unless the marinade itself is being used to cook the birds, it can be strained and stored for several weeks in the refrigerator for later use. Add fresh vegetables and flavouring ingredients when reusing.

Spiced Marinade

This quantity is sufficient for 2 kilograms (4 pounds) of game

2 teaspoons ground coriander
1 teaspoon ground cumin
3 teaspoons ground ginger
½ teaspoon salt
½ teaspoon garlic salt
½ teaspoon white pepper
½ teaspoon cayenne or red pepper
1 cup (9 fl oz) white vinegar
3 tablespoons vegetable oil

Use with venison, rabbit, and game birds, particularly those to be served with fruit or fruit sauces. This is also excellent for pork, lamb, and (especially) mutton.

Mix all the ingredients thoroughly in a blender or food processor. Pour over the game or meat and marinate for 1 hour or as directed by the individual recipe.

Batters

Crêpe Batter

This quantity is sufficient for twelve 18- to 20-centimetre (7 to 8 inch) crêpes

90 g (3 oz) plain (all-purpose) flour
½ teaspoon salt
3 eggs, lightly beaten
1 cup (9 fl oz) milk
1 tablespoon vegetable oil

Sift the flour and salt into a mixing bowl. Make a well in the centre, add the eggs, milk, and oil and whisk the ingredients together until smooth. Allow to stand for 20 minutes before using.

Brush a pan lightly with oil and heat. Cook 1½ to 2 tablespoons of the batter until lightly browned on the bottom. Turn and brown briefly on the other side. Continue cooking the rest of the batter in the same way.

Note: Crêpes can be cooked and frozen, separating each with freezer wrap. Reheat and use as required.

Savoury Coating Batter

This is a very light batter, ideal for coating small pieces of poultry or game, or a mixture of both, for fritters. The batter can be flavoured in a variety of ways.

125 g (4 oz) plain (all-purpose) flour
2 tablespoons vegetable oil or melted butter
¾ cup (⅓ pt) lukewarm water
¼ teaspoon salt
½ teaspoon onion powder
2 egg-whites, stiffly beaten

Sift the flour into a mixing bowl. Make a well in the centre and pour in the oil or butter, water, salt, and onion powder. Beat well with a wooden spoon until the batter is smooth and leave to stand for at least 30 minutes.

Just before using, fold in the stiffly beaten egg-whites.

Variation

Instead of the onion powder, substitute ½ teaspoon of dry mustard, garlic powder, or herbs.

Pastry

Most of the pastries included are the less usual and are particularly good with poultry and game.

With the exception of the hot-water crust pastries there is one golden rule; play it cool — hands, equipment, and ingredients.

Choux Pastry

250 ml (8 fl oz) water
125 g (4 oz) butter
125 g (4 oz) plain (all-purpose) flour
a pinch of salt
4 × 55 g (2 oz) eggs, lightly beaten

Put the water and butter in a saucepan and bring just to boiling-point. Remove the pan from the heat, tip the flour and salt into the liquid, and beat with a wooden spoon until the mixture is smooth and leaves the sides of the pan. Leave to cool slightly. Gradually add the eggs to the paste, beating thoroughly until the mixture is shiny and smooth. Use as the recipe directs.

Cream Cheese Pastry

This delicious short savoury pastry is very good for vegetable flans.

250 g (8 oz) plain (all-purpose) flour
½ teaspoon salt
60 g (2 oz) butter
60 g (2 oz) cream cheese
3–4 tablespoons iced water
lightly beaten egg

Sift the flour and salt into a mixing bowl. Cut the butter and cheese into small pieces and add to the flour. Using the fingertips, rub the butter and cheese into the flour until there are no lumps and the mixture looks like fine breadcrumbs. Add 3 tablespoons of the water and with one hand mix quickly together to form a dough. Use a little more of the water if the dough is too dry. Knead lightly for a few seconds, shape into a ball, and cover with plastic-wrap or greaseproof paper. Chill in the refrigerator for 30 minutes before rolling and use as the recipe directs. Brush with the egg before baking.

Shortcrust Pastry

Makes 500 grams (1 pound) of pastry

500 g (1 lb) plain (all-purpose) flour
½ teaspoon salt
250 g (8 oz) butter
cold water

Sift the flour and salt into a mixing bowl. Cut the butter into the flour with a knife and rub in with the fingertips until the mixture resembles fine breadcrumbs. Gradually add enough cold water to form the dough into a rolling consistency. Turn on to a board and knead lightly. Cover and chill in the refrigerator for 20 minutes before rolling. Roll the pastry on a lightly floured board and use as the recipe directs.

Note: Pastry that needs a great deal of flour on the board to prevent it from sticking has had too much water used in the mixture. Keep the liquid to a minimum.

Cobbler Dough

The texture of this raised dough is similar to that of scones (biscuits) and can be used cut into rounds as a savoury and dessert pie topping, or cut into crescents to serve with soup or as a garnish.

250 g (8 oz) self-raising (self-rising)
  flour
½ teaspoon salt
125 g (4 oz) butter
milk

Pre-heat the oven to moderately hot. Sift the flour and salt into a mixing bowl. Rub the butter into the flour until it resembles fine breadcrumbs. Use enough milk to form a soft, but not sticky, dough. Knead lightly and turn on to a board lightly sprinkled with flour.

Roll the dough to 1-centimetre (½ inch) thickness and cut into rounds using a 5-centimetre (2 inch) plain or fluted cutter. If you are making crescents, roll the dough to a thickness of 5 millimetres (¼ inch). Brush with milk or egg glaze (page 205) and bake for 20 to 25 minutes, or as the recipe directs.

Herb Cobbler

Add ½ to 1 teaspoon of dried mixed herbs to the dry ingredients before rubbing in the butter.

Coffee Cobbler

Use 1 tablespoon of strong black coffee and enough milk to mix the ingredients to a dough.

Cheese Cobbler

Sift ½ teaspoon of dry mustard with the salt and flour. Add 60 grams (2 ounces) of finely grated Cheddar cheese to the dry ingredients and reduce the butter to 90 grams (3 ounces). Rub in the butter and mix to a dough. Glaze and bake on lightly oiled trays.

Lemon Cobbler

Add the finely grated rind of half a lemon to the dry ingredients. Rub in the butter and mix to a dough with 1 tablespoon of lemon juice and light sour cream. Glaze and bake on lightly oiled trays.

Dessert Cobbler

Add 1 to 2 teaspoons of castor (superfine) sugar and ½ teaspoon of mixed spice to the dry ingredients before rubbing in the butter.

Suet Crust Pastry

375 g (12 oz) plain (all-purpose)
  flour
¼ teaspoon salt
1 teaspoon baking powder
185 g (6 oz) finely grated beef suet
1 cup (9 fl oz) water, less 2
  tablespoons

Sift the flour, salt, and baking powder into a mixing bowl. Add the grated suet and rub into the flour with your fingertips. Mix to a soft dough with the water. Knead lightly until the dough is smooth and elastic. Use as the recipe directs.

Turkey Cobbler, page 221; using Cobbler Dough

Puff Pastry

Makes 500 grams (1 pound) of pastry

500 g (1 lb) butter
*500 g (1 lb) plain (all-purpose)
  flour*
a pinch of salt
1 teaspoon lemon juice
cold water

Shape the butter into a neat block and chill in the refrigerator until firm. Sift the flour and salt into a bowl and mix to a dough of rolling consistency with the lemon juice and water. Turn on to a lightly floured board, knead lightly, and roll to an oblong shape.

Put the butter on the centre of the dough. Fold the bottom part of the dough over the butter, and then fold the top part down, so that the fat is completely covered. Press the open edges firmly together with a rolling pin and make a right-angled turn of the pastry. Press the rolling pin at intervals across the block of pastry to give it a corrugated appearance. Roll the pastry into an oblong shape, fold into three layers, and again seal the edges and corrugate the top. Chill for 10 minutes before rolling again.

Repeat the rolling and folding twice more, sealing each time with the rolling pin. Chill again for 10 minutes. Repeat the rolling three times and chill again.

Roll for the final time and use as the recipe directs. Rest the pastry in the refrigerator before baking.

Hot-Water Crust Pastry — Moulded

Hot water makes this a pliable pastry which is easy to mould. Use for hot or cold raised pies and prepare the filling before making the pastry. To make a raised pie in a mould, grease a 15-centimetre (6 inch) round or oval mould before making the pastry. A spring-form mould or cake tin is ideal.

*500 g (1 lb) plain (all-purpose)
  flour*
1 teaspoon salt
*³/4 cup (¹/3 pt) water mixed with ³/4
  cup (¹/3 pt) milk*
125 g (4 oz) lard, less 1 tablespoon
egg glaze (opposite)

Sift the flour and salt into a warm mixing bowl. Heat the water, milk, and lard in a small pan until the lard has melted. Stir and remove from the heat just before the mixture boils. Make a well in the centre of the flour and pour in the hot liquid. Working quickly, beat with a wooden spoon, gradually drawing the flour into the liquid from the edges of the well. Finish mixing the dough by hand as it becomes too stiff to mix with a spoon.

Turn the dough on to a lightly floured board, cut off one quarter, and leave the small portion covered in the mixing bowl. Lightly roll the remaining dough, lift into the mould and shape to fit, pressing well into the corners and making sure that there are no splits or creases in the pastry. Add the filling according to the recipe.

Roll the reserved dough to form a lid. Dampen the edges of the case with water, put the lid in position, and pinch the edges together to seal the pie. Decorate the top with pastry trimmings cut into leaves, brush with the egg glaze, and bake as the recipe directs.

Hot-Water Crust Pastry — Hand-Raised

I think that a hand-raised pie has more charm than the more elegant moulded ones. Make the hot-water crust as directed opposite and shape as follows. You can make the filling after preparing the pie.

Use a straight-sided container about 15 centimetres (6 inches) in diameter. Lightly oil the outside of the dish and dredge with flour. Set aside. Make the pastry, cut off the piece for the lid, and leave covered.

Put the dough on a sheet of foil and flatten the centre. Press the base of the oiled mould on the centre of the flattened dough and mould the pastry up the sides of the dish with your hands, pressing quite firmly and keeping the thickness of the pastry even. Overwrap the pastry with the foil, pleating where necessary to fit smoothly over the dough. Fold the foil over the rim of the container and chill in the refrigerator until the pastry is firm enough to hold its shape without the mould. In the meantime, make the filling.

Loosen the foil and carefully ease the container out of the pastry case. A gentle twist will loosen it quite easily. Leave the foil in place and trim just above the top rim of the pie. Carefully place the foil-wrapped case on a baking tray and fill with the prepared mixture. Pack the filling gently, but firmly, into the case so that it will hold its shape. Roll the remaining pastry to form a lid. Cover and dampen the edges together before pinching to form a seal. Trim neatly, cut a vent in the centre, glaze, and bake as the recipe directs. Remove the foil as soon as the pie is cooked.

Egg Glaze

One egg beaten with a small pinch of salt until the yolk darkens a little will give a beautiful glaze to pies, if brushed over the pastry before it is baked.

Swag Pastry

500 g (1 lb) plain (all-purpose) flour
1/2 teaspoon salt
1/2 teaspoon cayenne or red pepper
315 g (10 oz) butter
1 tablespoon lemon juice
3 tablespoons iced water

This is a very short, 'melt-in-the-mouth' pastry but resilient enough to withstand the jolts and jars of transport to picnics and outdoor lunches.

Sift the flour, salt, and cayenne or red pepper into a mixing bowl. Cut the butter into small pieces and rub into the flour. Mix to a fairly firm dough with the lemon juice and water. Chill for 30 minutes before rolling. Use as the recipe directs.

Stuffings

Basic Herb Stuffing

This quantity is sufficient for 2 kilograms (4 pounds) of poultry or game.

2 tablespoons butter
1 medium onion, chopped
1 teaspoon dried mixed herbs
125 g (4 oz) fresh breadcrumbs
salt
freshly ground black pepper

This basic recipe can be halved or doubled and added to in many ways.

Melt the butter and cook the onion until transparent. Sprinkle with the herbs (substitute the equivalent amount of a particular favourite if you prefer). Stir the breadcrumbs into the pan and mix thoroughly. Season with salt and black pepper to taste. This basic stuffing can be lightly bound with stock, water, wine, or lightly beaten egg.

Ham and Pecan Stuffing

This quantity is sufficient for a 2 to 2.5 kilogram (4 to 5 pound) bird

1 tablespoon butter
125 g (4 oz) chopped ham
2 large onions, chopped
250 g (8 oz) dry breadcrumbs
salt
freshly ground black pepper
125 g (4 oz) chopped pecans
2 tablespoons brandy

Use with turkey, chicken, guinea fowl, and pheasant. The quantity halves or doubles readily.

Melt the butter in a shallow pan and fry the ham until very lightly browned, adding a little more butter if there is negligible fat on the ham. Reduce the heat and cook the onions until transparent. Stir the breadcrumbs into the pan and mix well until all the pan-juices have been absorbed. Remove the pan from the heat and season with salt and black pepper to taste. Stir in the pecans and finally the brandy. Leave to cool before using.

Nut Stuffing

This quantity is sufficient for a 2 kilogram (4 pound) bird

90 g (3 oz) goose fat or butter
1 large onion, chopped
2 tablespoons finely chopped fresh coriander
1 teaspoon dried mixed herbs
¼ teaspoon ground mace
¼ teaspoon ground cloves
155 g (5 oz) fresh breadcrumbs
125 g (4 oz) chopped pecans or macadamia nuts
salt
freshly ground black pepper

This is a stuffing I particularly like for duck and goose. It is also very good with pork.

Heat the fat or butter in a large shallow pan and cook the onion until transparent. Sprinkle the herbs and spices over the onion and mix thoroughly. Stir the breadcrumbs into the pan with the nuts. Mix well until all the pan-juices have been absorbed. Season with salt and black pepper and remove from the heat. Leave to cool before using. Do not overstuff with this mixture because it swells with cooking.

Oyster Stuffing

This quantity is sufficient for a 2 kilogram (4 pound) bird

3 tablespoons butter
1 small onion, finely chopped
1 celery stalk, finely chopped
salt
freshly ground black pepper
250 g (8 oz) dry breadcrumbs
1 teaspoon dried thyme
24 fresh or bottled oysters, well drained
approx. 3 tablespoons stock or dry white wine

This is a traditional stuffing, often used for chicken. As it is basically pre-cooked it is also suitable for the smaller game birds. You can chop the oysters or leave them whole — I prefer them whole.

Melt the butter in a shallow pan and fry the onion and celery until softened but not brown. Season the vegetables lightly with salt and black pepper. Stir the breadcrumbs and thyme into the pan. Mix thoroughly until all the pan-juices have been absorbed. Remove from the heat. Add the oysters to the mixture with enough stock or wine to bind — it should hold together and not be too crumbly.

Spoon the stuffing loosely into the cavity of the bird and close the opening with poultry pins or coarse thread.

Pork and Apricot Stuffing

This quantity is sufficient for a 4 to 5 kilogram (8 to 10 pound) bird

2 tablespoons butter
1 medium onion, finely chopped
500 g (1 lb) very finely minced (ground) pork
30 g (1 oz) fresh white breadcrumbs
3 teaspoons dried mixed herbs
3 tablespoons ground almonds
3 tablespoons finely chopped dried apricots
1 teaspoon salt
½ teaspoon black pepper
3 tablespoons cream

This is a highly versatile mixture that is suitable for turkey, goose, duck, and chicken. Use the stuffing in the neck and body cavities of duck or chicken — both of which need only half the quantity of stuffing.

Melt the butter in a shallow pan and gently cook the onion until transparent. Add the pork, breaking up any lumps with the back of a fork, and cook with the onion for 5 to 6 minutes, until the meat changes colour. Stir the breadcrumbs and herbs into the pan, mix thoroughly with the meat, and remove from the heat. Stir in the almonds and apricots and season with salt and black pepper. Leave to cool before adding the cream. Fill the bird loosely with the stuffing just before cooking.

Wild Rice Stuffing

This quantity is sufficient for 1.5 to 2 kilograms (3 to 4 pounds) of poultry or game.

140 g (4½ oz) wild rice
½ teaspoon salt
3 tablespoons butter
2 tablespoons finely snipped chives
60 g (2 oz) finely chopped prosciutto
white pepper

Rinse the rice thoroughly with cold water, then put it in a pan with enough boiling water to cover. Simmer for 2 minutes, strain, and repeat the process twice more.

Cover the rice with boiling water again, add the salt, and simmer for 5 minutes. Strain and add the butter, chives, and prosciutto. Season with salt and pepper to taste and use as the recipe directs.

Garnishes

Orange Cogs

Slice one unpeeled orange thinly and with a sharp knife make small triangular cuts around the peel.

Citrus Twists

Slice unpeeled lemons or limes thinly and with a sharp knife make one straight cut from the centre of each slice to the peel and twist apart.

Radish Roses

Top and tail the radishes. Start at the base and make shallow slits in the skin to form petals. Soak the radishes in a bowl of iced water for 2 to 3 hours.

Celery Bon-Bons

Cut celery stalks into 10-centimetre (4 inch) lengths. Make several slits at each end. Soak in iced water for at least 2 hours.

Spring Onion (Scallion) Bon-Bons

Use the green ends of the spring onions (scallions) cut into about 7-centimetre (3 inch) lengths. Make 2.5-centimetre (1 inch) parallel hairline cuts at each end of the spring onions (scallions). Soak in iced water for 30 minutes.

Tomato Rosettes

Choose small firm tomatoes and with a small pointed knife make vandyke cuts around the middle and through to the centre, and carefully separate top from bottom.

Carrot Curls

Top, tail, and scrape firm young carrots and using a potato peeler cut them into long thin strips. Roll the strips and secure with cocktail sticks. Soak in iced water for 2 hours and discard the sticks before using.

Geisha Gherkins

Use midget gherkins. Hold firmly on a board and, starting 5 millimetres (¼ inch) from the flower end, make four lengthwise cuts. Spread the gherkins carefully into fans.

Turned Mushrooms

Use button mushroom caps. Make six equal, shallow curved cuts, radiating from the centre to the edge of each mushroom. Notch a shallow 'v' against the inner side of each curve. Serve raw or lightly simmered in lemon juice and butter.

Clockwise from top: Tomato Rosettes; Spring Onion Bon-Bons; Turned Mushrooms; Geisha Gherkins; Citrus Twists; Celery Bon-Bons; Orange Cogs; Radish Roses; and Carrot Curls

Accompaniments

The following two versions of fried bread are different in size but based on the same principle. Croûtons are small cubes of bread, croûtes are larger triangles. Serve croûtons with soup and casseroles, croûtes to garnish and add texture to small game and casseroles.

Croûtons

3–4 tablespoons butter
4 slices of bread, with crusts removed, cut into 1-cm (½ inch) cubes

Melt the butter in a shallow pan. Add the cubed bread and shake over moderately high heat until evenly browned and crisp. Drain on paper towels before serving.

Note: The butter can be flavoured with garlic, ginger, or herbs before the bread is added. Before serving, the croûtons can be sprinkled with parsley, paprika, or poppy, caraway, or celery seed.

Croûtes

Cut the crustless bread into triangles, or stamp with a cutter into fancy shapes. Sauté in hot butter until crisp and golden on each side. Drain and serve.

Fried Crumbs

Serves 4

60–90 g (2–3 oz) fine fresh breadcrumbs
2 tablespoons butter

These make a pleasant accompaniment not only to game. It is well worth preparing more than you need (they store well in an airtight jar) and use for sprinkling over vegetables, salads, and soup.

Melt the butter and fry the crumbs until golden brown and crisp.

Variations
The butter can be flavoured with garlic, herbs, fresh ginger, finely grated citrus rind, or spices.

Forcemeat Dumplings

Serves 4

60 g (2 oz) fresh breadcrumbs
30 g (1 oz) finely grated beef suet
2 tablespoons chopped fresh mixed herbs or 2 teaspoons dried mixed herbs
2 teaspoons finely chopped parsley
salt and pepper
1 egg, lightly beaten

These very light dumplings are a delicious accompaniment to poultry and game casseroles.

Mix the breadcrumbs thoroughly with the suet and add the fresh or dried herbs, parsley, and salt and pepper to taste. Use only enough of the egg to bind the mixture firmly — it should not be sticky. Form into walnut-sized balls and store on a lightly floured plate until ready to use.

Cook on top of a casserole for 1 hour, or as the recipe directs.

Matzo Meal Balls

Not only a light and delicious garnish for thick and thin soup, these matzo balls can be flavoured in a variety of ways and served as dumplings with casseroles and stews.

Serves 4–6

3 tablespoons goose fat or chicken fat or melted butter
3 eggs, lightly beaten
140 g (4½ oz) fine matzo meal
1½ teaspoons salt

Mix the melted fat (it should not be hot) with the eggs. Put the meal in a bowl with the salt, fork together, and make a well in the centre. Pour a little of the egg mixture into the matzo. Keep adding the egg and mixing until the ingredients are well blended.

Chill for 30 minutes before shaping, with wet hands, into twelve balls (they can be deep-frozen for later use, if you wish). To serve as a garnish for soup, poach the balls with 1 teaspoon of salt in gently simmering water for 35 minutes. Lift from the water and transfer to the soup 5 minutes before serving.

Matzo Meal Dumplings

Prepare the dumplings as described above and cook on top of a casserole or stew for the last 35 to 40 minutes of the cooking time.

Chopped Liver Dumplings

Mix one set of trimmed and finely chopped chicken livers and 1 teaspoon of finely snipped chives into the matzo with the egg mixture.

Mustard Dumplings

Mix 2 teaspoons of dry English mustard and 1 teaspoon of poppy seed with the dry ingredients before adding the eggs.

Hazelnut Dumplings

Roll twelve whole hazelnuts in butter, sprinkle with garlic salt, and roll the basic matzo mixture around each.

Apricot-Stuffed Apples

These tart apples are particularly good with roast goose and duck.

Serves 4

90 g (3 oz) dried apricots
¾ cup (⅓ pt) water
4 tart cooking apples, cored

Put the apricots in a small saucepan with the water and bring to the boil. Cover and simmer until the apricots are tender. Remove the lid and cook until most of the liquid has evaporated. Purée the apricots in a blender or food processor or rub through a sieve.

Make sure that pips and tough cores have been removed from the apples. Arrange them in a lightly oiled baking dish and fill the centres with the apricot purée. Bake in the oven, below the goose or duck, for 30 to 35 minutes. The apples should still be slightly firm when served.

LEFTOVERS

Left-over food does not have to be dreary. Many delicious dishes can be prepared from what may seem like boring remnants and very often from small quantities that you would not think of doing anything with.

It is often worth cooking more than you need for one meal in order to take advantage of these superb réchauffé dishes.

Chicken Divan, page 215

Egyptian Omelette

Serves 4

*1 medium eggplant (aubergine),
    quartered and thinly sliced*
salt
2 tablespoons butter
1 tablespoon olive oil
1 medium onion, coarsely chopped
1 large clove of garlic, crushed
½ teaspoon dried mixed herbs
*125–250 g (4–8 oz) shredded
    cooked poultry or game*
*75–155 g (2½–5 oz) cooked pasta
    (optional)*
freshly ground black pepper
6–8 eggs, lightly beaten

This is very like the Spanish tortilla — a thick cake of 'allsorts', using what you have on hand but definitely eggplant (aubergine) in place of the potato used in the Spanish version, eggs plus vegetables, cooked pasta, and herbs. Then add whatever you have in the way of cooked poultry or game. Serve hot or cold with vegetables or salad.

Put the sliced eggplant (aubergine) in a strainer, sprinkle lightly with salt, and leave for 20 minutes, until the juice starts to drain. Shake off any excess moisture and pat dry before using.

Melt the butter with the oil in a 23 centimetre (9 inch) omelette pan. Sauté the onion and garlic for 2 minutes. Reduce the heat, add the eggplant (aubergine), and cook until it is just softened. Sprinkle with the herbs and stir in the poultry or game, pasta, or any other vegetables. Season to taste and pour the eggs over the mixture. Cook until they are almost set and either brown the top under a very hot grill (broiler) or turn the omelette on to a plate and slide the unfinished side back into the pan to brown.

Cut into wedges and serve immediately or leave until quite cold before cutting.

Egyptian Omelette

Parsi Omelette with Chicken

This is a highly spiced omelette, lighter than a tortilla, more substantial than a French omelette. Serve with potato balls (page 185) and a crisp salad.

Serves 4

4 tablespoons ghee or butter
1 small piece of fresh ginger, peeled and sliced
1 large onion, chopped
375 g (12 oz) chopped cooked chicken
5 eggs
2 egg-yolks
2 tablespoons redcurrant jelly
1 hot green chilli, seeded and chopped
3 tablespoons very finely chopped coriander or parsley
juice of 1 large lemon
1 large clove of garlic, crushed
1 teaspoon salt

Melt the ghee or butter in a heavy-based frying pan (skillet). Add the ginger and fry over moderate heat for 1 or 2 minutes to flavour the fat. Discard the ginger. Add the onion and fry until golden. Reduce the heat, stir in the chicken, and mix with the onion. Cook gently for 2 or 3 minutes.

Beat the whole eggs lightly in a bowl. Mix the yolks thoroughly with the redcurrant jelly and stir into the beaten eggs with the remaining ingredients.

Increase the heat and when the fat is sizzling, pour the egg mixture over the chicken. Stir lightly for 1 minute, then shake the pan to level the mixture. Cook until just set and serve immediately, cut into wedges.

Variation
Although chicken has been used, any left-over poultry or game bird can be substituted.

Chicken Divan

There is nothing 'make do' about a divan — it fits happily for any occasion. Use fresh or frozen broccoli and serve with roast potatoes.

Serves 4

375 g (12 oz) pack of frozen broccoli, or 500 g (1 lb) fresh broccoli, trimmed
375–500 g (³⁄₄–1 lb) chopped cooked chicken
salt and pepper
60 g (2 oz) toasted slivered almonds
2 tablespoons grated Parmesan cheese
Sauce
1¹⁄₂ cups (14 fl oz) milk
1 small onion
1 bay-leaf
60 g (2 oz) butter
3 tablespoons plain (all-purpose) flour
salt
white pepper
¹⁄₂ cup (4 fl oz) cream
1 tablespoon dry sherry

Cook the broccoli in lightly salted water until just tender. Drain and arrange in a shallow ovenproof dish, with the flower ends against the rim of the dish. Pre-heat the oven to moderate.

Fold the chicken into the sauce, adjust the seasoning, and pour over the broccoli. Sprinkle with the almonds and cheese and bake in the centre of the oven for 25 to 30 minutes. Serve immediately.

Sauce
Put the milk, onion, and bay-leaf in the top of a double boiler and cook over simmering water for 15 minutes. Strain the milk and discard the flavouring ingredients. Melt the butter in a saucepan, stir in the flour, and cook gently for 2 minutes. Gradually add the strained milk, stirring constantly between each addition, until the sauce is thick and smooth. Season with salt and pepper to taste and simmer for 1 minute. Remove the pan from the heat and add the cream and sherry.

Variations
Substitute cooked goose, turkey, or duck for the chicken and cook in the same way.

Chicken Mille-Feuille

This is hardly a novel way to use leftovers but it is certainly very agreeable and far more interesting than cold slices of chicken. Serve with a tart salad — for example, lettuce and grapefruit segments charged with some chopped pimiento or capers.

Serves 4–6

500 g (1 lb) pack of frozen puff pastry, thawed, or 1 quantity of puff pastry (page 204)
1½ tablespoons butter
3 tablespoons plain (all-purpose) flour
1½ cups (14 fl oz) milk
½ cup (4 fl oz) cream
salt
white pepper
500 g (1 lb) chopped cooked chicken
125 g (4 oz) lean ham, chopped
4 spring onions (scallions), finely chopped
1 teaspoon pickled green peppercorns, drained
Spanish paprika

Pre-heat the oven to very hot. Roll the pastry to approximately 5 millimetre (¼ inch) thickness and cut into three rectangles, each about 25 by 10 centimetres (10 by 4 inches). Sprinkle baking trays lightly with water, arrange the pieces of pastry on them, and chill for a few minutes. Bake until well raised and golden. Leave to cool on wire racks before filling.

Melt the butter in a heavy-based saucepan, stir in the flour, and cook gently for 1 or 2 minutes without browning. Add the milk gradually, beating well between each addition, until the sauce is thick and smooth. Simmer for 2 or 3 minutes. Remove from the heat and cover the surface closely with plastic-wrap, to prevent a skin from forming. Leave to cool before adding the cream. Season with salt and pepper to taste, remove 3 tablespoons of the cream sauce, and reserve.

Mix the chicken with the ham, spring onions (scallions), and green peppercorns and fold into the sauce. Spread half of the chicken mixture over one sheet of pastry. Put another pastry layer on top and spread with the remaining chicken mixture. Cover with the last sheet of pastry, drizzle the reserved sauce over, and sprinkle with paprika.

Serve garnished with salad.

Chicken Mille-Feuille

Stuffed Bread Cases

These are crisp and delicious, they travel well for picnics, and you can even take the empty cases and fill them in situ. These are single-portion size but they can be made in a small 'finger-food' party size, and although a bit fiddly to make they do stand the time test by remaining crisp. Serve hot with a creamed vegetable or cold with assorted salads.

Use day-old sandwich bread and trim away all crusts with a sharp knife (preferably an electric carving knife). If the bread is too fresh and crumbles, freeze for an hour before trimming.

Cut the trimmed bread into 9 centimetre (3½ inch) cubes. Cut the outline of an inner cube from each piece of trimmed bread by cutting down, to within 1 centimetre (½ inch) of the base, on all sides. The trick lies in removing the inner cube without damaging the base. Insert the point of a small, sharp, pointed knife, 1 centimetre (½ inch) above the base of the shell and in the centre of one side. Keeping the knife parallel with the base, wiggle it around in a cutting motion. This will gradually release the centre. The small incision in the side will heal rapidly. Finally shave a little bread from each vertical corner.

Use the centres for crumbs or, if you are very keen, they are a perfect size to make into smaller bread cases, which can be dried and stored for later use.

Lightly brush the cases inside and out with melted butter and bake for 20 minutes in the oven pre-heated to moderately slow.

Use any of the following mixtures to fill the cases.

Chicken and Mushrooms in Pimiento Sauce

This quantity is sufficient for four to six bread cases or pastry horns

1 quantity of pimiento cream sauce (page 196)
1 tablespoon butter
1 bacon rasher, chopped, with rind removed
6 spring onions (scallions), chopped
125 g (4 oz) button mushrooms, sliced
375–500 g (¾–1 lb) diced cooked chicken
salt
white pepper
1 tablespoon finely chopped fresh coriander

Prepare the sauce and simmer in the top of a double boiler.

Melt the butter and cook the bacon, spring onions (scallions), and mushrooms until tender. Lift the mixture from the pan with a slotted spoon, mix with the chicken, and season to taste. Add to the sauce and heat thoroughly before filling the cases or horns. Serve garnished with the coriander.

To serve cold, chill the mixture thoroughly before using.

Turkey Club Sandwich

With little trouble the humble sandwich can be elevated to a culinary delight. This version must surely come into that category.

For each serving allow

2 slices of rye or other bread, buttered
1 teaspoon mayonnaise
2 crisp lettuce leaves
2 generous slices of turkey meat
1 crisp-cooked bacon rasher, crumbled
4 slices of tomato
2 stuffed olives, sliced
2 thick slices of avocado, lightly sprinkled with lemon juice
salt
freshly ground black pepper
1 teaspoon capers, drained
watercress

Spread the buttered bread lightly with the mayonnaise. On one slice of bread lay first a lettuce leaf, then a slice of turkey, then half the bacon. Cover with two slices of tomato, then some of the olives and one slice of avocado. Season with salt and black pepper. Cover with the second slice of bread and repeat the layers. Sprinkle the capers and remaining olives over and garnish with the watercress.

Turkey Club Sandwich

Swedish Turkey Fritters

Serves 4

1 quantity of savoury coating batter (page 200)
500 g (1 lb) coarsely minced (ground) cooked turkey
125 g (4 oz) coarsely minced (ground) lean ham
2 teaspoons chopped fresh mixed herbs or ½ teaspoon dried mixed herbs
¼ teaspoon ground mace
2 spring onions (scallions), finely chopped
6–8 bacon rashers, with rind removed
oil for deep-frying
freshly ground black pepper
lemon wedges

Serve these delicious fritters with game chips (page 184), crisp salads, and any standard tartare sauce.

Prepare the batter and leave to stand before adding the egg-whites.

Mix the turkey with the ham, herbs, mace, and spring onions (scallions). There will probably be enough salt from the ham and bacon. I find this mixture is usually moist enough to cling together without binding; if, however, it is very dry, add a teaspoon or two of the batter. Divide into six to eight portions and shape into thick patties. Wrap each patty, tournedos-fashion, with a bacon rasher and secure with a cocktail stick. Pre-heat the oil to 185°C (365°F).

Fold the stiffly beaten egg-whites into the batter. Coat each patty with the batter and deep-fry, three or four at a time, until crisp and golden. Drain on paper towels and serve garnished with the lemon wedges.

Pineapple Boats

Hot pineapple halves are filled with a savoury turkey mixture. Serve with potato balls (page 185) and assorted salads.

(page 185)

Serves 4

2 medium pineapples, halved
2 tablespoons butter
1 tablespoon vegetable oil
2 celery stalks, sliced
1 clove of garlic, crushed
60 g (2 oz) button mushrooms, sliced
1 small tomato, peeled, seeded, and chopped
1 canned pimiento, drained and chopped
1 teaspoon arrowroot or cornflour (cornstarch)
2 tablespoons dry sherry
500 g (1 lb) cubed cooked turkey salt
freshly ground black pepper
2 tablespoons finely snipped chives

Twist the spiked stalks from the pineapples and save a few of the leaves for decoration. Halve the pineapples. Cut away and discard the hard core. Carefully scoop out the flesh, leaving a 1-centimetre (½ inch) shell. Do this over a shallow dish to catch the pineapple juice. Dice the fruit and set aside.

Melt the butter with the oil in a saucepan and cook the celery over low heat until it begins to soften. Add the garlic, mushrooms, tomato, pimiento, and the pineapple juice. Cover and simmer for 3 or 4 minutes. Pre-heat the oven to moderate.

Mix the arrowroot or cornflour (cornstarch) to a smooth paste with the sherry and stir into the vegetable mixture with the diced pineapple and the turkey. Season with salt and black pepper to taste and simmer for 2 minutes longer. Put the pineapple shells on a baking tray, divide the turkey mixture between them, and bake in the centre of the oven for 15 to 20 minutes.

Arrange on a heated serving dish, garnish with the chives, and decorate with the reserved pineapple leaves.

Pineapple Boats

Turkey Cobbler

Serves 4

2 tablespoons butter
2 tablespoons vegetable oil
2 medium carrots, thinly sliced
1 large onion, chopped
2–3 sweet chillies, seeded and sliced
125 g (4 oz) button mushrooms,
    halved or sliced
salt
white pepper
1 tablespoon plain (all-purpose)
    flour
1 cup (9 fl oz) turkey stock or
    chicken stock
½ cup (4 fl oz) cream
500 g (1 lb) cubed cooked turkey
1 quantity of cobbler dough
    (page 203)
milk

The turkey is folded into a saucy vegetable mixture and topped with cobbler dough. Serve with crisp Brussels sprouts, lightly sprinkled with almonds and lemon juice.

Melt the butter with the oil in a flameproof baking dish. When the fat is sizzling, add the carrots and onion and brown lightly. Reduce the heat, add the chillies and mushrooms, and stir with the other vegetables. Season lightly with salt and pepper, sprinkle with the flour, and mix thoroughly. Cook for 1 or 2 minutes before gradually adding the stock. Stir until thickened and smooth. Remove the dish from the heat and pre-heat the oven to moderate.

Stir the cream into the vegetable mixture with the turkey. Adjust the seasoning and bake for 20 to 25 minutes. Roll the cobbler dough to a thickness of 1 centimetre (½ inch) and cut into 5-centimetre (2 inch) circles. Arrange on a baking tray, brush lightly with milk, and bake on a shelf above the turkey for 12 to 15 minutes, until golden (they can be cooked directly on top of the turkey mixture for 20 to 25 minutes but are more crisp when cooked separately). Arrange the cooked cobbler over the turkey and serve hot.

Chicken Cobbler
Substitute for the turkey an equal quantity of cooked chicken, or a mixture of chicken and ham. Prepare and cook as described.

Goose Brûlée Attunga

Serves 4

375–500 g (¾–1 lb) sliced cooked
    goose
1 cup (9 fl oz) chicken stock
3 tablespoons orange juice
finely grated rind of 1 orange
2 tablespoons redcurrant jelly
salt
freshly ground black pepper
1 orange, peeled and cut into
    segments
90 g (3 oz) seedless raisins
2 tablespoons brown sugar

This is a minimum-effort réchauffé dish. Serve with a mixed salad for lunch or add vegetables for a main course.

Simmer the sliced goose in the chicken stock for 7 or 8 minutes. Mix the orange juice and rind with the redcurrant jelly. Pre-heat the grill (broiler).

Remove the goose from the stock and arrange in a shallow heatproof serving dish. Pour the orange juice mixture over the goose and season with salt and black pepper to taste. Pattern the orange segments and raisins over the top and sprinkle with the brown sugar. Grill (broil) until the sugar bubbles and glazes the surface. Serve immediately.

Goose Brûlée Attunga

Turkey Brioche

Hot or cold, this is a good way to use a relatively small amount of left-over turkey. Serve hot with a creamy vegetable or cold with salad. Use a bought brioche or make one from any standard recipe.

Serves 4

1 large brioche
3 tablespoons hot milk
60 g (2 oz) butter
1 red (bell) pepper, seeded and
chopped
6 spring onions (scallions), coarsely
chopped
¼ teaspoon celery seed
1 tablespoon plain (all-purpose)
flour
3 tablespoons cold milk
salt
white pepper
a pinch of chilli powder
375 g (12 oz) chopped cooked
turkey
½ cup (4 fl oz) cream

Remove the top of the brioche and set aside. Hollow the centre of the brioche, leaving a shell about 2.5 centimetres (1 inch) thick. Put the scooped-out crumbs in a bowl, pour the hot milk over, and leave to soak.

Melt the butter and gently cook the pepper and spring onions (scallions) until softened. Sprinkle with the celery seed and flour, cook for 1 or 2 minutes, and gradually add the cold milk, stirring constantly until a smooth sauce is formed. Beat the soaked crumb mixture into the sauce and season with salt, pepper, and chilli powder to taste. Fold the turkey into the sauce, add the cream, and adjust the seasoning.

To serve the brioche hot, brush the centre lightly with butter, and put in a moderately slow oven for 10 minutes. Fill with the hot turkey mixture, put the lid on, and serve, cut into wedges.

If serving cold, chill the mixture before filling the cold brioche.

Turkey Brioche

Enchiladas

These are the filled tortillas of Mexico. Traditionally, they are made with cornmeal or flour painstakingly kneaded and patted into shape. This recipe shortcuts that lengthy process with good results, The filling can be built around any cooked poultry or light game and these very spicy pancakes need only a salad as a side dish.

Serves 4

1 quantity of crêpe batter
(page 200)
oil
1 cup (9 fl oz) milk
1 egg
1 ½ teaspoons Hungarian paprika
1 teaspoon chilli powder
125 g (4 oz) grated mozzarella
cheese

Filling

1 tablespoon olive oil or vegetable
oil
1 large onion, chopped
2 cloves of garlic, crushed
1 red (bell) pepper, seeded and
chopped
2 × 425 g (15 oz/No. 300) cans
peeled tomatoes, crushed
2 tablespoons tomato paste
1 teaspoon powdered oregano
½ teaspoon cayenne or red pepper
1 teaspoon Mexican chilli powder
250–500 g (½–1 lb) chopped
cooked poultry or game
salt

Prepare the crêpe batter and leave to stand while you make the filling.

Make thin pancakes in a lightly oiled pan, cooking both sides lightly without browning. Stack the pancakes as they are made. Pre-heat the oven to moderate.

Beat the milk and egg with the paprika and chilli powder in a shallow dish and leave to chill. Dip each pancake in the egg mixture before refrying until browned on both sides.

Divide the filling between the pancakes and roll them. Arrange them in a lightly oiled baking dish. Pour any remaining sauce around the pancakes and sprinkle them with the grated cheese. Bake in the centre of the oven for 15 to 20 minutes, until the cheese has melted and is lightly browned.

Filling

Heat the oil in a large frying pan (skillet) and brown the onion quickly. Reduce the heat and cook the garlic and pepper gently until the pepper is just softened. Stir in the tomatoes, their liquid, and the tomato paste. Sprinkle with the oregano, cayenne or red pepper, and Mexican chilli powder. Simmer for 5 or 6 minutes. Add the poultry or game, stir well, and season with salt to taste. Simmer gently until the sauce has thickened.

Enchiladas

Hare Croquettes

There is always a surprisingly large amount of meat left on a hare carcass after serving. Made into small croquettes, it is an excellent appetiser. Larger ones make a substantial meal, served with potatoes rosemary (page 186), a crisp green vegetable, and Cumberland sauce (page 196).

Serves 4

375–500 g (³/₄–1 lb) hare from roast saddle
1 medium onion, finely chopped
1 small clove of garlic, crushed
2 tablespoons grated Parmesan cheese
45 g (1¹/₂ oz) fresh breadcrumbs
¹/₂ teaspoon salt
¹/₄ teaspoon white pepper
¹/₄ teaspoon ground ginger
¹/₄ teaspoon mixed spice
3 eggs
1 tablespoon milk
125–185 g (4–6 oz) dry breadcrumbs
2 tablespoons butter
3 tablespoons olive oil or vegetable oil
freshly ground black pepper

Cut all the meat from the hare carcass and mince (grind) coarsely. Mix thoroughly with the onion, garlic, and cheese. Toss the fresh breadcrumbs with the salt, white pepper, and spices. Add the seasoned breadcrumbs to the hare, mix well, and bind with one of the eggs, lightly beaten. Shape the mixture into small round balls or larger cork-shaped croquettes.

Beat the remaining eggs lightly with the milk and pour into a shallow dish. Spread the dry breadcrumbs over a sheet of greaseproof paper. Dip the croquettes in the egg and roll in the crumbs. For a very crisp coating, the egg-dip and crumbing can be repeated.

Heat the butter with the oil in a shallow pan and fry the croquettes, rolling them in the fat until crisp and evenly browned. Drain on paper towels, arrange on a heated serving dish, and grind a little black pepper over before serving.

Hare Mayonnaise

The smallest quantity of left-over hare can be turned into a tempting summer lunch or first course. Serve with an assortment of salads or individually on lettuce leaves.

Serves 4–6

1 quantity of game mayonnaise (page 225)
250–375 g (¹/₂–³/₄ lb) diced cooked hare
1 small bulb of fennel, trimmed and chopped
1 small green (bell) pepper, seeded and chopped
90 g (3 oz) cooked long-grain rice
20 pimiento-stuffed olives
lettuce leaves
1 tablespoon finely snipped chives

Prepare the mayonnaise and put it in a large bowl. Mix the diced hare with the fennel, pepper, rice, and half of the olives, finely sliced.

Fold the hare mixture into the mayonnaise and pile on to lettuce leaves on a serving dish or on individual plates. Garnish with the remaining olives and sprinkle with the chives.

Venison Mayonnaise

Cold roast venison is revitalised with a game mayonnaise that is quickly made in a blender. Serve with a potato salad and chilled fennel peas (page 181).

Serves 4–6

cold roast venison, thinly sliced
small dill pickles

Game Mayonnaise
6 juniper berries
8 spring onions (scallions), chopped
juice and finely grated rind of
    1 lemon
2 egg-yolks
1 cup (9 fl oz) olive oil
salt
white pepper
2 hard-boiled eggs

Arrange the sliced venison on a serving plate, coat with the mayonnaise, and garnish with the pickles.

Game Mayonnaise
Mix the juniper berries with the spring onions (scallions), lemon juice and rind in a blender or food processor until smooth. Add the egg-yolks and blend thoroughly. Gradually add the oil and seasoning, blending until the mayonnaise is thick and creamy. Finally blend the chopped eggs with the mayonnaise and adjust the seasoning.

Venison Patties with Kirsch Butter

This is a 'no-fuss' way to produce a very sophisticated dish. Make and chill the Kirsch butter first and serve with potatoes rosemary (page 186) and peas.

Serves 4

500 g (1 lb) minced (ground)
    cooked venison
125 g (4 oz) finely minced
    (ground) pork
1 medium onion, finely chopped
1/4 teaspoon ground mace
1/4 teaspoon ground oregano
salt
freshly ground black pepper
1 egg, lightly beaten
plain (all-purpose) flour
oil

Kirsch Butter
4 tablespoons softened butter
approx. 2–3 teaspoons Kirsch
1 teaspoon finely chopped parsley

Mix the minced (ground) meats thoroughly with the onion, mace, oregano, salt, and black pepper. Bind with the egg and divide the mixture into equal portions. Shape into cakes and dust with flour. Heat the oil in a heavy pan (a mixture of vegetable oil and goose fat is good) and shallow-fry the patties until crisp and browned.

Slice the Kirsch butter into pats, and serve on top of the hot patties.

Kirsch Butter
Beat the Kirsch gradually into the butter, using a little more or less to taste. Add the parsley and shape the butter into a roll. Enclose in plastic-wrap or foil and chill until very firm.

APPLIANCE COOKERY FOR POULTRY AND GAME

Most of us have some of the items that stores are pleased to call 'small appliances'. Chosen with care they are a boon in, and out of, any kitchen — time-saving, economical, convenient, or just plain fun.

There are scores to choose from but my choice rests on those which are kindest to poultry and game, have multiple uses, and earn their keep.

Clockwise from top right: *fan forced oven; grill (broiler); electric frying pan; clay pot; electric barbecue; rotisserie; vertical grill (broiler); centre: deep fryer*

Clay-Pot Cookery

The clay pot may seem out of place next to space-age appliances but it was probably one of the earliest 'small appliances'.

The Australian Aboriginals, who were among the first people to cook with clay, wrapped edible reptiles in it. The Romans later cooked in unglazed clay pots similar to our own.

It is this lack of glazing which allows food cooked in a clay pot to retain moisture while it browns. Casseroles, too, are given a distinctive character.

Clay-Pot Chicken

Without qualification, this is my favourite chicken casserole. It has everything — simplicity, succulent flavour, and superb appearance. Add crisp beans or snow peas (mange-tout) and it is just perfect.

Serves 4–6

10 spring onions (scallions), green and white parts, coarsely chopped
3 celery stalks, sliced
1 large onion, chopped
2 medium carrots, thinly sliced
1 small clove of garlic, finely chopped
salt
white pepper
60 g (2 oz) butter
1 kg (2 lb) chicken pieces
3 tablespoons chicken stock
1 cup (9 fl oz) cream

Toss the spring onions (scallions) in a large mixing bowl with the celery, onion, carrots, and garlic. Sprinkle with salt and pepper. Pre-heat the oven to moderately hot. Put the butter in the pot in one piece, add a handful of the mixed vegetables, and top with a layer of chicken. Then add more vegetables and more chicken until the pot is full. It does not matter if you end with vegetables or chicken. Pour the stock into the pot, cover, and cook in the centre of the oven for 1¼ hours. Check the seasoning and adjust if necessary. Pour the cream into the pot, cover, and cook for 15 to 20 minutes longer. Serve from the pot with vegetables of your choice.

Clay-Pot Chicken

Chicken Normandy

Serve with crisp French beans and jacket-baked potatoes (page 186).

Serves 4

375 g (12 oz) dried apple rings
4 chicken Maryland joints
2 teaspoons dried tarragon
2 tablespoons melted butter
salt
white pepper
2 tablespoons Calvados or whisky
3 tablespoons cream

Soak the clay pot and lid in cold water for 10 minutes; drain. Line the base with the apple rings. Put the chicken on top of the apples, skin side up. Mix the tarragon with the butter, pour over the chicken, and season to taste. Cover the pot and put it in the centre of the oven. Set the temperature to moderately hot and cook for 1 to 1¼ hours, until the chicken is tender and golden.

Transfer the joints to a heated serving dish and keep hot. Strain any excess fat from the surface of the apples and put them in a saucepan. Beat lightly with a wooden spoon, stir in the Calvados or whisky, and bring to the boil. Reduce the heat, stir in the cream, and adjust the seasoning. Spoon the sauce over the chicken and serve immediately.

Imperial Duck

An early Roman recipe in a Roman vessel. Originally sour wine was used but wine vinegar is a suitable substitute. Serve with pasta or rice and a green salad. The quantity given can easily be halved.

Serves 8

2 × 2 kg (4 lb) ducks, quartered
8 small onions, peeled and each
   studded with 2 cloves
1 cup (9 fl oz) duck giblet stock or
   chicken stock
3 tablespoons wine vinegar
salt
freshly ground black pepper
¼ teaspoon dried sage
¼ teaspoon dried oregano
24 green olives

Soak the clay pot in cold water for 15 minutes; drain. Put the duck pieces in the pot with the onions, stock, and wine vinegar. Season lightly with salt and pepper and sprinkle with the herbs. Cover the pot and put in the centre of the oven. Set the temperature to moderately hot and cook for 1¼ to 1½ hours, until the duck is tender.

Transfer the duck and onions to a heated serving dish and keep hot. Remove the fat from the surface of the pan-juices and strain the liquid into a saucepan. Add the olives and simmer for 3 or 4 minutes. Adjust the seasoning and pour over the duck.

Rotisserie, Barbecue, and Grill (Broiler)

For simplicity's sake I have joined the rotisserie, barbecue, and grill (broiler) — folding or otherwise — together. They are all virtually interchangeable and all foods cooked in them need fairly regular basting.

Grilled Quails

The quails are basted with lemon butter and simply grilled. Serve with snow peas (mange-tout) for complete luxury.

Serves 4

8 quails, flattened
juice of 1 lime or 1 small lemon
60 g (2 oz) butter, melted
salt
freshly ground black pepper
lime twists or lemon twists
(page 209)

Split each quail through the backbone and trim the spinal bones away. Carefully open the birds, lay them cut side down on a board, and press along the breastbone with the heel of your hand. Fold the legs yoga fashion and secure in place with a small skewer.

Mix the lime or lemon juice with the butter and brush liberally over each side of the quails. Pre-heat the grill (broiler) and cook the birds at medium to high heat for 12 to 15 minutes, basting once during this time with the lemon butter.

Season with salt and black pepper before serving garnished with a citrus twist.

Grilled Quails

Venison Shashlyk

These can be barbecued or cooked on a rotisserie kebab attachment. Serve with jacket-baked potatoes (page 186) and salads.

Serves 4–6

1 kg (2 lb) venison, cubed, and trimmed of all fat
12 tiny pickling onions
12 button mushrooms
1 large red (bell) pepper, seeded and cut into 12 chunks.

Marinade

juice of 1 lemon
2 tablespoons olive oil or vegetable oil
1 large onion, roughly chopped
1 teaspoon salt
1/21 small clove of garlic, crushed
3 juniper berries

Make the marinade. Thread the venison and vegetables alternately on skewers and lay them in a shallow dish. Pour the marinade over and leave for 2 to 3 hours before cooking.

Prepare barbecue coals or pre-heat an electric barbecue or rotisserie. Cook the shashlyk for 20 to 25 minutes, turning them on a barbecue. Baste occasionally with the marinade.

Marinade

Blend the marinade ingredients in a blender or food processor and leave to stand at room temperature for 30 minutes before using.

Venison Burgers

Why not venison burgers? There are prime cuts on every beast but the trimmings can also be put to good use. Served with mushroom sauce (page 197) or béarnaise sauce (page 195) and salad they are very good.

Serves 4–6

1 kg (2 lb) venison, marinated
2 tablespoons reserved marinade
1 1/2 teaspoons dried mixed herbs
salt
freshly ground black pepper
oil

Drain the venison and pat dry. Mince (grind) the meat coarsely and mix with the reserved marinade. Form the mixture into thick burgers and sprinkle on each side with the herbs, pressing them lightly on to the meat. Season both sides with salt and black pepper. Chill until ready to cook.

Pre-heat the griddle (or barbecue hot-plate) until very hot. Just before cooking, brush the plates lightly with oil and sear the burgers on each side. Cook for 8 to 10 minutes in a folding griddle or 6 to 8 minutes on each side if using a barbecue.

Slow Cookers/Deep-Friers

Enough has been written about very slow cookers, so I have used a three-in-one, all-purpose pan which acts — with a stone insert — as a slow cooker, saucepan, and deep-frier.

The dial setting and cooking time may vary slightly with the age of the meat used or between different brands of appliance.

Chicken Wings Quattrocento

This most delectable chicken dish is perfect for cooking in a controlled-heat pan. Serve with an egg pasta and salad.

Serves 4–6

2–3 tablespoons olive oil
2 large onions, chopped
1 kg (2 lb) chicken wings
3 cloves of garlic, crushed
salt
freshly ground black pepper
2 × 400 g (14 oz/No. 300) cans
    peeled tomatoes, crushed
2–3 teaspoons dried tarragon
3 tablespoons tomato paste

Heat the oil with the control on medium. Add the onions and fry gently until transparent. Push the onions to one side and brown the chicken wings very lightly on all sides. Add the garlic and stir the ingredients together, seasoning well with salt and black pepper. Pour the tomatoes over the chicken and sprinkle with the tarragon. Increase the heat until the tomatoes are bubbling. Add the tomato paste and mix well. Reduce the heat, cover, and simmer the chicken for 50 to 60 minutes, although the chicken will not spoil if cooked for longer. Adjust the seasoning before serving over pasta.

Chicken Wings Quattrocento

Maple Chicken

Deep-fried chicken is coated with a crisp batter and then drenched with maple syrup. Hot or cold, it is delicious. Serve with potato chips, crisps, or salad.

Serves 4

1 quantity of savoury batter
*   (page 200)*
1·5 kg (3 lb) chicken pieces
salt
oil for deep-frying
185 g (6 oz) maple syrup

Prepare the batter. Sprinkle the chicken lightly with salt and steam over rapidly boiling water for 15 minutes. Remove from the heat and leave to cool.

Pre-heat the oil to 190°C (375°F). Fold the egg-whites into the batter and coat the chicken. When the oil is hot, deep-fry the chicken, three or four pieces at a time, until crisp and golden. Drain on paper towels. When all the chicken is cooked, return to the frying basket and dip briefly in the hot oil. Lift to drain the excess oil and, holding the basket of chicken over a tray, immediately pour the maple syrup over.

Maple Chicken

Deep-Fried Crisp Chicken

This is double-cooked chicken: first deep-fried and then baked. Serve with potato balls (page 185) or chips.

Serves 4–6

1 teaspoon salt
¼ teaspoon white pepper
1½ teaspoons baking powder
185 g (6 oz) plain (all-purpose) flour
½ cup (4 fl oz) water
1 large egg, lightly beaten
oil for deep-frying
2 kg (4 lb) chicken pieces
extra plain (all-purpose) flour
lemon twists (page 209)

Sift the salt, pepper, and baking powder with the flour. Mix the water and egg together and beat into the flour mixture to form a smooth batter. Pre-heat the oil to 190°C (375°F), between 9½ and 10 on the dial. Pre-heat the oven to moderate.

Dust the chicken lightly with flour and coat with the batter. Dip the frying basket into the hot oil and deep-fry two or three pieces of chicken at a time until crisp and golden. As the chicken is fried, put the pieces on a rack standing on a baking tray. When all the chicken is done, bake for 15 minutes.

Arrange on a hot serving dish and garnish with the vegetables of your choice and lemon twists.

Crumbed Turkey Mayonnaise

Not cold turkey again. The mayonnaise is used in quite a different way. Serve with sautéed potatoes and coffee pot asparagus (page 178) or peas.

Serves 4

4 small turkey drumsticks, skinned
90 g (3 oz) dry breadcrumbs
¾ cup (⅓ pt) mayonnaise
salt
freshly ground black pepper
3 tablespoons butter
3 tablespoons vegetable oil
3 tablespoons finely snipped chives or finely chopped spring onions (scallions) tops
2 tablespoons plain (all-purpose) flour
1¼ cups (11 fl oz) chicken stock
juice of 1 lemon
lemon twists (page 209)

Steam the drumsticks for 10 minutes over simmering water. Remove and leave to cool. Spread the breadcrumbs over a shallow dish. Brush the drumsticks liberally with mayonnaise, then roll them in the crumbs, pressing them on firmly. Season with salt and black pepper to taste.

Melt the butter with the oil in an electric frying pan (skillet) set on medium heat. Add the drumsticks and cook, turning frequently, until the juices run clear when a thigh is pierced with a skewer. Transfer the drumsticks to a heated serving dish and leave to stand in a warm place.

Drain off all but 2 tablespoons of the fat remaining in the pan. Reduce the setting to low, add the chives or spring onions (scallions), and cook for 1 minute. Sprinkle the flour into the pan, mix thoroughly, and cook for 1 or 2 minutes without colouring. Increase the heat and gradually add the stock, stirring constantly until the sauce is smooth. Simmer for 2 minutes. Stir the remaining mayonnaise into the sauce with the lemon juice. Heat through, without boiling and adjust the seasoning. Spoon the sauce over the turkey. Garnish with lemon twists just before serving.

Crumbed Spatchcock Mayonnaise

Substitute two halved spatchcocks for the turkey. Steam without removing the skin. Coat and cook in the same way.

Turkey with Marsala

This is a delicious way to cook a jointed turkey hindquarter. Any of the small dumplings on page 211 can be cooked on top of the turkey for the last hour of the cooking time. Serve with a crisp green vegetable.

Serves 4–6

1 turkey hindquarter, jointed
30 g (1 oz) plain (all-purpose) flour
½ teaspoon salt
½ teaspoon white pepper
¼ teaspoon dried oregano
3 tablespoons goose fat or ghee
12 small pickling onions, peeled
125 g (4 oz) small button mushrooms
1 large clove of garlic, crushed
3 tablespoons chicken stock
3 tablespoons Marsala
juice of ½ lemon

Separate the drumstick and thigh from the breast of the turkey. Cut the thigh and the breast meat into two or three portions and dust with the flour seasoned with the salt, pepper, and oregano.

Heat half of the fat or ghee in a frying pan (skillet) and quickly brown the turkey on all sides, transferring the pieces, as they are browned, to the stone insert of a slow cooker. Add the remaining fat to the pan and shake the onions over moderate heat until lightly browned. Add the onions to the turkey with the mushrooms, garlic, stock, wine, and lemon juice. Cover and cook on dial setting 5 for 20 minutes. Reduce the setting to 1 and cook for 4½ to 5 hours longer.

Note: This dish, prepared in the same way, can be cooked in a casserole for 1½ to 2 hours. Pre-heat the oven to moderate.

Guinea Fowl Rosé

Serve with game chips (page 184).

Serves 4

1 tablespoon butter
2 tablespoons vegetable oil
1 medium onion, coarsely chopped
1 celery stalk, finely sliced
2 guinea fowl
250 g (8 oz) zucchini (courgettes), sliced
125 g (4 oz) button mushrooms, halved
salt
freshly ground black pepper
¾ cup (⅓ pt) dry rosé
1 egg-yolk
2 tablespoons cream

Heat the butter with the oil in a frying pan (skillet) and quickly sauté the onion and celery until lightly browned. Transfer to the stone insert of a controlled-heat pan. Brown the guinea fowl, one at a time, on all sides. Put the birds on top of the vegetables. Add the zucchini and mushrooms to the pan (skillet), turn for 1 or 2 minutes until lightly coated, and transfer to the pot with the birds. Season to taste with salt and black pepper and add the wine. Cover and cook for 3½ hours with the dial set on 1½.

When the birds are almost tender, remove 2 tablespoons of the pan-juices and mix with the egg-yolk. Stir back into the pot and finish cooking. Just before serving, add the cream and adjust the seasoning.

Note: This dish, prepared in the same way, can be cooked in a casserole for 50 to 60 minutes in a pre-heated moderate oven.

Pheasants Felicity

Clearly any food can be ruined but you would be hard pushed to spoil pheasants when cooking them in a slow pot. These are cooked on a low setting (1½ to 2 on the dial) for 4 hours. Serve with tiny new potatoes or crusty bread.

Serves 4

2 tablespoons butter
2 tablespoons vegetable oil
1 large onion, halved and sliced
½ head of celery, trimmed and cut into 5 cm (2 inch) lengths
2 pheasants
2 oranges
1 cup (9 fl oz) chicken stock
1 teaspoon Angostura bitters
salt
freshly ground black pepper
125 g (4 oz) button mushrooms, sliced
3 tablespoons dry white wine

Heat the butter with the oil in a large frying pan (skillet) until just sizzling. Lightly brown the onion and celery. Using a slotted spoon, transfer the vegetables to the slow cooker and spread them over the base. Brown the pheasants on all sides in the frying pan (skillet) and place them, breast side up, on the bed of vegetables. Set the slow cooker on low and cover.

Using a vegetable peeler or very sharp knife, remove two thin 5-centimetre (2 inch) strips of rind from one of the oranges and squeeze the juice from the other. Put the rind, juice, stock, and bitters in a small pan, bring to the boil, and pour over the pheasants. Season lightly with salt and black pepper, cover, and leave without stirring for 3 hours. Add the sliced mushrooms and wine and cook for 1 hour longer. Adjust the seasoning before serving.

Chicken or Guinea Fowl Felicity
Both can be cooked in the same way as pheasant Felicity. Choose small chickens or spatchcocks.

Pheasants Felicity

Country House Pigeons

Serve with potatoes rosemary (page 186) and peas.

Serves 4

4 large pigeons
1 quantity of pigeon marinade
  (page 199)
1 tablespoon goose fat or ghee
2 bacon rashers, cut into strips, with
  rind removed
2 medium onions, halved and sliced
2 medium carrots, sliced
2 small tomatoes, peeled, seeded,
  and chopped
salt
freshly ground black pepper
12 juniper berries, bruised

Marinate the pigeons for 6 to 8 hours. Remove from the marinade, reserving ½ cup (4 fluid ounces). Heat the fat or ghee in a frying pan (skillet) and sauté the bacon until the fat starts to run. Reduce the heat and add the onions, carrots, and tomatoes. Turn in the fat for 4 or 5 minutes, until they begin to soften. Transfer the mixture to the stone pot and season lightly.

Put three juniper berries in the cavity of each pigeon. Tie the legs together and fold the wings neatly under the body. Season lightly with salt and pepper. If there is not enough fat remaining in the frying pan (skillet), add a little more before browning the pigeons quickly on all sides. Arrange the birds on top of the vegetable mixture and pour the reserved marinade over. Cover and cook for 10 minutes on medium setting. Reduce to 1 and cook for 3 to 3½ hours, until the birds are tender.

Transfer the pigeons to a heated serving dish and keep hot. Beat the vegetables with a wooden spoon until smooth, or quickly put through a blender or food processor. Reheat and adjust the seasoning. Spoon a little over each bird and serve the rest separately.

Note: This dish, prepared in the same way, can also be cooked on top of the stove, for 40 to 45 minutes.

Quails in Almond Batter

Deep-fried quails cook in the time it takes for the coating to become crisp and golden. Serve with Portuguese cucumber (page 181) and a crisp green salad.

Serves 4

1 quantity of savoury coating batter
  (page 200)
60 g (2 oz) ground almonds
8 quails
salt
freshly ground black pepper
oil for deep-frying
lemon twists (page 209)
redcurrant jelly or cranberry sauce

Prepare the savoury batter, adding the ground almonds to the mixture with the flour. Leave to stand for 20 to 30 minutes before adding the beaten egg-white.

Trim the wing-tips from the quails and tie the legs loosely together. Season lightly with salt and black pepper. Pre-heat the oil to 185°C (365°F), dial setting 8½ to 9.

Fold the beaten egg-white into the batter and, holding the quails by the legs, dip the birds in the batter (it does not matter if some goes into the cavity of the bird). Dip the frying basket quickly into the hot oil, put four of the quails in the basket, and deep-fry until crisp and golden. Drain on paper towels and keep hot. Cook the remaining quails, drain, and arrange all the birds on a heated serving dish. Garnish with lemon twists and serve the redcurrant jelly or cranberry sauce separately.

Pressure Cookers

My early experiences with pressure cooking were so disastrous that they put me off using 'that wretch' for years, and I eventually threw it out.

Since then the 'hit-and-miss' aspect has vanished with the addition of automatic timers, making pressure cookers trouble free and wonderfully time saving.

As with all appliances the maker's directions must be followed.

Jugged Hare

The hare is marinated overnight and normally takes in excess of 3 hours to cook. Using a pressure cooker, the hare is ready in a quarter of the time. Moreover, one of the essentials of successfully jugging hare is to seal the casserole completely: pressure cookers certainly do that. Cook for 40 minutes on high pressure (15 pounds). Serve with creamy mashed potatoes. Carefully remove the shiny membrane before jointing the hare.

Serves 6

1 hare, jointed
¾ cup (⅓ pt) dry red wine
3 tablespoons wine vinegar
1 small onion, sliced
6 black peppercorns
2 bay-leaves, crumbled
2 fat bacon rashers, sliced, with rind removed
1 tablespoon vegetable oil
1 large onion, sliced
2 celery stalks, sliced
2 medium carrots, sliced
½ teaspoon ground allspice
5 cm (2 inch) strip of lemon rind
juice of 1 lemon
salt and pepper
¾ cup (⅓ pt) game stock or beef stock
2 tablespoons redcurrant jelly
1 tablespoon plain (all-purpose) flour
1 tablespoon butter

Put the hare joints in a plastic bag with the wine, vinegar, onion, peppercorns, and bay-leaves. Seal the bag and marinate for several hours, turning the bag occasionally. Remove the marinated hare, and pat dry. Strain and reserve the marinade.

In the open pressure cooker, fry the bacon with the oil until the fat runs. Brown the hare on all sides. Add the onion, celery, carrots, allspice, lemon rind, and lemon juice. Season with salt and pepper. Stir in the stock and ¾ cup (⅓ pint) of the reserved marinade. Cover the pan and bring to pressure. Lower the heat, and cook for 40 minutes.

When the hare is ready, reduce the pressure rapidly. Remove the cover and, using a slotted spoon, transfer the hare and vegetables to a heated serving bowl. Stir the redcurrant jelly into the sauce. Work the butter into the flour and whisk small pieces into the sauce until it is thickened to your liking. Adjust the seasoning and pour the sauce over the hare.

Bistro Rabbit

A few simple ingredients combine to make this a flavoursome and attractive dish. Serve with boiled rice and a salad.

Cook for 20 minutes at high (15 pounds) pressure.

Serves 4

1 rabbit, jointed
2 tablespoons melted goose fat or butter
2 medium onions, thickly sliced
2 teaspoons brown sugar
3 cloves of garlic, finely chopped
3 canned pimientos, drained and sliced
1¼ cups (11 fl oz) dry white wine
salt
white pepper

Put the rabbit on a foil-covered grill (broiler) rack. Brush with the goose fat or butter and lightly brown under the grill (broiler). Transfer to a pressure cooker. Spread the sliced onions over the foil, sprinkle with the sugar, and brown quickly under the grill until the sugar bubbles. Layer the onions over the rabbit with the garlic and pimientos. Add the wine and season with salt and pepper. Cover the pan and bring quickly to pressure. Lower the heat immediately and cook for 20 minutes. Reduce the pressure rapidly.

Transfer the rabbit and vegetables to a heated serving dish. Adjust the seasoning of the sauce and spoon over the rabbit. The sauce can be thickened with a little beurre manié if you like but it does seem to take the edge off the flavour.

Bistro Chicken
Substitute six chicken thighs and cook in the same way as the rabbit.

Venison Flamande

This Belgian dish normally takes several hours to cook. Using a pressure cooker, the whole of the cooking is finished within an hour and the result is in no way inferior. Cook on high (15 pounds) pressure for 45 minutes and serve simply, with boiled potatoes.

Serves 4–6

3 tablespoons butter
1 tablespoon vegetable oil
1 kg (2 lb) cubed lean venison
2 large onions, coarsely chopped
2 cloves of garlic, crushed
1 teaspoon dried thyme
2 teaspoons chopped parsley
1 small bay-leaf
½ teaspoon ground cloves
1 teaspoon Hungarian paprika
2 tablespoons redcurrant jelly
1 cup (9 fl oz) beef stock
1 cup (9 fl oz) port
salt
freshly ground black pepper
3 teaspoons plain (all-purpose) flour

Melt the butter with the oil in the open pressure cooker. Quickly brown the cubed venison on all sides. Reduce the heat a little, add the onions and garlic, and cook until they are the colour of pale straw. Add the herbs, bay-leaf, cloves, and paprika, stirring to mix thoroughly with the meat. Add the redcurrant jelly, stock, and port. Season with salt and black pepper to taste.

Cover and bring to full pressure before timing. When full pressure is reached, reduce the heat under the cooker. When the cooking time is finished, reduce the pressure rapidly.

Remove the cover. Mix the flour to a smooth paste with a little cold water and add some of the cooking liquid to it. Stir into the cooker and simmer for 2 or 3 minutes until the sauce has thickened. Adjust the seasoning before serving.

Venison Chilli

The sudden need to improvise has created many great dishes as well as making the difference between a good or superb recipe. This, then, is Brewster's magnificent chilli, the simple result of adding baked beans as make-weight to a kidney bean shortage. If the venison has been marinated, drain and pat dry before mincing (grinding) and cook for 12 minutes at high pressure. Cook unmarinated venison at the same pressure for 16 minutes. Serve as usual with salted crackers.

Fry the smoked pork or spek quickly in the open pressure cooker until the fat starts to run and it is lightly browned. If necessary, add a little oil with the onions, pepper, and celery and cook for 1 or 2 minutes, until just softened. Stir the venison into the vegetable mixture, breaking up any lumps with a fork, and turning until the meat changes colour. Add the tomatoes and liquid, tomato paste, and chilli powder (remember that you can always add more later). Season with salt to taste, cover, and cook on high pressure for the times given above.

Reduce the pressure quickly and add the beans. Adjust the seasoning and simmer until the beans are hot.

Note: Dried kidney beans can be used in place of canned: soak them overnight and cook with the venison. If you do not have a pressure cooker, prepare the chilli in the same way and simmer for 1 to 1¼ hours before adding the beans.

Serves 6–8

250 g (8 oz) diced smoked pork or spek
1–2 tablespoons vegetable oil
2 medium onions, coarsely chopped
1 large green (bell) pepper, seeded and coarsely chopped
2 celery stalks, chopped
1 kg (2 lb) coarsely minced (ground) venison
2 × 400 g (14 oz/No. 300) cans peeled tomatoes, pulped, with their liquid
4 tablespoons tomato paste
2–4 teaspoons Mexican chilli powder
salt
440 g (16 oz/No. 303) can red kidney beans, rinsed and drained
440 g (16 oz/No. 303) can baked beans in tomato sauce

Venison Chilli

Fan-Forced Ovens

The difference in temperature evenness of a fan-forced oven, whether in your regular oven or a portable model, is quite marked.

The portable ones are most useful if you have only one oven, providing extra space at 'stress times', as well as being able to be used almost anywhere (therefore keeping a lot of heat out of the kitchen).

Again the individual manufacturer's directions should be followed.

Pastry Horns

Perhaps we are more used to seeing these attractive whorls of pastry filled with fruits and cream. Pack them with a savoury mixture and they become crisp and interesting cornucopias. Serve with a creamed vegetable and salad.

Use pastry horn moulds or, far more easily, mould the pastry over foil horns, which are readily removed when the horns are cooked. To make foil moulds, cut sheets of foil into 25 centimetre (10 inch) squares. Fold the squares into triangles and, holding the longest edge, roll the triangles into cones. Tuck the joining points evenly inside the cones so that they will stand upright.

Serves 4–6

1 quantity of swag pastry
(page 205) or shortcrust pastry
(page 201)
egg glaze (page 205)
Filling
1 quantity of béchamel sauce
(page 196)
1 tablespoon vegetable oil
1 medium onion, chopped
1 celery stalk, chopped
500 g (1 lb) cubed cooked poultry
or game
1 canned pimiento, drained and
chopped
salt
white pepper

Prepare the pastry and chill before rolling. Pre-heat a conventional oven to hot. Set a fan-forced oven to 190°C (375°F).

Roll the pastry thinly and cut into 2 centimetre (¾ inch) strips. Starting at the point of the cone, roll the pastry around the moulds, overlapping each layer by 5 millimetres (¼ inch). Pinch the end firmly and stand the cones on a baking tray. Brush lightly with the egg glaze and bake for 30 to 35 minutes, until crisp and golden.

Remove the moulds from the horns, spoon the filling in, and serve immediately.

Filling
Make the sauce and set aside. Heat the oil in a small pan and cook the onion and celery until softened and lightly browned. Mix with the cubed meat and pimiento and set aside. Fold the meat mixture into the sauce, simmer gently until very hot, and season with salt and pepper to taste.

Chicken and Leek Pie

This is a creamy old-fashioned double-crust pie. The addition of one hot chilli adds a nice touch. Serve with crisp green vegetables.

Serves 4–6

1·5 kg (3 lb) chicken thighs
3 cups (¹/₃ pt) chicken stock or water
1 quantity of shortcrust pastry (page 201)
3–4 leeks, split and sliced
1 hot red chilli, seeded and thinly sliced
2 tablespoons butter
2 tablespoons plain (all-purpose) flour
¹/₂ cup (4 fl oz) cream
salt
white pepper
egg glaze (page 205)

Poach the chicken in the stock or water until tender. Make the pastry; cover and chill before rolling. Lift the cooked chicken from the stock and set aside to cool, reserving the cooking liquid.

Blanch the leeks for 1 minute in some of the boiling stock; strain and set aside. Remove and discard the skin and bones of the chicken and cut the meat into chunky pieces. Sprinkle with the sliced chilli and set aside.

Melt the butter, stir in the flour, and cook for 1 or 2 minutes without browning. Gradually add 1¼ cups (11 fluid ounces) of the reserved stock, stirring between each addition until the sauce is smooth and thickened. Simmer for 2 or 3 minutes and remove from the heat. Add the cream and season well with salt and pepper.

Pre-heat a conventional oven to very hot and set a fan-forced oven to 200°C (400°F). Roll out half of the pastry to line a 23 to 25 centimetre (9 to 10 inch) pie-plate. Spread the chicken and leeks over the pastry. Roll the remaining dough. Add some of the sauce to the chicken and brush the pastry edge lightly with water. Cover the pie, trim, and seal the edges firmly. Cut a small slit in the top of the pastry and decorate with the trimmings if you wish. Brush lightly with the egg glaze and bake in the centre of a conventional oven or at any level of a fan-forced oven for 30 minutes, until the pastry is crisp and golden.

Chicken and Leek Pie

Chicken Liver and Ham Gougère

This Burgundian dish is traditionally made with a cheese-flavoured choux paste, but with this rice filling I prefer to use a plain choux. The even heat distribution of a convection or fan-forced oven cooks choux pastry well. Serve with crisp green vegetables.

Serves 4–6

1 quantity of choux pastry
   (page 201)
1 tablespoon fried crumbs
   (page 210)
1 tablespoon finely chopped parsley
Filling
60 g (2 oz) butter
250 g (8 oz) chicken livers, skinned
   and trimmed
1 large onion, halved and sliced
60 g (2 oz) mushrooms, sliced
1 ½ tablespoons plain (all-purpose)
   flour
1 ¼ cups (11 fl oz) chicken stock
3 tablespoons dry red wine
125 g (4 oz) coarsely chopped lean
   ham
2 medium tomatoes, peeled, seeded,
   and cut into eighths
8 green olives, stoned and quartered
salt
freshly ground black pepper

Prepare the choux pastry and arrange in spoonfuls in a lightly oiled circular dish, leaving the centre free. Bake on any level of a fan-forced oven set at 190°C (375°F) or in the centre of a conventional oven pre-heated to hot. Bake for 30 to 40 minutes, until the pastry is crisp and golden. Cook the filling while the pastry is cooking. Pile the livers into the centre of the pastry, sprinkle with the crumbs and parsley, and serve hot.

Filling

Melt half the butter in a large shallow pan, and quickly sauté the chicken livers on all sides until sealed. Remove from the pan. Reduce the heat, add the remaining butter, and cook the onion until transparent. Add the mushrooms and turn in the pan-juices until they are coated but still firm. Sprinkle with the flour, stir well, and cook for 1 minute. Gradually add the stock, stirring constantly until the sauce is smooth. Fold the reserved livers into the sauce with the wine, ham, tomatoes, and olives. Simmer for 2 or 3 minutes and season with salt and black pepper to taste.

Game and Ham Gougère

Substitute 500 grams (1 pound) of diced, cooked game for the chicken livers and add to the sauce with the ham.

GLOSSARY

Angostura bitters	Trademark for a bitter aromatic tonic made in Trinidad from bark, roots and herbs, etc.
aspic jelly	A savoury jelly made from the bones of meat, game, poultry or fish. Available in ready-to-prepare packets.
bard	A piece of larding bacon or fat placed on game while roasting to prevent drying out of flesh.
bird's eye chilli	Very small, very hot chillies, often used in pickles. Handle with caution.
brioche	Sweet bun or roll, raised with egg and yeast, available from patisserie.
cabana sausage	Also called Kransky sausage. Readily available.
cayenne pepper	Hot, biting, condiment made from the ground pods and seeds of different varieties of capsicums (bell peppers).
Chinese plum sauce	Preparation of mashed plums and spices used as a dipping sauce or in stir-fried dishes. Available at Asian food stores. Hoisin sauce may be substituted.
chocolate, bitter	Unsweetened, bitter, dark chocolate used originally by the Aztecs.
chillies, sweet, green	Use the same as red chillies. Available at Asian food stores.
chorizo sausages	Very spicy, Spanish sausages, with chillies added. Use with caution.
coconut cream	Creamy liquid made from the grated flesh of the coconut, not the liquid inside the nut. Readily available.
cornmeal	Meal made from maize or grain.
cracked wheat (bulgar) Turkish (burghul) Arabic	Hulled wheat steamed and partly cooked, available coarse or fine.
cumin seed	Seedlike fruit of small plant, essential in curry powder. Similar in appearance to caraway seeds but they cannot replace each other.

Roast Pheasant, page 110; with Game Chips, page 184

Curaçao	Liqueur flavoured with the peel of the bitter Curaçao orange.
Dijon mustard	Made from white and black mustard seeds mixed with the acid juice from unripened grapes.
dill	Feathery and thread-like leaves similar to fennel, gives a distinctive slightly aniseed flavour to dishes.
fenugreek	Small flat seeds with a slightly bitter flavour essential in curry powder. The green leaves are used in Indian cooking.
five spice powder	Reddish-brown powder made up of star anise, fennel, cinnamon, cloves and Szechwan pepper, essential in Chinese cooking.
garam masala	Mixture of spices often used in Indian cooking. Usually made from coriander, cumin and cardamom seeds with peppercorns, cinnamon sticks, cloves and nutmeg. Readily available.
ghee	Clarified butter. Readily available.
giblets	Heart, liver, or gizzard from a bird.
Hoisin sauce	Sweet, spicy sauce, essential in Chinese cooking. Readily available.
juniper berries	Purple berries used in cooking or in making gin.
Kirsch	Brandy distilled from black cherries.
lima beans	Several varieties of bean with a broad, flat, edible seed.
lychees	Fruit of a Chinese sapindaceous tree having a thin shell with a sweet pulp.
Madeira	Strong white wine similar to sherry.
matzo meal	Ground grain used in dumplings and scones (biscuits).
Melba toast	Narrow slices of dry toast named after Dame Nellie Melba, the Australian operatic soprano.
pâté	Paste or spread made of finely ground liver, meat or fish.
persimmons	Astringent plumlike fruit, becoming sweet and edible when ripe.
pimiento	Red Spanish pepper with a sweet pungent flavour.
proscuitto	Cured ham from Italy.

rock salt	Common salt in coarse rock-like masses.
saffron (threads)	World's most expensive spice, obtained from the dried stamens of the saffron crocus. Available as dark orange strands with a strong perfume or as a powder.
sake	Pronounced 'sahk-ay'. Japanese rice wine usually served warm.
sambals	Combinations of chillies and spices used as accompaniments to rice and curries. Available at Asian food stores.
sauerkraut	Fine cut cabbage, salted and allowed to ferment. Readily available.
sesame oil	Oil extracted from sesame seeds available at health food stores.
shirataki noodles	Translucent noodles used in 'sukiyaki', made from the starch of a tuberous root. Sold in packets or cans.
soy sauce	Very salty sauce indispensable in Chinese cooking. Available light or dark at all Asian food stores.
Tabasco sauce	Trademark of a very hot red sauce made from matured capsicums (bell peppers).
tamarillos	Ovular red fruit similar to a large plum with a sweet/sour edible pulp.
terrine	Pâté of meat or game served in an earthenware cooking dish.
trail — woodcock	Intestine of the woodcock. Woodcocks are marsh dwellers and do not have a stomach in the usual sense. Considered a delicacy.
truffle	Edible fungi with a tuberous appearance. Great delicacy.

INDEX

ACKNOWLEDGEMENTS

This book represents the time, work, and support of many people and organisations and I would like to express my sincerest thanks to them all — to the many friends who lent me precious books and old, handwritten family documents, particularly Joyce McCallum, Rachel McCarthy, Ellen Rowe, and Jonathan Hallmer; Judy and Peter Warren of Attunga Goose Farm, Forster, who supplied me with valuable information about geese.

I also wish to thank Professor J. B. Hennessey, Department of Middle Eastern Archaeology, University of Sydney, who was exceedingly helpful to me in providing answers to the more obscure historical questions.

Walter Boles, Acting Curator of the Australian Museum's Department of Ornithology and his colleague, Associate Curator Wayne Longmore, shared their knowledge concisely and generously and I thank them both.

Among other people who gave me help and much-needed information are Julia Limbury who worked long hours typing my manuscript, thus enabling me to complete the book on time; Paddy Fitzgerald of Shamrock Meats for his very practical help; the staff members of the Sydney consulates of Austria, Brazil, Czechoslovakia, Denmark, Egypt, Germany, Hungary, Mexico, New Zealand, Sweden, and the United States of America; members of the Country Women's Association of New South Wales, the Jewish Folk Centre, and the Turkish Islamic Culture Association. I am indebted to all of you.

A special mention must be given to my editor Deirdre Adamek who gave her time unsparingly to this book and whose insistence on editorial niceties, guidance, and encouragement is greatly valued and appreciated.

The photography for this book is the result of teamwork for long hours over many, many weeks. The skill of photographer Andrew Warn is evidenced by the pictures; I thank him as well for his unfailing good humour, sustained enthusiasm, and patience. Marie McDonald completed the studio team, helping me to prepare the food and contributing her experience, her talent, and her friendship.

'Props' for photography came from all quarters: the Royal Doulton company supplied a vast array of their outstandingly fine china and glassware; Inini, Bill Johns' wonderful shop in Neutral Bay, is a paradise for cooks and homemakers and he opened his doors to me, as did Mrs Grace of Charisma, Mosman, who dressed the tables with her elegant napery. My thanks go also to Nicky and David Prentice of Accoutrements, Mosman; the old Furniture Warehouse, Balmain; and the countless friends who packed up their treasured possessions and lent them to me for a long period.

Many suppliers sought, obtained, and delivered to my kitchen the ingredients and equipment for testing and photographing the recipes. Their generosity, not only of products but also of valuable advice and information, was overwhelming, particularly John Meredith of Thirlmere Poultry Supplies, Thirlmere, New South Wales, with his twice-weekly deliveries of perfect game and game birds.

I would also like to thank the following organisations and their representatives for the help and co-operation they have given me in the preparation of this book:

Alcan (Aust.) Ltd; Anchor Foods Pty Ltd; H. G. Brown and Sons Pty Ltd and Roger Brown; Francesco Cinzano and C.I.A. (Aust.) Pty Ltd; Edgell/Birds Eye (Division of Petersville Ltd) and Barbara Lowery; Honey Distributors; John West Foods Ltd; Lavery Dairy Products Ltd; Master Foods of Australia; Nabisco Pty Ltd and David Wills; Peters Milk (Division of Petersville Ltd); Rice Grower's Co-operative; Seagers (Australia) Pty Ltd and Michael Talbot-Price; Steggles Pty Ltd and Leslie Berge and Doug Kitchen; Vegetable Oils Pty Ltd; White Wings Ltd and Pat Patterson; Monier Consumer Products; Prestige Group (Australia) Pty Ltd; Rank-General Electric Housewares Pty Ltd; Sunbeam Corporation Ltd; Thorn Kenwood.